Angora Matta

Angora Matta

Actos Fatales de Traducción Norte-Sur

Angora Matta

Fatal Acts of North-South Translation

Marta E. Savigliano

Wesleyan
University Press
Middletown,
Connecticut

Published by Wesleyan University Press,
Middletown, CT 06459

Printed in the United States of America
Designed by Chris Crochetière
Set in Bodoni, Stone, and Myriad Tilt types by B. Williams & Associates
Illustrations by Marta E. Savigliano
Inked drawing of Angora Matta by Miguel Nanni

Library of Congress Cataloging-in-Publication Data
Savigliano, Marta.
    Angora Matta : fatal acts of North-South translation = actos fatales de traducción
  norte-sur / Marta E. Savigliano.
      p. cm. — (Music/culture)
    Text in English and Spanish.
    Includes bibliographical references (p.).
    ISBN 0-8195-6598-9 — ISBN 0-8195-6599-7 (pbk.)
    1. Buenos Aires (Argentina)—Drama.   2. Beverly Hills (Calif.)—Drama.
  3. Women murderers—Drama.   4. Murder for hire—Drama.   5. Exiles—Drama.
  I. Title.   II. Series.

PS3619.A86A85 2003
812'.6—dc21

                                                                    2003041187

5   4   3   2   1

A Jeff Tobin, con amor y squalor

Table of Contents/Indice

Illustrations

Author's Note
(On Tangophilia and Ethnographitis)

Adventurous readers with the time, patience, and love required to engage in writerly experimentation should skip this note. I am afraid these lines will ruin the potential pleasure involved in discovering your own version of what this book is about, of the author's intentions, and of its failures and accomplishments. If, however, you choose to continue, this is what I think you should know: You have opened a book that challenges the conventions of fiction and scholarly writing, and that demands an interest in both. This text counts on the readers' imagination, curiosity, and a certain ability to jump over and/or swim between fictional and scholarly interpretations of impossible realities in searching for a sense of truth. It will only work when in the hands of readers who consider playfulness and a sense of humor as legitimate tools for approaching serious understanding of tragedies.

Angora Matta is a translingual, intercultural, and interdisciplinary work that adopts performative writing to reflect on north-south politics of culture. The centerpiece of the book is an operatic libretto that situates the complex lives and identities of contemporary Argentine characters as displaced (exiles, émigrés, travelers) or as locally bound but globally conscious citizens. These characters conflictively share a time of post-dictatorial mourning and re-democratized squalor. The leitmotif of the opera and of the book is the Memory of Power, a collective narrative that attempts to make sense of disjointed episodes of past violence by taking hold of the consciousness of different agents involved in the making of history. The main purpose of the work is to question the representational practices of ethnography, performance and film that have fetishized Argentine "culture" (taken to be a sorrowful, nostalgic, and passionately tangoesque culture) by isolating it from contemporary history and the global flow of international politics.

This mixed-genre work reflects the influence of contemporary Argentine fiction writers Luisa Valenzuela (*The Lizard's Tail*), Norberto Piglia (*Artificial Respiration*), and Tununa Mercado (*La Madriguera*). These authors conjure painful historical memories of past political events meant to be forgotten. Writing appears in their texts as a dangerous machinery that, in remembering, threatens to bring back to life that which we would prefer had never happened. And because they remember nightmarishly, reality (past and present) becomes bolder and clearer through the writers' impressionistic interpretations than through classical academic accounts delineated by disciplinary norms of objectivity. Thus, post-dictatorial fiction writers enliven true experiences and events that go otherwise unaccounted for. Witnesses and participants of the dictatorships of the 1970s connect to these memories as survivors. Unlike these works, however, *Angora Matta* focuses on the transmission of experiences of post-dictatorial mourning to foreign audiences who are prone to spectacularize political violence in the so-called third world through mechanisms of exoticism. It dwells in the difficulties of translating the culture of the "other" into universalized disciplinary discourses such as anthropology and art. In doing so it problematizes the limits of current understandings of identity and representation in line with the works of Hélène Cixous, Trin Minh-ha, Dorinne Kondo, Gloria Anzaldúa, Gayatri Spivak, and Kamala Visweswaran. These scholars have engaged in performative writing and/or fiction and playwriting in order to call attention to and to step out of the limits imposed by established academic discourses affecting the representation of others' "cultural" practices and understandings. Taking a politically invested ethnographic viewpoint that claims "native" knowledge as it questions its legitimacy to represent an "other" close to "home," this book calls attention to how difference and indifference work together in producing (mis)understandings across "cultures," and to the dangers of culturalism. It does so by exploring the linguistic and corporeal traffic of difference (coded as culture) as well as the attempts to overcome otherness through translation and co-presence. It attempts to grasp what lies between established identities, carved differences, and representations mounted so as to bridge identified differences. For this purpose, the book attends to the moments and processes when one identity is inhabited by another, one language transforms into the other, and one corporeality is provoked by the temporal and spatial co-presence of the one it simultaneously alienates and intends to understand. The concepts of identity and representation are thus set into motion as fluid articulations and endless transformations and as the effects of reconfigured instabilities. By setting writing into performance, and thus knowledge into laboring practice, this book looks at cultural contact as live, failed encounters in which differences are negotiated through mobilized and vociferous bodies.

Historically and existentially situated at the crossroads of generalized paradigmatic exhaustion coupled with global ostentatious exploitation, *Angora Matta* taps into the potency of a shattered yet reconfigurable memory (the Memory of Power). It uses performance to enliven connections between politics and poetics. The book has three parts. Part I is a doubled introduction authored by a *tangópera* librettist and a central character in her libretto (a medium qua ideologue) offering two contending versions of how this book came into being. Part II is the libretto for the musical drama *Angora Matta*, a tangópera conceived as a thriller. It contains fourteen scenes, illustrated in twenty-five drawings, that relate a political murder mystery undertaken by a ex-*guerrillere* turned hit woman in exile. The plot moves between Los Angeles, Buenos Aires, and Miami during one week in 1999. This libretto is the subject of dispute that generates the authorial claims presented in Part I. Part III contains scholarly essays written by (that is, in the voices of) three other characters who appear in the libretto. Their essays reflect interests and positions that dispute or supplement the ways they are represented in the libretto. Elvira Díaz is an ethnographer disenchanted with her profession who investigates nocturnal identities; Manuela Malva is a biting foreign-film critic invested in demystifying exotic renderings of the Argentine tango world and its associations with national identity; Angora Matta, the assassin for hire, closes the book with philosophico-poetic meditations about her profession.

Part I, "An Uneasy Pact," presents an authorial dispute between the librettist and one of the main characters in her tangópera, a professional medium who is enraged over the inaccuracy, and even the accuracy, of the ways she believes herself to be depicted in the tangópera. The medium decides to launch a class-action suit against the librettist on behalf of herself and the others who are (mis)represented in the libretto. For this purpose, the medium searches for the other characters that appear in the libretto, taking for granted that they, too, will be annoyed over their disfigurations, which, because of the political undertones of the drama, put them at risk. The medium never meets any of them, but she manages to collect some of their writings, which she plans to publish as a collection of essays alongside the libretto with an introduction in which she claims that the libretto is anonymous. In sum, she plans to steal the libretto and at the same time to sue the librettist. The tangópera's author learns about these maneuvers and tries to reach a settlement with the medium. The librettist, who insists that the characters are fictive, is nonetheless unable to resist the temptation to take a look at the documents allegedly produced by her characters. The medium agrees to give her these materials on the condition that the librettist serve as her apprentice, thus immersing the librettist in the medium's esoteric ways of knowing (preoccupations with identity and corporeality that she addresses through trance, translation, and transubstantiation). Ethnographers' obsessions with the textual representation of others and themselves are a subtext of this detectivesque story that moves literally through translations—translations that do not accept one original language. Walter Benjamin's work on truth and the materiality of words is central to this dispute.

Part II, "The Contested Object," consists of the libretto itself. The plot is as follows: Angora Matta, the main character, is an Argentine ex-*guerrillere* and exile from the military dictatorship of the 1970s, who, as the drama begins, has settled in Beverly Hills and is earning her living as a hit woman. She is hired to commit a crime in Buenos Aires. As usual, she is unconcerned with the identity of the victim and the interests involved. She is told that more precise instructions will be delivered upon her arrival. Act 1 shows Angora, always disguised, moving from the airport to her hotel and through various typical downtown Buenos Aires scenes (the Past and Present bookstore, The Emigré café, and the tango club The Dump) where she holds dramatic and equivocal encounters with characters (Elvira Díaz, Manuela Malva, and Mariano Monteamor being the most crucial) that connect her to buried memories and repressed desires entangling personal grief with moral and political post-dictatorial mourning. In Buenos Aires, Angora thus faces her militant past and defeated revolutionary ideals as she witnesses a general social climate of dystopia over re-democratization. Through tangos, *murgas*, *milongas*, creole waltzes, and *candombes*, Angora reinserts herself in a social fabric that both draws and repels her, enlivening the conflicts between those who stayed and those who left (such as exiles and émigrés) during the dictatorship and its aftermath. She cannot halt this traumatic process, for she is in pursuit of the successive, partial instructions that will guide her to her unknown victim. Act 1 ends at the tango club, where Angora meets Mariano Monteamor—a *macho posmo*, in contemporary Argentine slang, that is, a self-centered, self-defeated, but charming and romantic man. He senses Angora's aura of death and is convinced (or hopes) that he is her passionate victim.

Act 2 finds Angora ready to accomplish her fatal task, now having in hand all the necessary information. She moves swiftly, professionally, avoiding Mariano, who unknowingly stands in her way. She disappears from the scene as the death of the President is announced in the news. An emergency cabinet meeting is held to discuss the assassination: the perpetrator has escaped; all they know is that it is a woman. They must inform the public nevertheless that the Politicians are in full control of the situation. Having no real clues to follow, they send the secret police to consult a famous medium and Witch in town. Elvira, Manuela, and Mariano, who are also looking for Angora (but each for different reasons), consult the same Witch. The Witch, who counterrepresents Angora's denial of personal and sociopolitical history, monumentalizes the Memory of Power. Falling into successive trances, the Witch is possessed by the victimizers and victims of the past military repression, who struggle to take over her voice with threats, false accusations, confusing confessions, and a relentless chronicle of violent events that occurred between 1976 and 1983, the years of the dictatorship. In the nightmarish atmosphere of the Witch's office, all the main characters encountered by Angora in her trip to Buenos Aires arrive one by one. The Witch receives them without asking any questions; the Memory of Power must continue unfolding. Having worked the Witch to exhaustion, the Memory moves on to the others present at her office, who continue relating the consequences of the military rule in current times of failed re-democratization. The Witch, recovered, closes act 2 as an acute ideologue who will deliver the structural reasons for the current economic and political turmoil. She will not respond to her clients' inquiries about whether Angora is responsible for the President's murder. The Memory of Power judges these details irrelevant.

An epilogue follows: In Miami, in a room with a big desk, someone with his back to the audience sits at a computer writing an e-mail message. The message says that the assassination is a farce: the President plotted the whole thing in order to run away from his responsibilities, taking with him his illegal gains. He happily instructs his cronies to pay Angora for doing such a diligent job. As he composes the message, Angora irrupts into the scene, surprising the President in his hideaway. She has followed him beyond her paid instructions, having decided to take justice into her own hands. Black-out; a struggle. On the still-flickering computer screen, the President's message is replaced by a transfer of funds to a Swiss bank account in Angora's name. Simultaneously, Mariano receives a phone call from abroad. The music of the "Memory of Power" loudly marks the finale.

My interest in exploring the operatic genre stems from the multiartistic possibilities it has to offer. Opera's use of a multiplicity of artistic devices (narrative, poetry, music, song, theater, choreography, scenography, costuming, and lighting) and its concomitant ability to convey complex information through redundancy as well as simultaneous divergence, works in multiple sensorial registers (aural, visual, and kinesthetic) and their corresponding symbolic horizons. This wealth of resources, capable of generating intellectual-aesthetic experiences involving all the senses, as well as opera's adscription to a stuffy high culture bordering the grotesque, seemed promising for the task at hand: telling a story of Latin American tragic *and* magic realism. *Angora Matta* plays seriously with and against stereotypes that allocate to and generate in Latin America, and in particular in Argentina, a destiny of femme-fatality.

Part III, "The Controversial Evidence," consists of three "exhibits" made up of the documentation collected by the Witch as proof of the real existence, not only as persons but also as authors, of those represented as fictional characters in the libretto. These documents show how the complex lives, identities, concerns, and even skills of Elvira, Manuela, and Angora have been flattened, decontextualized, and misinterpreted in order to fit into the narrative concocted by the librettist—the artist as ethnographer. Exhibit A presents writings attributed to Elvira Díaz, a relentless *milonguera* (tango dancer) by night who is also an ethnographer of the contemporary tango world. "Nocturnal Ethnographies: Following Cortázar in the Milongas of Buenos Aires" and "Gambling Femininity: Wallflowers and Femmes Fatales" are two complementary readings of the *milongas* (tango dance halls) of Buenos Aires that include a series of methodological qualms and failed experimentations in the rendering of ethnographic writing. The first essay offers the concept of "nocturnal identities" to account for the necessary but unwelcome misrepresentation of the subjects under study. A tangophilic ethnographer from the present encounters an observant tangophobic character of the past (Cortázar's Dr. Hardoy in "The Gates of Heaven" [1949]) and a dance of contested readings of the heavily heterosexual, sexist, and fetish-driven tango world follows. The changing articulations of sex, race, and class in the milongas of downtown Buenos Aires are discussed in terms of sociohistorical reconfigurations of passion, the crux of the tango cult. The second essay advances a "gambling theory" to account for the participation of women in the patriarchically ruled tango clubs. It is an attempt to counter the usual feminist interpretations that resort to Freudian sadomasochistic models. A detailed description of tango steps and corporeal attitudes seeks to explain milongueras' addiction to a dancing game that requires wallflowering subjection while promising exhilarating femme fatality as a reward. Tango women thus engage in gambling femininity in their nightly milonga incursions, betting on gaining the status of an irresistible object of collective desire unavailable to them in their safely subjected daily lives.

Exhibit B contains two works attributed to Manuela Malva, an aspiring tango singer drawn to drinks and cafés who earns a decent living as a foreign-film critic. Manuela's essays ("*Evita*: The Globalization of a National Myth" and "Cinematic Sex Tours: On Potter's *The Tango Lesson* [1997] and Saura's *Tango, no me dejes nunca* [1998]") discuss the films *Evita* (Parker 1996), *The Tango Lesson* (Potter 1997), and *Tango, no me dejes nunca* (Saura 1998) in terms of the violence of cultural appropriation, addressing specific instances of politico-ideological work at play in the making of art that spectacularizes otherness. Tangophilia and ethnographitis, as well as complementary "diseases" at work in generating the fascination of the north with the passionate culture of the south, appear overwhelmingly in the masterful techniques of representation of intercultural sexualized intercourse presented in these films. The tango world, characterized as an alluring dance and music that takes hold of bodies and emotions, is represented (and cinematically marketed) as a victimizer of the main characters (in Potter's and Saura's cases, the foreign directors; in Parker's, a Madonnified Evita) of the films, rendering them vulnerable to exotic otherness—and thus confounding the terms of cultural imperialism. Artists-as-ethnographers-as-victims of tangophilia is the formula for displacing the work of representation onto the represented.

Exhibit C, "Edgy Meditations," closes the book with a series of aphorisms, fables, and other short pieces of poetic prose attributed to Angora Matta—who when not at work ruminates on death, evil, and ambition while obsessing about the knife kept under her pillow that has taken over her life. Who is Angora Matta (a.k.a. Angora Kils) *really*? The enigmatic feline killer woman will not explain herself. She acts a Latin American story of femme fatality with a vengeance. She can be represented but cannot be known. We just have to follow her unpredictable steps, her geophysical and political translocations between the north and the south, her memory losses and reconstructions, her outbursts of translingual consciousness. The librettist represents a crucial slice of her life. The medium (to the librettist, a Witch) refuses to believe it. As far as I know, Angora Matta never existed. But I needed to make her up, contained in a doubled case of legalistic and clinicalized wrappings, hoping she can cut her way out.

MARTA ELENA SAVIGLIANO
Los Angeles, July 14, 2001

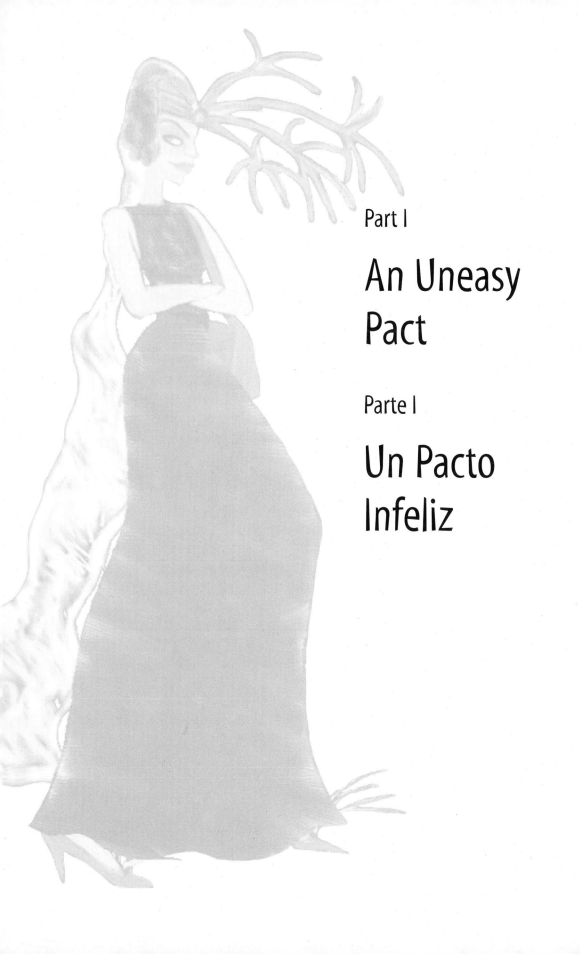

Part I

An Uneasy Pact

Parte I

Un Pacto Infeliz

Translingual Trances and Authorial Claims

by the Librettist and XYa

Reclamos de Autoría y Trances Translinguales

por la Libretista y XYa

The Librettist's Claims/Reclamos de la Libretista

Original: Cowardice and pettiness allow me to declare myself as the author of this book. The ambition to appear in bibliographic indexes and to promote my professional career, in addition to the potential material benefits (modest ones according to certain standards but significant for a cultural worker), finally won out over my will. I begin, thus, with this confession. I cannot live up to that grandiose desire of mine to release these writings solely under fictive signatures. I am not resigned, however, to the logical consequences. I believe that even though my name is stamped on the cover, securing me all profits, I can insist on the multiple, apocryphal, and disfigured authorship of this collection of works that, I repeat, I wrote. I am taking this liberty. *(Punto y aparte.)*

I know that the demands I impose on those witnesses who are my readers are disproportionate. I dare to do so probably because for the most part I do not know them. I have tried to put myself in their generous position, that of the potential audience for my shameless elaborations. I have not been able to, or else it has not intimidated me. I have provided this service on numerous occasions for others. I recall the pleasures involved, not always because of the product that was being delivered but certainly in relation to my magnanimous role of enabling spectator. I appeal to this complicity. *(Otro punto y aparte.)*

Translation: De cobarde y mezquina me adjudico la autoría de este libro. La ambición de figurar en los índices bibliográficos y de promover mi carrera profesional, con las consabidas ganancias materiales (exiguas según ciertos estándares pero significativas para una trabajadora de la cultura), ganaron finalmente mi voluntad. Empiezo, entonces, por esta confesión. No me atrevo a cumplir con ese deseo de grandeza que tengo de dar a conocer estos escritos sólo bajo firmas ficticias. No me resigno, sin embargo, a las lógicas consecuencias. Creo que aunque mi nombre figure en la tapa, asegurándome los beneficios, puedo insistir en la múltiple, apócrifa y desdibujada autoría de esta colección de trabajos que, repito, escribí yo. Me tomo esa libertad. *(Full stop.)*

Sé que exijo desmesuradamente a esos testigos que son mis lectores. Me atrevo tal vez por desconocerlos en su mayoría. He intentado ponerme en ese lugar generoso de audiencia potencial de mis descaradas elucubraciones. No lo he logrado o no me ha logrado intimidar. Yo misma he prestado ese servicio en numerosas oportunidades para otros. Recuerdo el placer involucrado, no siempre en el producto que se me entregaba pero sí, claramente, en mi papel magnánimo de espectadora posibilitante. Apelo a esa complicidad. *(Another full stop.)*

Original: La creación apela a la lealtad. Contrariamente a lo que se cree, la creación no es un acto individual de expresión inspirada *(enraptured)* que emerge del aislamiento ensimismado. Es un pedido de auxilio; un testimonio del miedo a la locura. Y la locura sí, considero, es un estado próximo (aunque no completamente) a la soledad radical. Donde la locura actúa la resignación al desencuentro con los otros, la creación apuesta sino a la comprensión al menos al reconocimiento del cruce existencial. En ese sentido la creación—el arte—busca el momento efímero de lealtad. La lealtad implica; es un pacto. Los pactos no libran ni borran las sospechas. Las saltean con conocimiento de causa. La creación es un abuso de confianza. Los hay más o menos desvergonzados. Juzgar la magnitud del abuso, en este caso, queda en manos del sometido (del que se presta al papel de receptor y testigo). La escritora o artista, entonces, es ejecutante (¿verduga?) a la vez que víctima del lector o audiencia que, en principio, desde un lugar vulnerable de sometimiento, pasa a juzgar. (La linearidad que imponen las convenciones literarias no me permite capturar la compleja simultaneidad de estos procesos.) El placer que genera este intercambio aparentemente incomprensible de locura compartida (que por ser compartida, como intento explicar más arriba, empuja el límite de la locura al tiempo que huele su proximidad) es un enigma de seducción irresistible. (Aquí debería iniciar otro párrafo pero temo perder . . . me perdí. *(Full stop.)*

Traducción: Creation asks for loyalty. Contrary to common knowledge, creation is not an individual act of enraptured expression (*inspiración*) that emerges from a state of focused isolation. It is a cry for help, a testimony to the fear of madness. And madness, I believe, is a state of being more proximate (although not fully) to radical solitude. Where madness performs resignation regarding the impossibility of the encounter with others, creation bets that recognizing existential crossings is possible—even if understanding is not. In this sense creation—art—searches for that ephemeral moment of loyalty. Loyalty implicates; it is a pact. Pacts do not liberate or erase suspicions. They knowingly skip over them. Creation is an abuse of trust. There are more and less shameless ones. The judgment regarding the magnitude of the abuse in this case falls into the laps of the subjected (of those who play the role of witnesses and receptors). The writer or artist, then, is the performer (executioner) and at the same time the victim of the reader or audience that, in principle, from a vulnerable position of submission, passes to one of judging. (The linearity imposed by literary conventions does not allow me to capture the complex simultaneity of these processes.) The pleasure engendered in this apparently incomprehensible exchange of shared madness (that because of its shared nature, as I attempt to explicate above, pushes off the limits of madness as it smells its proximity) is an irresistibly seductive enigma. (I should initiate another paragraph here but I am afraid of losing . . . I lost it.) *(Punto y aparte.)*

Original: Esta interrupción me viene bien, entonces, para explicar el formato inusual que han ido tomando estas notas. Encontrar un lugar, habitarlo con una voz y, obviamente, expresarse en un idioma son premisas que atiende cualquier narrador potable. El lector ya se topó con muestras de las dificultades que tengo para atenerme a esta receta. Yo vivo colgada entre lugares, voces e idiomas. Hay muchos como yo, y tal vez siempre los hubo, pero lo cierto es que tendemos a esconder nuestra condición perturbadora. Nos arrancamos, nos transponemos, nos translinguamos obligados a elegir, lo más rápido posible, la pertenencia. En este texto se desata este ajuste que, supuestamente, da inteligibilidad a la narración. Aquí se exponen la fragilidad y la arbitrariedad de las mencionadas elecciones. Me explico: anuncio "original" or "traducción" al iniciar cada párrafo para indicar precisamente que lo que se leerá a continuación nació, para bien o para mal, a veces en inglés y otras veces en castellano; y que lo traduje, inmediatamente, a la otra lengua (castellano o inglés, según el caso) no sólo para que me sigan los lectores monolingües (entre los que se cuentan esos que quiero y que se quejan de no poder leerme) sino también para explorar el confuso y arduo movimiento de palabras/sentidos en el que estamos inmersos los que vivimos en estado de traducción. Estoy cansada de que este esfuerzo de mediación cultural no se reconozca. Los idiomas nos poseen, y el prolijo silencio rara vez nos visita.

Traducción: This interruption comes in handy, then, for explaining the unusual format that has been shaping these notes. Finding a place, inhabiting it with a voice, and, obviously, expressing oneself in a language are premises to be followed by any tasteful narrator. Readers have already encountered signs of the difficulties I have faced in trying to follow this recipe. I live suspended between places, voices, and languages. There are many others like me, and probably there have always been; but in truth we tend to hide our disturbing condition. We uproot, transpose, and adopt translingualism, forced into choosing, as soon as possible, where and to whom/what we belong. This text undoes this tightening adjustment that supposedly makes narration intelligible. Here the arbitrariness and fragility of the aforementioned choices are exposed. Let me explain: I announce "original" and "translation" at the beginning of each paragraph to indicate precisely that what will be read right after was born, be it for good or ill, sometimes in English and other times in Spanish; and that I translated it immediately into the other language (Spanish or English, as needed) not only for the sake of monolingual readers (including those whom I love and who frequently protest because they cannot read me), but also to explore the arduous and confusing movement of words and meanings in which we who live in a state of translation are immersed. I am tired of this effort at cultural translation not being recognized. Languages possess us, and tidy silence seldom pays us a visit.

Original: Me atraen los enigmas. Las paradojas y los dilemas. Las redes enmarañadas. Me mantienen ocupada. Me aterroriza el vacío. Nunca sufrí de claustrofobia. No aguanto la simple claridad. Me inquieta el amanecer. La visibilidad no me interesa; soy miope de nacimiento. El tacto, el olfato y los sonidos siempre fueron mis guías. Los oftalmólogos me atemorizan más que los dentistas. Cultivo el barroco antropológico y el surrealismo naïf. Quisiera heredar el *green thumb* de mi madre. No quisiera morir sin haber aprendido árabe. (Y leer las *Mil y Una Noches* en el original.) Todavía lloro con algunas músicas, con algunas lecturas; lagrimeo en algunas películas y a veces cuando escribo. (Esto último dos veces en mi vida.) Admiro la maldad como quien admira un traje lujoso de noche, imposible de comprar. Admiro a poca gente y siempre envidié a los que se dan la libertad de admirar. No entiendo bien la envidia. (Esta emoción me visita muy poco, tal vez por el aspecto pragmático de mi personalidad.) Solía temer la venganza; eso ya pasó. La dificultad con la que he ido descubriendo la forma de identificar las emociones me hace pensar que, más allá de las terminaciones nerviosas y sinopsis cerebrales, los afectos son socioculturalmente adquiridos. Aprendemos a sentir ésto o lo otro. Y de allí el poder de las palabras. Sentir en otro idioma requiere rigurosa traducción. (El humor es lo más frustrante de todo. Esa es mi experiencia, tal como he aprendido a hablar de ella.) La energía no me fluye; me sale a borbotones. Ergo, la sangre y la energía son cosas distintas. (Estoy tomando unas gotas homeopáticas para mejorar esta condición. No me preocupa, pero estoy dispuesta a seguir los consejos del Dr. Wu, recomendado por mi colega de Minnesota con la mejor buena intención de aliviar mis raptos de fatiga). No me gusta tachar; prefiero borrar y en lo posible pasar en limpio. (Esto se lo debo a la escuela de monjas y a la disciplina impuesta por los empleados administrativos de las oficinas estatales argentinas. Algunos opinan que es un legado de la Doctrina de Seguridad Nacional.) Me disgusta ese ser en el que me convierto cuando se requiere de mí que establezca orden e instrucciones a seguir. Me aburren las listas de prioridades. Bostezo poco, pero en momentos claves. Dicen que por los bostezos, suspiros y estornudos entran y salen los espíritus. Que la sal gruesa corta el tráfico de ánimas especialmente durante el sueño. Desparramar la sal bajo la cama. El cuchillo, bajo la almohada.

Traducción: Enigmas attract me. Paradoxes and dilemmas. Entangled nets. They keep me busy. Voids terrify me. I have never suffered from claustrophobia. I spend my days spotting traps. I cannot stand simple clarity. I am restless at dawn. I am not interested in visibility; my myopia is congenital. Touch, smell, and sounds have always been my guide. Eye doctors scare me more than dentists. I cultivate the anthropological baroque and naive surrealism. I would like to inherit my mother's green thumb. I would not like to die without having learned Arabic. (And before reading the *Thousand and One Nights* in the original.) I still cry with some music, and with some readings; I weep in some movies and sometimes when I write. (The last only twice.) I admire meanness as one who admires an unaffordable fancy nightgown. I admire a few people, and I always envied those who enjoy the liberty to admire. I do not understand envy very well. (This emotion visits me very seldom, perhaps due to the pragmatic aspect of my personality.) I used to fear vengeance; that is over now. The difficulty with which I have been discovering the ways of identifying emotions makes me think that, beyond nervous endings and cerebral synapses, affects are socioculturally acquired. We learn to feel this and that. Hence the power of words. Feeling in a different language demands rigorous translation. (Humor is the most frustrating of all. That has been my experience—as I have learned to talk about it.) My energy does not flow; it comes out in bursts. Ergo, blood and energy are not the same thing. (I am currently taking some homeopathic drops for bettering this condition. I am not worried about it but I am willing to follow the advice of Dr. Wu, recommended by my colleague from Minnesota with the best intentions for alleviating my outbursts of fatigue.) I dislike strikeouts; I prefer to erase and better yet to make clean copy. (I owe this to the school of nuns and to the discipline imposed by the administrative employees of Argentine state offices. Some believe that we owe this to the National Security Doctrine.) I dislike that being I become when I am required to establish order and impart instructions. Listing priorities bores me. I yawn rarely, but at key moments. They say that through yawns, sighs, and sneezes the spirits enter and exit. That coarse salt cuts the traffic of souls especially when at sleep. Spread salt under the bed. The knife, under the pillow.

Original: I realize now that the former lines are rather erratic, but I am in a rush. I do not know how long it will take for the next one to arrive. All coming voices must be recorded. I am aware that actually this might already be yet another one and not me. I continue nevertheless. Some crucial matters demand explanation. I was involved in a distasteful legal dispute that fortunately is now over. I was the unhappy victim of an accusation hurled by a medium of sorts. I write and teach for a living and I know perfectly well the legalities, rights, and wrongs of my profession. Anyway, this woman was convinced that a character of my creation, absolutely fictitious, featured in one of my recent and most imaginative works, not only resembled her but actually described her and some recognizable circumstances in which she was involved in real life. *Su convicción era férrea y su actitud obstinada.* [Her conviction was strong and her attitude obstinate.] Believe me. I tried to manage the crisis using every and all reasonable techniques as a resource. I developed arguments from the most simple to the most sophisticated, to no avail. I cited renowned authorities on the subject of authorship; I tried to joke about it with her. Nothing. Her mind was set. She would argue that she sensed or felt (not that she thought or believed) that my Witch— the character in my libretto and object of our dispute—appropriated her being and affected her integrity. Representation and misrepresentation for her were one and the same thing. She insisted that the nonconsensual use of her persona for research and/or creative purposes (she would make no distinctions here either) was particularly preposterous when I misquoted her or attributed to her an ideology she never professed. Neither my lawyer nor I could persuade her of the blatant contradictions and misinterpretations carried through her arguments: She was troubled as much by the accuracy as by the inaccuracy of my depictions of her. I was able to use these irrational statements in my defense. *(Otro párrafo.)*

Translation: Me doy cuenta ahora que las líneas previas son un tanto erráticas, pero estoy apurada. No sé cuánto demorarán en llegar las próximas. Todas las voces visitantes deben ser registradas. Advierto que tal vez ésta ya sea una más de esas otras y no yo. Con todo y así, continúo. Algunos asuntos cruciales exigen explicación. Estuve involucrada en una desagradable disputa legal que afortunadamente ya llegó a su fin. Fui víctima infeliz de una acusación esgrimida por una especie de médium. Yo escribo y enseño como medio de vida y conozco perfectamente bien las legalidades, derechos y deberes de mi profesión. Como sea, esta mujer estaba convencida de que un personaje de mi creación, absolutamente ficticio, que figura en una de mis obras recientes y más imaginativas, no sólo se le asemejaba sino que virtualmente la describía, a ella y a algunas circunstancias reconocibles en las que decía haber estado involucrada en la vida real. (Original:) Su convicción era férrea y su actitud obstinada. (Translation continues:) Créanme. Intenté manejar la crisis recurriendo a todas las técnicas razonables. Desarrollé desde la más simple hasta la más sofisticada argumentación sin éxito. Cité a conocidas autoridades sobre el tema de la autoría; traté de bromear con ella al respecto. Nada. Su idea, fija. Esgrimía que sentía o percibía (no que pensaba o creía) que mi Bruja—el personaje de mi libreto y objeto en disputa—se apropiaba de su ser y afectaba su integridad. Para ella, la representación y la desfiguración eran una misma cosa. Insistía en que el uso inconsulto de su persona para fines de estudio y/o creativos (aquí tampoco hacía diferencias) era particularmente absurdo y pernicioso cuando la citaba fuera de contexto o le atribuía una ideología que jamás profesara. Ni mi abogado ni yo pudimos persuadirla de las contradicciones y falsas interpretaciones que conllevaban sus razonamientos: le molestaban tanto las precisiones como las imprecisiones de mis formas de retratarla. Pude emplear estas aseveraciones irracionales en mi defensa. *(Another paragraph.)*

Original: XYa (the Witch's adopted name that in her view captures the universal coordinates of the feminine principle) mobilized earth and sky, day and night, searching for fellow characters (whom she believed to be persons) mentioned in my libretto. Her idea, I believe, was to pursue a class-action lawsuit. Luckily they did not respond to her delusional proposition (since they did not exist), but I gather that somehow, aided by her high contacts, she was able to collect a series of writings of uneven value and sophistication allegedly authored by people who bore the names of my characters. An unnecessary but perhaps welcomed clarification: My characters were not conceived as writers of any genre; they are never portrayed writing or even mentioning that activity (except for one love letter). XYa did not accept this fact as sufficiently exculpating and argued that I had rendered unfairly flat impressions of my characters' personalities. Hence, my artistic limitations had nothing to do with the truth and moreover proved her point concerning my slandering representations. I had failed to provide even the most rudimentary information: How did my characters make a living? What did their houses look like? Who were their parents? What were their culinary preferences? Et cetera. She accused me, then, of focusing solely on their "nocturnal identities" (a term she said she borrowed from one of my characters' writings; I was able to corroborate this later). The documentation she had collected would partially remedy my carelessness. At this point, I admit, my curiosity overcame my anger. I had been wondering for a long time about the details of my characters' lives and even about what they looked like. I knew I could only include so much information in my *tangópera*, but as I worked on their lyrics and styles, their movements and settings, their emotions, to be conveyed through the music, I found myself daydreaming about their lives. I wanted XYa's documents. I paid a tremendous price for them. Regret? Unthinkable. Oh, that cold sweat again . . . write more later. *(Aquí otro paréntesis indicando un nuevo párrafo.)*

Translation: XYa (alias adoptado por la Bruja ya que, según ella, captura las coordenadas del principio femenino) movilizó cielo y tierra, día y noche, en busca de los otros personajes (que para ella eran personas) mencionados en mi libreto. Su idea, creo, era iniciar un juicio colectivo. La suerte quiso que no respondieran a su propuesta delirante (¡no existían!) pero de alguna manera, supongo que ayudada por sus altos contactos, pudo colectar una serie de escritos de valor y sofisticación despareja que, alegó, eran de la autoría de gente que llevaba los nombres de mis personajes. Una aclaración innecesaria pero quizás bienvenida: Mis personajes no fueron pensados como escritores de género alguno; jamás se los presenta escribiendo y ni siquiera mencionan dicha actividad (a excepción de una carta de amor). XYa no aceptó este hecho como exculpación suficiente y sostuvo que yo había representado con injusta chatura sus personalidades. Mis limitaciones artísticas nada tenían que ver con la verdad y, más aún, ésto era prueba de su acusación respecto del carácter defamatorio de mis representaciones. Yo ni siquiera había suministrado la información más rudimentaria: ¿cómo se ganaban la vida mis personajes? ¿Qué aspecto tenían sus viviendas? ¿Quiénes eran sus padres? ¿Cuáles eran sus preferencias culinarias? Etcétera. Me acusó, entonces, de ocuparme solamente de sus "identidades nocturnas" (término que dijo haber tomado prestado de los escritos de uno de mis personajes; hecho que corroboré luego). La documentación que ella había recopilado subsanaría parcialmente mi descuido. Llegado este punto, admito que mi curiosidad sobrepasó mi furia. Yo había pasado largas horas contemplando los detalles de las vidas de mis personajes e inclusive sus aspectos físicos. Sabía que sólo podía incluir contada información en mi tangópera, pero a medida que trabajaba en sus canciones y estilos, sus movimientos y puestas en escena, sus emociones a ser comunicadas a través de la música, continuaba fantaseando sobre sus vidas. Yo quería los documentos de XYa. Pagué un precio tremendo por ellos. ¿Me arrepiento? No, impensable. Ay, ese sudor frío otra vez . . . sigo escribiendo más tarde. *(Here another set of parentheses indicating a new paragraph.)*

Original: Estimo estar aún en plena posesión de mis facultades. Dejo constancia de mis dudas; tal vez sea otra la voluntad que me posee. La verdad suele crear tanta sospecha como el engaño. Lo importante es la relación, la conexión ética, la confianza o desconfianza creadas entre los que intervienen en un diálogo, situación o acto. Más que un contrato, ésto es un voto de fe. Las rúbricas suelen ser invisibles, aunque es sabido que en ciertas culturas la tinta o la sangre, como fluidos sagrados, son el agente ritual cuya mancha sobre superficies preciadas y homogéneas—el papel, la piel—marcan indeleblemente el vínculo juramentado. Las palabras escritas son como las cicatrices que dejan las heridas infligidas por los pactos de lealtad. Los escritos, sin embargo, son invitaciones abiertas a un pacto que propone el escriba a todo aquel que lo lee. La escribidora se tajea en la presencia vacía de una audiencia deseada. De allí el horror a la página en blanco que precede a todo primer trazo. De allí la situación de trance que supone el acto de escribir. De allí las alusiones a la escritura como *performance* o actualización de una intencionalidad ajena que posee al escritor y lo convierte en su instrumento. El autor anónimo y la multiplicación apócrifa de la autoría son desplazamientos perversos que espectacularizan esta situación.

. . . Creo reconocer aquí cierta familiaridad con otros pensadores mejores y más famosos . . . sobre la corporalidad de la escritura . . . desde la menstruación al semen . . . pero me atengo por el momento a mi propio hilo, ya por demás entreverado dado mi estado semi-racional.

Traducción: I assess I am still in full control of my mental abilities. I make a note of my doubts; perhaps another will possesses me. Truth often creates as much suspicion as deceit. What matters is the relationship, the ethical connection, the trust or mistrust cultivated between those who participate in a verbal exchange, situation, or act. More than a contract, this is a leap of faith. The signatures tend to be invisible, although it is well known that in some cultures ink and blood, like sacred fluids, are the ritual agents whose stains on precious and homogenous surfaces—paper, skin—permanently mark the sworn bond. Written words are like scars left by the wounds inflicted by loyalty pacts. Writings, however, are open invitations to pacts that the writer proposes to anyone who will read her. The writer slashes herself in the void presence of the desired audience. Hence the horror of facing the blank page that precedes all first traces. Hence the situation of trance presupposed in the act of writing. Hence those references to writing as performance or actualization of an alien intentionality that takes possession of the writer and transforms him/her into its instrument. The anonymous author and the apocryphal multiplication of authorship are perverse displacements that spectacularize this situation.

. . . I believe I recognize here a certain familiarity with other, better and more famous, thinkers . . . on the corporeality of writing . . . from menstruation to semen . . . but for the moment I will stick to my own thread, already too entangled for a semi-rational state of mind like mine.

Original: Anyway. I agreed to serve as her apprentice. We signed a contract. XYa would pass me all the collected documents, including her introduction as editor of the planned volume (given that she was one of my opera's characters, whose personalities I was determined to investigate). The writings would be given to me at the spasmodic pace of a page a day. It took me 257 days to gather them all and initiate the work of reconstruction. Several intervening factors complicated the process. First, the pages for each article or essay were delivered to me in reverse order, starting with the last, then the next to last, and so on, until the title page finally arrived with the name of the author. It was only then that I could start making sense of who, which character's namesake, was writing what. Second, as time went by, my apprenticeship progressed and thus my ability to serve as a vessel for the visitors conjured by XYa at the request of her clients improved. My lapses of lucidity—at least of the kind of consciousness that I could trust as being mine—concurrently shortened. My thoughts for the most part seem to me to flow quite coherently, but I sense changes in speed, associative patterns, issues of interest, and even memories. Now I had to sort out not only the order and voices present in those pages but also the ones who inhabited me, or more precisely the one who had risked her sanity (who knows if this is me right now) in pursuit of these elusive characters. I still know I created them. I am certain of that. Furthermore, as my working through their writings advanced, I started sensing, tentatively at first, and then at that incredible reverse speed of light that we have come to call insight, I *knew* I had read them before. I could anticipate the word choices, I could confidently guess the arguments, I was convinced by the conclusions before I laid my eyes on the preceding discussion. *(Aquí hubiera querida evitar el punto y aparte.)*

Translation: En fin. Acepté servirle de aprendiz. Firmamos un contrato. XYa me pasaría los documentos recopilados, incluyendo su introducción como editora del planeado volumen (dado que ella era uno de los personajes de mi ópera cuyas personalidades yo había decidido investigar). Los escritos me serían entregados al ritmo espasmódico de una página por día. Me llevó

257 días juntarlos en su totalidad e iniciar el trabajo de reconstrucción. Diversos factores intervinieron complicando el proceso. Primero, las páginas de cada artículo o ensayo me fueron entregadas en el orden inverso de progresión, empezando por la última, seguida por la penúltima, y así hasta llegar finalmente a la página titulada y con el nombre del autor. Sólo entonces pude empezar a entender quién, cuál tocayo de mi personaje, era el que lo había escrito. Segundo, a medida que transcurría el tiempo, mi entrenamiento de aprendiz progresaba y con ello mi habilidad de servir como receptáculo de los visitantes conjurados por XYa a pedido de sus clientes. Mis lapsos de lucidez consecuentemente se acortaron, al menos del tipo de conciencia que podía confiar fuese mía. Mis pensamientos en general parecen fluir con bastante coherencia, pero percibo cambios de velocidad, y en la estructura asociativa, los temas de interés, e incluso los recuerdos. Ahora debía establecer no sólo el orden y la identidad de las voces presentes en esas páginas sino también las de aquellas que me habitaban a mí o, más precisamente, a quien había arriesgado su salud mental (quién sabe si esa soy yo ahora) en busca de estos personajes elusivos. Todavía sé que los he creado. De eso estoy segura. Pero, a medida que avanzaba mi trabajo sobre los escritos comencé a percibir, *supe* en un principio tentativamente, y luego a esa increíble retro-velocidad de la luz que hemos dado en llamar *insight*, que los había leído con anterioridad. Podía anticipar las palabras escogidas, podía adivinar con confianza los argumentos, las conclusiones me convencían antes de posar mis ojos en la discusión que las precedía. (*Here I would have liked to avoid a full stop and the ensuing break.*)

Original: In order to confirm these uncanny certainties I wrote down the subtitles, beginnings, and endings of paragraphs that I anticipated finding in each installment. I waited with trepidation, measuring my sobriety, for that time of the day at which XYa would hand me the next page. She whiffed I was up to something; I faked my states of confusion or pushed them even further so as to gain some time. On a spring day, I think it was March or was it September (was I in the southern or the northern hemisphere when I came to this realization?), during breakfast (the time of the day I could freely devote to these works of thoughtful retro-compilation), I *remembered*. Different images of me in different scenarios, for the most part academic ones, delivering these different papers, and despite all these differences, a sense of a *me* that pulled everything together like a magnet. This confidence did not last, but I retained a memory of it. By the time I got to the last of the pages (I estimated I had only one or two pages to go before arriving at the beginning) of XYa's brief introduction to the planned publication, I harbored no doubts about whose hands had written all of the documents included. My body recognized them and claimed its possessive rights of identity.

These writings were the product of the labor of an identifiable corporeal *I* who in questioning authorship had set herself up for a troubling journey of unforeseeable results. An author of renowned fame can safely afford to engage in identity plays; publishers and audiences will keep him together. This was definitely not my case, and I would have lost my works and my self to XYa's manipulations had it not been for my cowardice and ambition. I feared madness too much; I wanted too much the profit of my work. This simple revelation came to me with a very particular rush of boredom, a clear sense of aging.

(O.) I communicated my finding to XYa in what turned out to be a brief, low-key conversation. She laughed, high pitched, nodded at me, and immediately relieved me of my duties. Before sending me off from her office for the last time, she handed me the remaining first pages of her introduction. She said she would not interfere with my publication of the volume or question my authorship so long as I included her introduction. I accepted. When I read what you are about to read I marveled at her wicked imagination (although she still needs to develop her writing skills, and which, in my view, resemble too many acclaimed authors). How could she come up with such a twisted account of the facts? How could she have plotted to erase me altogether from the picture, claiming that my libretto was anonymous? Are vengeance and dramatized victimization the sources or the effects of evil?

LOS ANGELES, MAY 3, 2000

Translation: Para confirmar estas certezas inquietantes tomé nota de los subtítulos, principios y finales de párrafos que anticipaba encontrar en cada entrega. Esperaba sobresaltada, midiendo me sobriedad, ese momento del día en el que XYa me pasaría la próxima página. Ella husmeaba algo; yo fingía mis estados de confusión o los provocaba desmesurados para ganar tiempo. Un día de primavera, creo que fue en marzo o era septiembre (¿estaba en el hemisferio Norte o Sur cuando me di cuenta?), durante el desayuno (momento que podía dedicar libremente a estos trabajos de cuidadosa reconstrucción), *recordé*: diferentes imágenes mías en diversos escenarios, la mayoría académicos, presentando esos varios artículos, y a pesar de todas esas diferencias tuve la sensación de un *yo* que juntaba todas las partes como un imán. La certeza no me duró, pero pude retener el recuerdo de la certeza. Para cuando llegué a las últimas páginas (estimaba que me faltaban sólo una o dos para alcanzar el principio) de la breve introducción de XYa a la planeada publicación no me quedaban dudas. Sabía de quién eran las manos que habían escrito todos esos documentos. Mi cuerpo los reconocía y reclamaba sus derechos posesivos de identidad. Estos escritos eran producto del trabajo de un yo corpóreo identificable, quien al cuestionar la autoría se había lanzado a un viaje perturbador de resultados imprevisibles. Un autor de fama reconocida podía darse el lujo de entretenerse en juegos de identidades con tranquilidad; editoriales y audiencias lo mantendrían entero. Sin duda éste no era mi caso, y hubiera perdido mis trabajos y mi ser gracias a las manipulaciones de XYa si no fuera por mi cobardía y ambición. Temía demasiado a la locura; deseaba demasiado las ganancias de mi obra. Esta simple revelación me llegó con una oleada muy particular de aburrimiento, una sensación clara de envejecimiento.

(T.) Le comuniqué mi hallazgo a XYa en lo que resultó ser una conversación breve, sin altisonancias. Sólo una carcajada, en tono agudo, un cabeceo indicando asentimiento. Inmediatamente me relevó de mis funciones. Antes de despedirme de su consultorio por última vez me entregó las restantes primeras hojas de esta (su) introducción. Dijo que no interferiría con mi publicación del volumen ni cuestionaría mi autoría siempre y cuando incluyera su introducción. Acepté. Cuando leí lo que están por leer me maravillé de su imaginación malevolente (aunque precisa aún desarrollar sus dotes de escritora ya que, en mi opinión, emula demasiado y demasiados autores aclamados). ¿Cómo podían ocurrírsele semejantes relatos tortuosos de los hechos? ¿Cómo pudo haber pergeñado mi completa desaparición de la escena al declarar que mi libreto era anónimo? La venganza y la victimización dramatizada ¿son fuentes o efectos del mal?

LOS ANGELES, 3 DE MAYO DEL 2000

[Original: Nota de la Libretista como Traductora/Editora: *A continuación, y cumpliendo con lo prometido, incluyo la introducción que escribiera la Bruja a la planeada publicación de los documentos compilados. Aclaración: he tomado algunas decisiones editoriales para aliviar el trabajo de los lectores. El texto original, tal como me lo pasó XYa, incluye algunas secciones en español y otras en inglés. Me atrevo a interpretar que los cambios de idioma siguen las instancias de posesión a las que se vio sujeta en el transcurso de la producción de este escrito. Admito, sin embargo, que ésta es una especulación basada en mi propia experiencia como escritora a partir de la etapa de aprendiz de médium a la que me sometí por su exigencia. Es bien sabido que los poseídos suelen hablar en lenguas varias, incluso desconocidas y hasta muertas. Las encarnaciones de los diferentes visitantes explicarían este curioso fenómeno. De allí tal vez las referencias de XYa a una supuesta asociación entre el trance, la transubstanciación y la traducción, esta última como translocación de conductos, vías o vehículos de comunicación encarnados en el lenguaje. Deduzco que estas extrañas inferencias se aplican también a la escritura. Las alusiones que hace XYa a la corporalidad así lo hacen suponer. Mi nota como traductora bilingüe (por parte doble), entonces, es la siguiente: los originales de XYa, que aparecerán en inglés o español según sea el caso, estarán identificados por una O. entre paréntesis (O.) a comienzo del párrafo correspondiente; mis traducciones, del español al inglés o viceversa, aparecerán precedidas por una T. entre paréntesis (T.). Además, y con el mismo fin de facilitar la lectura, me*

he permitido reorganizar el texto de manera de presentar primero el texto completo en inglés y, a continuación, en español (ver página 34). No he pedido autorización a la autora (XYa) para ejecutar este trastocamiento que considero plenamente justificado. Ahora sí, la versión de XYa de los hechos.]

[Traducción: Librettist qua Editor/Translator's Note: *Following and in keeping with my promise, I include the Witch's introduction to the planned publication of the compiled documents. Clarification: I have made some editorial decisions in order to lighten the readers' work. The original text, as handed to me by XYa, includes some sections in English and some in Spanish. I dare to interpret that the language switches follow the instances of possession to which she was subjected while producing these writings. I admit, however, that this is a speculation based on my own experience as a writer since I undertook an apprenticeship as a medium, which she demanded of me. It is well known that the possessed often speak in tongues, including unknown and even dead languages. The incarnations of different guests would explain this curious phenomenon. Thus, perhaps, XYa's references to a supposed association between trance, transubstantiation, and translation, the latter as a translocation of ducts, conduits, or vehicles of communication incarnated in language. I suppose that these strange inferences also apply to writing. XYa's allusions to corporeality have led me to believe this. My note as bilingual translator (in a redoubled sense) is then as follows: XYa's originals, appearing in English or Spanish as might be the case, will be identified by an O in parentheses (O.) at the beginning of each corresponding paragraph; my translations, from Spanish into English and vice versa, will appear preceded by a parenthetical T (T.). In addition, and with the same purpose of facilitating the reading, I have permitted myself to reorganize the text so as to present in a block, first, the complete text in English, and then, the complete text in Spanish (see page 34). I have not requested the author's (XYa's) authorization for executing this translocation since I consider it fully justified. And now XYa's version of the facts.]*

XYa's (Planned) Introduction/La (Planeada) Introducción de XYa

(T.) I take advantage of this moment of lucidity (it might be a trance, and it is definitely transient) to clarify that I ignore the origin, or more precisely the author of the libretto of this *tangópera* (an infelicitous name for what seems to be a new genre of entertainment). This is not so regarding the characters that appear represented in it, with a certain amount of creative license. Not only do I recognize them, but I know them rather well, almost better than I would have liked. (I will attempt to keep my desires at the margins of these lines.) And here I must specify that even though they have been in my presence, in flesh and blood so to speak, on a few opportunities (in some cases only once), I have acquainted myself with their destinies, with their histories, and even with their personalities. This has come through their notes and writings, which I have been recuperating—documents authored by these characters (whom in their roles as authors I should actually address as persons). I attempt to explain the following: Angora Matta (a.k.a. Angora Kils), Mariano Monteamor, and the rest are persons of my acquaintance. They have been present in my office on Pringles Street. I have gotten to know about their pasts, about their presents, and in broader strokes about their futures while in states of trance, my work technique. My memories of the occurrences during those moments of trance or possession are fragmentary. By this I mean that I do not exactly remember all I get to know or learn during working hours. Not all consultations generate in me this particular interest. Actually there have not been that many occasions on which I have decided to recuperate, complete, or define the details of a history or person arrived in my office. This time, however, something different happened.

(T.) On a scorching afternoon I was handed through the mail and with no return address an envelope containing a libretto titled *Angora Matta:* Tangópera-*Thriller* . . . et cetera. I set it aside, assuming that it was a mistake. That same day, at a different time, the name "Angora" triggered a cascade of associations. I remembered or believed I recognized, imprecisely, a certain familiarity. In a moment of respite between clients, I returned, stung by curiosity, to the envelope and its contents. The text was presented in two columns in Spanish and English. Not without a couple of interruptions I began learning about a dramatic plot that included me. I appeared there as the Witch or the *Poseída (la Bruja)*, in a scene in the second act: "At the Witch's Office" (*En el Consultorio de la Bruja*). At first, of course, I thought that the Witch or Bruja was one of those, let us say, generic foreseers, healers, or mediums, any of those types that frequently pepper a story, just like nuns, virgins, orphans, bastards and other liminal characters. Little by little, however, the images and circumstances evoked started producing in me more-concrete feelings of recognition than the ones usually generated by pure imagination. I will not describe the exact genealogy of this process. Suffice it to say that at some point I understood that this fiction was no such thing (actually, an irrelevant issue and a corroboration of something well known to literary experts, although still a matter of dispute among ethnographers).

(T.) What is interesting, then, is that I discovered that the reality hidden in this work of fiction contained me as a referent and, more precisely, as a reservoir of memory, and to my horror, of the Memory of Power. I do not know how crucial it is to clarify for my readers (the fact that the work is bilingual makes my assessment of the audience's knowledge difficult) the danger to which such an irresponsibility on the part of the author or authors exposed me. Outraged by this lack of sensitivity, oversight, or deliberate manipulation, I launched the necessary investigations in order to reveal the author's identity and initiate a suit for wrongs and damages that would clear me of guilt, charges, and suspicions. Very well. And so we arrive at how I undertook the labor of tracing one by one all the other characters in this infamous work. I suspected that they had been victims of the same bad faith. Briefly: I was not able to establish personal contact; I succeeded in taking hold of the writings some of them had left in the hands of friends and relatives; and I never found out the name or identity of the author. And that is where begins the story of this book, which, on the advice of my lawyer, I decided to publish as an anthology.

(T.) I thus include the tangópera in its totality, as it fell into my hands, along with some author's notes, and a selection of the writings and documents produced by some of its protagonists. These are Elvira Díaz, ethnographer; Manuela Malva, film critic; and Angora Matta, poet and philosopher. I appreciate the kind collaboration of their families and acquaintances. They provided some invaluable data, in particular concerning the complex identity of the above-mentioned that, with their explicit consent, I will deliver. The information at my disposal indicates that each of these persons (like most inhabitants of this world) carries out a double (if not multiple) life. Hence their identities are complex. Their acquaintances in particular were interested in discussing what we might call their nocturnal identities, which, in certain cases, coincide with illicit or at least unacceptable activities. (In this regard, see Elvira Díaz's work in this volume.)

(T.) Readers can appreciate such existential complexities when comparing some of the characters' diverse facets as they appear represented in the tangópera's libretto and through the interests they proclaim in their writings. Thus, we encounter Elvira Díaz, a relentless *milonguera* who simultaneously writes her ethnographic observations about this nocturnal practice; Manuela Malva, drawn to drinks and cafés, who dreams of becoming a tango singer but who earns a decent living as a foreign-film critic; and Angora, who sometimes adopts Matta as her last name and at other times goes by Kils (a fact that raises my suspicions concerning the truthfulness of either name), about whom we learned very little. It would seem that Angora is an urban ex-guerrilla, who went into exile probably in Europe or Mexico in the 1970s. The events of life led her to reside in Los Angeles, where she enjoys a rather comfortable situation. The aforementioned libretto would indicate that she works as a hit woman. The brief writings I have recuperated, with great effort, make me think that perhaps this is true, given her obsessive references to a knife, death, and evil. Mariano Monteamor, another one whom I had great interest in contacting, remains obscure. I could not obtain direct, trustworthy information or documentation. I gathered only gossip: that he is a crook, that he is cute, that he is a bum, that he is a poor devil, that he is a hustler, and other such things that are quite characteristic in nocturnal and tango environments. Regarding the rest of the men, most of them powerful (the President, the Detectives, the Politicians), I will state the obvious: they had others deny their presence or they personally denied all relationships between fact and fiction. Among the many who contributed to elucidate these matters that kept me awake, milongueros and milongueras were the most valuable, despite their discreet nature. I continue in their debt, repaying them to the extent to which I am able with my professional services.

(T.) Finally, I wish to thank my literary agent, and I also would like to tackle the problematic issue of my motivation so as to avert ungenerous speculations. This publication is not the product of wills to riches or fame, but a gesture, which some will deem contemptuous, toward vengeance. In what follows I will qualify this drive in order to orient those drawn by analytic exaggeration. I believe I have the right to contextualize this tangópera by adding the documentation that I have deemed pertinent. That is all. I consider that just as the author (male or female) took the liberty of making use of me and of my work as simple objects around which to interweave imaginary, "creative" interpretations, without my knowledge or consent, and without stopping to consider the potentially nasty effects this could have on my reputation and even (and I tremble at the thought of it) on my existence, I believe myself, I repeat, to be justified when I dare to respond with this act. My response in no way measures up to the covert arrogance of the artist or academic at issue, who had no shame in making of me (and, I suspect, of the rest of the protagonists) a strange dramatic parody with clearly compromising ideological bents. In so many words, the author created an exotic manifesto in which, despite my brief intervention (more precisely, in scene 13 of act 2), I carry the leading voice of a so-called Memory of Power.

(T.) In sum, mine is an attempt at reappropriation of identity, an exercise of my own creative freedom, as much as a call for attention. What do we understand by artistic responsibility? Discussing this point entails revisiting the issue of power in relation to this anonymous work and, of course, to the reconfiguration of it that I am pursuing. I understand that this will sound rather enigmatic, but I proceed nevertheless. This compilation assumes a deliberate and overly ambitious intent. I seek, in a word, to reappropriate my fate. In order to do so I rely on a technique of re-presentation and framing that, preserving the original (in this case the texts themselves, without any intervention whatsoever on my part, for I would consider that a profanation), manages to transfigure the meaning and the signifying locus. The essence, thus, is maintained intact and at the same time changes, as in a magic trick, when one who was only a character (an other) is situated as the figure of authority, as the voice and viewpoint. As a coherent and unquestioned body. (This at least at the moment when the reader or spectator submits herself or himself to experience the work in any form: by buying the ticket or book, the mere gesture of moving to the library, bookstore, or theater, of opening the pages or taking a seat in the dark, and so on, regardless of the ulterior decision to interrupt or abandon the reading or the locale in anticipation of the end established by the author or director. The same could be said for the preestablished intentions of the subject or receptor, who, to give an example, enters the experience of someone else's work with resistances or suspicions and nevertheless places himself or herself in the hands of this leadership, perhaps for no other reason than to confirm his or her suspicions or to exert a biting critique.) I interrupt now. I recognize a dilettantism of sorts in these last reflections. It tends to be the symptom that evidences the beginning of a new wave of trances, jointly with the loosening of the tongue.

(T.) It would be irresponsible of me not to confess my efforts to keep myself attached to this light coherence.

(O.) Librettist qua Editor/Translator's Note: *After careful consideration I have decided to include the following essay where XYa placed it, that is, as a part of her planned introduction. It definitely reads like an independent piece, a whole other genre, but it is informative here in several regards. (T.) First, XYa was absolutely fixated on differentiating herself from my tangópera's character, who, in her view, dangerously distorted her intentions, interests, and even her being. In that work, as you will see in part II of this volume, the Witch plays the part of an influential ideologue, a historian as well as an analyst of power, of the exertion of domination and exploitation. I estimate that XYa wrote the following sketchy philosophical essay in order to counter potential political contaminations and to reassert her reputation as a serious professional, one fully devoted to studying the traffic of substances and potencies. Second (to go beyond pondering her manipulations or her duplicity), this short essay shows her making incursions into deep philosophical issues that, although somehow* unrigorous, reflect a sincere commitment to the understanding of old anthropological questions. *Apparently prompted by the exigencies of her practice, and regrettably without the necessary tools, she sets herself to work on the enigmas or aporias that lie at the crossroads of what she calls* corporeality, *which, after ruminating coarsely on the pitfalls of this concept, she proposes to address through* transubstantiation. *Thus, she considers it advantageous, from what I can tell, to focus on a process ("mechanics," to use her word) rather than on a thing. Her practice as a witch relies fundamentally on possession or mediumlike techniques. (She often makes reference to "visits" that seem to take her over, or at least to confound her identity by instilling other viewpoints, sensations, and memories into her . . . and here is when the questioning begins: Into her body? Into her mind? Into her consciousness? Into her soul?) These activities apparently place her corporeality and her identity at risk—the tone of her observations denotes some fear. Her profession does not allow her to find easy refuge in those accepted (though, to her, artificially drawn) severed connections between mind, body, soul, consciousness, corporeality, subjectivity, identity, rationality, and experience. Her visitors transform her; they never quite take over, and they never quite leave. Her writings, supplemented by the observations I was able to make during my own brief apprenticeship, suggest that it is necessary to make a paradigm shift in order to account for these kinds of phenomena. XYa is not so interested in capturing the transformations of each body, soul, subjectivity, or identity in isolation, so to speak, as they enter, they go through and terminate contact with one another. That atomistic model would miss the point.*

(O.) *In XYa's view, I think, we must grapple with the contact itself and the trafficking of substances involved. She seems to concern herself with the quantities, qualities, speeds, directionalities, and other properties and behaviors that pertain to transubstantiation per se, and not so much with the discrete entities involved. Things and beings connect with each other and to each other and exchange substances, in the process transforming themselves and their surroundings. Nobody and nothing would be strictly the same as it was before entering in contact (and thus establishing a traffic of substances and potentialities). Several key factors remain unclear; I will mention only a few. In my opinion, "contact" is a misleading designation for the process XYa is attempting to grasp. "Co-presence," as she proposes at some point, alludes more precisely to the apparently constant and uncontrollable traffic that includes the real and the imagined, the visible and the invisible, solids as well as nonsolids, the living and the inert, the conscious, the indifferent, and the aloof. (I can see, however, that "co-presence" might in turn convey a rather static picture, where the traffic itself runs the risk of getting lost.) A treatment of the shape and configuration of the beings, things, and forces involved before, during, and after undergoing this process, is also missing from her account. The crucial relationship between form and content, and their specific ways of responding to co-presence remains obscure. I would be interested, for example, in knowing how to address the aggregation of entities (social and individual, and at both the corporeal and the psychological levels) that momentarily conforms to one forceful directionality combining diverse intentionalities. A revolution or a movement of social resistance comes to mind, as well as conformism and generalized apathy. Following this thought I would speculate that physically discrete bodies with a sense of singular consciousness come together to configure a massive intentional force that might or might not be sharing the same space at the same time, and yet make up a social (moral and political) corporeality that nevertheless contains different factions or clusters of interests in a volatile and viscous state of negotiation. Prominent political philosophers have dealt with these issues and advanced analytical and explanatory models concerning how this process operates (Antonio Gramsci [1971], Antonio Negri [1999], Ernesto Laclau and Chantal Mouffe [1985], and others). I wonder if XYa's speculations point to what specifically happens in that moment of coming together, a close-up, as it were, on the crisscrossing not of interests but of senses, a term that would allow for contemplating irrational inclinations as well as rational choices, decisions and indecisions, unexpected interventions (memories and desires as well as a sudden storm, a flat tire, a back pain, a fallen tree on the road), and tangible as well as intangible aspects of what makes up thoughts and feelings. I realize that XYa's conceptual choices follow a quite different agenda. She is clearly wary about entering into the field of politics. She seems to be interested in legitimizing her practice in a way that will distinguish it from nonsense and madness. Her writings (more than our verbal exchanges) show that her ways of knowing do follow reasoning paths, but not a strict logic.*

(O.) XYa thinks that thoughts are particular kinds of feelings (we know/say we are thinking and not dreaming because we feel it is different, she says; we also say we remember and we sense, distinguishing them from thinking because we make distinctions within codifications of feelings). We discussed phenomenology a bit, but XYa is taken aback by the prescribed practice of epoge, the distancing technique that she learned from a visiting Argentine ethnographer trained at the Universidad de Buenos Aires during the dictatorship of the 1970s. (The visitor alluded to commented that her teacher, an Italian fascist refugee, applied phenomenology to the study of myths among native populations who insisted on polluting his work with everyday information, insignificant in a scholarly sense, concerning material livelihood. He was invested in preserving their culture, not their lives.) She would not venture any further into transubstantiations in that direction. (She believes that books, words, and the act of

*reading participate in the traffic of substances—thus the so-called
affinity, which others address in aesthetic terms, at play in our theoretical
choices.) When pressed to establish some working definitions of what she
understood by "feelings," "thoughts," "words," and "concepts" (I wanted
to map a common ground), XYa dismissed me under the pretense of undergoing post-trance stress. I was able to reshuffle and piece together,
however, some of her thoughts, feelings, and beliefs on these matters.*

*(O.) To semanticist arguments, which she seems to embrace, she responds
(personal communication, June 2000) with Hannah Arendt that "they are
absolutely right: in the final analysis all problems are linguistic problems;
they simply do not know the implications of what they are saying"
(Arendt 1969: 49). (T.) I think she meant that, at least in what concerns
her practice, it just cannot be left at that. Words are things with sensorial
and affective properties and ethical repercussions. (O.) In this essay, in
an incomplete note, she discusses citation in this regard to some extent.
She relies on Hannah Arendt's introduction to Walter Benjamin's* Illuminations *(1969). Regrettably, she fails to engage with Jacques Derrida
(1988), Gayatri Spivak's reading of Derrida (1980), and Judith Butler's
reading of Derrida and omission of Spivak (1993). (In this regard, see
Jeff Tobin 1999.) Those readings (and concomitant transubstantiations
might have led XYa to some interesting reflections. For example, she could
have elaborated on the differences at stake between considering citation
from the viewpoint of iteration—the physics of repetition, as it were—and
her own preoccupation with the exchange of substances at play in the
same operation.*

*(O.) I have in mind her concerns with viscosity, for example (an issue she
brought up precisely as a proof of my misrepresentations of her in the
tangópera, given that in scene 13 the Witch makes use of viscosity to analyze the workings of power). How does that property of clinging and
sticking that substances possess in certain states—neither solid nor liquid,
that move at a rather low speed, generating a certain expectant and re-
volting reaction one might say due to their seeming indecisive behavior—
how does it intervene in the making and unmaking of corporealities, the
blurring and shaping of identities, and the circulation of words? (To this
effect she could have conjured Jean-Paul Sartre (1956, 1964) and Mary
Douglas (1984), as well as Eduardo Savigliano, a nuclear engineer who,
at my request, contributed the following from the viewpoint of experimental physics: (T.) "According to the mechanics of fluids, viscosity is the resistance to displacement shown by some molecules of the fluid in respect to
others. Actually all fluids [gases and liquids] are, to a greater or lesser
degree, viscous. A fluid with null viscosity is a mathematical abstraction
and it does not exist in reality. As a consequence of viscosity, when a fluid
is agitated, the rubbing between the molecules, which displace themselves*

*at different speeds, generates heat, and the fluid increases in tempera-
ture. Solids are different from gases and liquids in that their intercorpus-
cular forces resist relative displacements and generate their relative im-
penetrability. (A certain diffusion of one solid into another can be
produced under great pressures, as is the case in cold lamination)" (personal communication, June 2000). I am working on how to apply these
findings to cold and heated communications, encounters and disencoun-
ters. This neglected viscous property could revolutionize our understandings of subjectivity and corporeality by emphasizing our actual connections, our "clinging" and sticking to each other, despite all efforts to
silence and dismiss these pulls. It could transform conceptualizations of
self-centered subjectivity that assume discrete separateness between bodies, bodies that coincide with selves. It could make us aware of the efforts
invested in creating differentiation and separation, challenging the notion
that communication follows individual singularity. It would show, much
to the contrary, that we come into being viscously connected with others
and are ideologically pressed into cultivating a sense of corporeal and
subjective discreet, discriminated and discriminating, separation that can
be overcome only with attempts at rational communication. The ethico-
political import of these reflections, including potential controversies, is
truly promising.*

*(O.) She could have discussed how citation and iteration bring along, then,
not only the cited thing but the fact of the visitation, the traffic of substances at play in the connection. This in turn would have allowed her to
confront current ideas on identity and "performativity," perhaps because
she could have redirected—revitalized, as it were—concerns with the
process (by now sanitized) of subject formation and identity constitution
by focusing not solely on differentiation but also on how permeable those
boundaries are, constantly crossed by substances that in different states,
at different speeds, and with different properties transit between beings
and beings, beings and things, the real and the imagined, the conscious
and the unconscious. And they do so gently or aggressively, poisoning and
blessing, with or without intentions and interests, transforming regardless
of the composition and state of that and those involved in the contact. (If
we were on speaking terms, I would have suggested she read Baruk Spinoza [1989], Gilles Deleuze on Leibnitz and Spinoza [1988, 1989], and
Macedonio Fernández [1990].) And when I write "contact" I do not mean
exclusively touch, but presence. And when I write "presence" I do not
mean that it is exclusively cotemporaneous or even cospatialized. This
uncanny traffic—and a seasoned witch like XYa could explain it better
than I—happens at long distances and between past and present times
and even between the living and the dead.*

(O.) This is not about perception and how or where or between what and

what it happens; it is also not about experience processed or recorded in minds or bodies; it is not about the memory of things lived directly or through empathy (as when transmitted through teachings or tradition). I agree with XYa that we learn how to feel and name our feelings. That is not the point I am trying to make. But the point is hers, not mine, although it has been transubstantiated now and sticks in between as it transforms the two of us and itself. And this long note is now inserted, implanted into the body of her text and the texture of her argument. And when I translate it, as I promised her I would, yet another transformation (destruction and revitalization) will occur. And something will drip, falling in between, that will get lost and in that fall will transform its state and perhaps its nature, now matter moving around or in stasis without words attached to it. Is this what she means by corporeality? Or is it what I mean, trying to cling to a word sonorous enough to make a space for translation as a mode of living? And here I mean translation not as the task of the translator engaged in transmitting someone else's senses put into words—the translator who methodically juggles linguistic literalness and poetic intervention so as to capture the choreography and the specific components of an alien writing, which must be mastered as if it were her own and yet kept at that distance that enables respect for an other's opinions, choices, and positions. (For those interested in this kind of translation I suggest reading Idelber Avelar [1999], Gayatri Spivak [1993, 1999], Walter Benjamin [1969], and Jacques Derrida [1985, 1998].)

(O.) The translator I have in mind perhaps deserves another name. She lives in translation. She constantly translates others and herself, back and forth between two languages that pertain to different cultural universes; and when she writes, she anticipates the translation to come. (T.O.T.O.T.) And the original might make its appearance in either language, and the ensuing translation—because it is a product of autotranslating herself and not of translating an alien other (although the self-translator might be taken for an other that translates herself, but not as other as others)—will be set to correct, embellish, question, and further the original rather unproblematically. And thus the translation becomes the original that, in turn, is prepared to be translated back. (T.) This obsessive, relentless translator (and I swear I am simplifying her task) senses there is something lost in the words that come and go, something substantial to her practice that is not a thing but a movement aimed at connecting, transmitting, or accomplishing a transit, a traffic of substances and energies. I wish I could write about it without recourse to anthropomorphisms, metaphysics, models borrowed from physics, and even the humanities (whether humanistic or antihumanistic). But what bothers me most is the clinicalization, the clinical judgment that keeps creeping in. I fear this is madness.

(O.) Back to XYa's essay on corporeality. Her words (which preceded mine) follow.]

(T.) I study the body, but I am not an anatomist. My interest in corporeality has driven me to a topic that is neither the soul in the religious sense, nor the spirit of the occultists, and also not the psyche of the psychologists and psychoanalysts. Corporeality is relevant to the bodies that have a certain consciousness of themselves (consciousness is an overly loaded, much philosophically used and abused concept, thus my "certain" consciousness), simultaneously false and precise, depending on whether particular spatiotemporal articulations—here and now, there and then, and so on—or whether specific isolated dimensions of complex relationships—class, gender, race, and so on—are adopted as frames of reference. Corporeality is a ubiquitous sense that positions the subject and generates orientation, like a compass. Things, others, and "the lived" [*vivencias*] (the reality principle) organize around it. Corporeality and identity are two conceptual elaborations that attempt to explain the same (thing) and fail at it: that feeling of unicity (uniqueness and unity) that distinguishes individual singularity. We know how important the intervention of others is in establishing the limits of that contour. We know that there is a clear physical referent, despite its substantial transformations in the course of that which we call life. We do not know the exact proportions in which language and the social, biology and the sensorial participate in this combination. We also do not know specifically how they articulate in order to create that which is me or an other. Misunderstandings proliferate (for instance, that others are bodies that develop their own consciousness; that there is no language without the biological base that allows its articulation; that without thought [without words] bodies do not know that they know they are; and that without sociality there is no corporeality, and without language [that is, without thought] there is no sociality.)

(T.) Language is socialized thought; and we know of thought only through the language that shapes it. If there is thought prior to or outside of language, we are supposed to call it emotion, feeling, or affect. (This is without attempting to produce exact definitions, given that specificity would require language.) Corporeality (the concept) is thus a maneuver aimed at recuperating what escapes the nets of language, and it resists (actually, some are interested in making it resist) accepted nominalism and even, in some cases, nominalisms to come. Those devoted to undoing the mind-body divide run up against these basic difficulties and fall into idealism or materialism—the notions of corporeality and identity, experience and discourse—in order to continue on their speculative or interpretative roads. This drives some disappointed (at times defeated) ones to question the validity of the intellectual (analytic or critical) tradition. Devotees of spirituality, artists, and even some scientists and humanistic thinkers that adhere to one or another kind of pragmatism prefer to leave these interrogations aside and set their bearings in other directions. They say they are uninterested in this play of mirrors. It is known that some cut off ropes, follow their own ways, and live more or less happily. This is not my case. I continue.

(T.) The corporeality that interests me is also not that connection or cultivation of mind-body balance sought by yogis or through transcendental meditation (generally combined exercises that, as in an ambush maneuver, play on two fronts—physical training and control of the mind—in order to harmonize energies into a holistic universe). I am not interested in revealing mysteries; there are no mysteries, only ignorance. I do not believe in ghosts; (O.) I do think that beings adopt different substantial states (different chemical and physical properties), fully composed of matter and its transformations.

(T.) What non-coopted concept could I apply, then, to this tangibility (I do not want to say "tangible reality" because I am not an empiricist either) of the unexplained (which I do not consider unexplainable)? I am fascinated by the traps of language, and even though I tend to accept that words draw us closer to "things" (including experiences) at the same time as they take us away from them, I do not live that way on an everyday basis. (In everyday life and away from professional obligations, I use all the approaches I have just discarded.) Why then that obsessive interest in corporeality, the reality of which I do not question but which I consider impossible to verbalize (and in saying that I include "to think")? I do not wish to find shelter in that pluglike concept that is "experience," that mixture of pagan vitalism, materialist intentionality, apparently pragmatic idealism, and heretical spiritualism. Phenomenology horrifies me. I find it impossible to trust metaphysics as a basis for my professional practice. I have carefully studied the ways in which these principles are juxtaposed and cover up for each other. We know that without subjectivity there is no sense of experience (loose experiences, without subjects to which to attach themselves, are unthinkable) and that subjectivity is the sum of acts of subjection, of forced definitions, of violent delimitations. If the insistence on corporeality is an act of protest against rationality and its limitations (that is, a politico-philosophical act), how do we discuss its particularities with coherent arguments? How do we revindicate the body without strengthening the body-mind division that situates the body in a place of marginalized difference? And how do we work on the non-difference (without falling into indifference)? For a specialist in the manipulation of incorporations, who refuses to believe in spirits, these questions are crucial and obsessive.

Hence my interest in transubstantiation or the transformation of substances, not in the alchemists' sense, but in the sense of the spatiotemporal borrowings, implants, dislocations and translocations that affect corporeality and its senses, its cultural and historical memories.

(T.) Readers should consider that in this office we practice what in vulgar lingo goes by the name of "possession," a term that in my view distorts the facts by obtrusively introducing a metaphysical bias. Our daily routine consists in a traffic of substances, of materialities of diverse composition and characteristics (weights, densities, temperatures, etc.) with different behavioral natures. We recompose, let us say, corporealities. We have not been able to establish with precision to what extent those contacts affect the state of the visiting and visited entities. We definitely observe the transformations, the fluidity or rejection with which the contacts develop—in sum, the more or less positive or negative effects. The duration (persistence or ephemerality) of these transubstantiations is unclear. Undoubtedly there are residual effects, symptoms of the "occupation," which, I insist, does not amount to a simple replacement of one being's interiority by another. This, sirs, is not to set an alien fruit into the empty shell of a nut. It is not the metamorphosis of the wolfman either. Personally, I am interested in the materiality rather than in the logic of these processes; but I cannot work without those shy steps that characterize rationality (that fantasylike system with which we believe we tame the ignored). (Others explain this much better than I.) How do I get at those physical principles already infested themselves by the language that defines and constrains them? I repeat that I trust neither experience nor rationality. When it comes to explicating something, orally or in writing, words are there with their tyranny. I ask myself, then, could there be a rest of something (sensible or nonsensical) that escapes between the cracks of one language and another, something that leaks in between two languages that attempt to refer to or to construct the same? Translation. Would it be helpful to reflect on translation? Translation as transubstantiations of emotional places, shaped by words that speak would-be thoughts. A whole play of masked masks.

(T.) My blood freezes (or my thoughts congeal) when I imagine (and what is that?) the scared reactions and, even worse, those of boredom. . . . Certainly others have discussed these topics before and much better than I do. Some have visited me and I have even read them, and I believe I recall some of them in this . . . but if I return to those memories and texts now, to track down with care what I have assimilated that I do not remember, I will have to go into their thoughts (those strong and enigmatic feelings) as I once did, and now I do not wish to submit myself voluntarily to that transubstantiation of the quotation.

[(T.) XYa's Note: I cannot but betray myself. Walter Benjamin visits me through Hannah Arendt: (O.) "Quotations in my works are like robbers by the roadside who make an armed attack and relieve an idler of his convictions" (Benjamin, in Arendt 1969: 38). (T.) Quotations (which I resist) in his view have the ability to awaken, to cut the fluidity of arguments by inserting themselves with concentrated and in the last instance destructive force. For Benjamin the power of quotations is (O.) "not the strength to preserve but to cleanse, to tear out of context, to destroy" (Arendt 1969: 39). Bibliomaniac turned collector of quotations, he aspired to write an entire text composed of quotations. His project was revolutionary. (T.) It elicits my interest because of its complications and because his proposed methodology is opposite mine, although both converge in keeping faith in a rather unconventional materiality. I continue.

(T.) In Benjamin, and to some extent in the brilliant reading that Arendt devotes to him, quotation's destructive force operates at two opposite ends. (In order to follow them I here make use of my familiarity with corporeal trafficking.) On the one hand, quotation poisons the discursive body where it is inserted; on the other hand, it cuts out the original context or body from which it is torn off. The quote would extrapolate a concentrated and valuable aspect of a past body into a present one. In this process of revitalization through destruction, quotes would be agents of contact between the past and the present. Thus, tradition would reconfigure itself as the memory of an alien body that is also familiar, and even owned. (I would add here that this uncanny diachronic aspect should be complemented by the synchronic one pertaining to interculturality, the avatars of co-temporal contacts of different traditions and the devastations and revolutionary potentials that mark the bodies subjected to various deterritorializing traffics: exiles, immigrants, refugees, tourists, travelers, all set to their own particular dynamics of assimilation, preservation, and re-creation of cultural memories—millions of simultaneous destructions and revitalizations that change signs even during each singular life. I am thinking of those who leave and dream of returning, of the one who wants to go away and cannot, of the one who left and comes back and cannot find herself, of the one who comes and goes as if nothing had happened. How many bodies, strange and yet one's own, appropriated and rejected with such diverse intensities, with such disparate consequences, incoherent and inconsistent, diligently destroying others and themselves so as to remain alive? I make them present with this quotation.)

(T.) Here I make yet another aside to explain that Benjamin did not trust communication, and that for him the force of quotations had nothing to do with the interpretations or explanations that often precede or follow

them. Quotation in itself—the mechanics at play in quoting—is what matters; but also quality. And at this point we face the problem of identifying that which is worth citing, not for the sake of communicating but rather for the sake of transmitting. How do we detect the citable? And how can citation transmit despite the destruction it generates?

(T.) Benjamin offers truth as a guide; he trusts the consistence of truth. Once again (as I see it) we are placed in the domain of the properties of substances. "Tradition transforms truth into wisdom, and wisdom is the consistence of transmissible truth" (Arendt 1969: 41). I understand those many who dwelled and still dwell on the origins of that truth and its arrival in the world of humans, and the concomitant problem of authority, but here I am interested in the issues of the consistence of truth and of the identifier of consistencies. What constitutes the consistence of truth? Should we look into the constitutive substance of truth or in its properties and movements, such as in transmissibility? To which I add—and I apologize for piling up so many questions—who and what is the one, the she or he, that assumes the task of identifying the truth?

(T.) The responses, as could be foreseen, come back all mixed up. Arendt writes that Benjamin, like a good collector, "entrusted himself to chance as a guide on his intellectual journey of exploration" (1969: 43). This thinking method, in her view, follows Benjamin's disposition toward flanerie, the privileged activity of those professional observers who would stroll the streets of the world's capital cities with the sole responsibility of taking intellectual delight in the high or low impressions that their socially confounded fellow citizens inflict upon the flaneur's exquisite sensibilities. This occupation of the chosen unemployed was already extinct in Benjamin's time, though he longed to practice it in the agitated Europe of the first half of the twentieth century. Apparently—and following Arendt, who deserves my trust and respect—Benjamin refused to become a part of the army of society's useful members, and thus he refused to define his function as an intellectual (and to use their methods). On one occasion, however, a phrase betrayed him indicating that he would have liked to be (O.) "the only true critic of German literature" (his friend Scholem tells about it in a letter). And in the introduction to Elective Affinities (1924, 1925), his essay on Goethe, he writes that "critique is concerned with the truth content of a work of art. . . . The critic ask[s] the basic question of all criticism—namely, whether the work's shining truth content is due to its subject matter or whether the survival of the subject matter is due to the truth content. For as they come apart in the work, they decide on its immortality. In this sense the history of works of art prepares their critique, and this is why historical distance increases their power" (in Arendt 1969: 4–5).

(T.) To this brilliant wandering path of thoughts (which I avoid editing and tailoring even further for my own sake so as to retain Benjamin's curious exploratory movement and to practice his teachings on citation—I destroy his, he destroys mine—mediated in this case by my translation of another translation and hence by a chain of transubstantiations, and all of the above without losing—is it not amazing?—the subject matter that keeps all of us involved in this busy, and that, I dare to remind you, just in case, is "truth") I will add now another piece that I cut out from a previous citation. This pertains to the comparison Benjamin establishes between the critic and the commentator—a comparison that allows him to say what he wishes regarding the role he is determined to attribute to the critic. (O.) I cite:

> If, to use a simile, one views the growing work as a funeral pyre, its commentator can be likened to the chemist, its critic to an alchemist. While the former is left with wood and ashes as the sole objects of his analysis, the latter is concerned only with the enigma of the flame itself: the enigma of being alive. Thus the critic inquires about the truth whose living flame goes on burning over the heavy logs of the past and the light ashes of life gone by. (in Arendt 1969: 5)

Arendt (the cited citer) comments on and/or critiques Benjamin's passage as follows:

> The critic as an alchemist practicing the obscure art of transmuting the futile elements of the real into the shining, enduring gold of truth, or rather watching and interpreting the historical process that brings about such magical transfiguration—whatever we may think of this figure, it hardly corresponds to anything we usually have in mind when we classify a writer as a literary critic. (Arendt 1969: 5)

It seems clear that the critic, who is more of an alchemist than a chemist (and not exactly like either of them), is a transmuter and transmitter, and not one who pretends to understand. (O.) This critic, who identifies as he transforms in order to effect the transmissibility of truth (all this through the practice of citation, to which I add translation), "preserves 'the intention of such investigations [the cited studies],' namely, 'to plumb the depths of language and thought . . . by drilling rather than excavating' (Briefe I, 329), so as not to ruin everything with explanations that seek to provide a causal or systematic connection" (Benjamin, in Arendt 1969: 48). (T.) Benjamin (and Arendt cites him in this regard but I will skip that) recognizes a certain pedantry and obscurantism in this proposal, but he prefers it to interpretive falsifying.
(T.) I admit that I am attracted by this method of thinking and way of life (my experience with flaneurs is rather limited but I am well acquainted

with their close relatives: the ethnographers who often come to me either conjured or as clients). But given my limitations (historical, social, and personal), I have to work for a living. Frankly, I make ends meet day by day with what this practice—which is almost a vocational one—provides me. These times of economic stringency and of unemployment stampedes have notoriously affected the flux of clients, so it might be worth clarifying that my practice relies to a great extent on chains of recommenders. In sum, my circumstances dictate not so much practical as practicable reflections and, whenever possible, effective ones. Now I go back to the issue of consistency, having given my readers some tools for evaluating my preference for the road of transmissibility. Truth, like the nugget of gold or the market's preferred stock, takes its consistency through its mode of circulation or transmissibility.

(O.) *Benjamin, in Arendt's reading, regards truth as an acoustic phenomenon, and privileges the word and especially the quoted word (rather than the sentence) as that which zeroes in on truth. Words, written or silent, as in thoughts, carry through the "consistence" of truth and to my taste (which is different from Benjamin's and Arendt's) make truth possible and impossible.]*

[(T.) Librettist qua Editor/Translator's Note: *The introduction through which XYa planned to guide the readers of these collected writings stops here, interrupted. Some loose paragraphs follow this note, more incoherent than the previous ones. I suppose they are notes, ideas on which she thought she would continue working. Or maybe they are discarded material. Or perhaps they are interventions by "visitors" whose opinions did not elicit her interest. You will notice some inconsistencies and contradictions with the above. I include them here in order to comply in full with my promise to publish her introduction in its entirety.*
Her brief notes follow.]

1. (T.) I wish to make a pact, however, that will sedate those worried with academic conventions to whom I voluntarily submit this book. I must be accountable to someone and now. Very well. I propose that this text be read in its entirety as a long succession of paraphrases, and I renounce any claim to originality. This does not apply to creativity. (On this matter see my reflections above, and I insist that they will resemble others, past and future, and better ones.)

2. (T.) I invite all those who so desire to visit my voluminous library and to check my underlinings and notes in the margins, supplemented on more recent texts with those little yellow Post-It stickers (the invention of a genius) that admit more elaborate comments. I admit that this solution

is scarcely pedagogical, in the sense that the distant circulation of this information remains restricted to personal contact, but I take refuge in the advantages of corporeality. I would not like to declare publicly this tickling doubt that emerges at vulnerable times, and in truth I do not know if it is mine or the internalized voice of authority. (I am referring to laziness and indulgence.) But having finally named these shameful weaknesses, I wish to clarify that I do not ask for clemency. Neurosis, in its adaptive and transgressive movements, prevents me from reaching the bottom of my motivations with absolute honesty.

3. (T.) It is not unusual for the professionally possessed to detect these changes in mood that accompany, literally, the replacement of one animus by another. This transubstantiation, contrary to general opinions, is not altogether left to chance.

4. (T.) Given that my lapses into coherence seem to become shorter and shorter, I have decided to continue these brief introductory notes before I regain full control of the flux of my ideas. I am experiencing the typical exhaustion that precedes abandonment by the visiting entity.

5. (T.) I fear losing these precious moments in which I believe I recognize a voice of my own while going through previous lines. I decide to continue on this note. Time has become my obsession. Urgency, even a sense of emergency, sustains my enterprise. I believe I remember mentioning this recurrent impulse.

6. (O.):

"Thus they lived among three impossibilities . . . : the impossibility of not writing" as they could get rid of their inspiration only by writing; "the impossibility of writing in German"—Kafka considered their use of the German language as the "overt or covert, or possibly self-tormenting usurpation of an alien property, which has not been acquired but stolen, (relatively) quickly picked up, and which remains someone else's possession even if not a single linguistic mistake can be pointed out"; and finally, "the impossibility of writing differently," since no other language was available. "One would almost add a fourth impossibility," says Kafka in conclusion, "the impossibility of writing, for this despair was not something that could be mitigated through writing"—as is normal for poets, to whom a god has given to say what men suffer and endure. Rather, despair has become here "an enemy of life *and* of writing; writing was here only a moratorium, as it is for someone who writes his last will and testament just before he hangs himself." (Kafka, in Arendt 1969: 31–32)

7. (T.) I herewith deliver the first page of this introduction (and hence complete the transference of such document) in Buenos Aires, May 14, 2000.

[(O.) Librettist qua Editor/Translator's Final Note: I believe I have finally figured out what XYa had in mind when she asked me to include her own drafted introduction as the sole condition for passing on to me the right and responsibility to publish this volume. One obvious reason: to implant doubt. (At this point you may well be wondering whether this whole volume, including the tangópera's libretto, and even I myself are all products of XYa's industrious imagination.) Another one: as a keen observer of contemporary readers' habits, she counted on the quick skimming of most of the text up to the end of this introduction and, consequently, on the reader's taking her words for the last (and true) word. Finally, I have to say I even suspect that XYa wrote these ruminations to humor me, my attempts at understanding and my efforts at translating her, that in the end have generated an opening to this volume cumbersome enough to put off even the most patient and friendly reader. (Los Angeles, 6/15/2000).]

(O.) Aprovecho este momento de lucidez (que tal vez sea un trance, que es definitivamente transitorio) para aclarar que desconozco el origen, o más precisamente el o la autora del libreto de esta tangópera (nombre desafortunado para lo que parece ser un nuevo género de espectáculo). No así a los personajes que aparecen allí representados, con cierta libertad creativa. No sólo los reconozco, sino que los conozco bien, casi mejor de lo que hubiera querido. (Intentaré mantener mis deseos al margen de estas líneas.) Y aquí debo precisar que si bien han estado en mi presencia, en carne y hueso por así decirlo, en pocas oportunidades (en algunos casos sólo una vez), me he compenetrado con sus destinos, con sus historias y hasta con sus personalidades. Esto a través de las notas y escritos que he ido recuperando; documentos de la autoría de estos personajes (a los que en su carácter de autores debiera en realidad referirme como personas). Intento explicitar lo siguiente: Angora Matta (alias Angora Kils), Mariano Monteamor, y los demás, son personas de mi conocimiento. Han estado presentes en mi consultorio de la calle Pringles. Yo supe de sus pasados, de sus presentes y, a grandes rasgos, de sus futuros en estado de trance, mi técnica de trabajo. Mi memoria de lo transcurrido durante los momentos de trance o posesión es fragmentaria. Con esto quiero decir que no recuerdo exactamente todo lo que sé o aprendo en horas de trabajo. No todas las consultas generan en mí este particular interés. En realidad no han sido muchas las oportunidades en que me he propuesto recuperar, completar, o definir los detalles de una historia o persona que llega a verme en tren de consulta. Pero esta vez ocurrió algo distinto.

(O.) Una tarde calurosa llegó a mis manos, por correo y sin remitente, un sobre cuyo contenido era un libreto titulado *Angora Matta: Tangópera-Thriller . . .* etcétera. Lo dejé de lado asumiendo que se trataba de una equivocación. Ese mismo día, en otro momento, el nombre "Angora" desencadenó una cascada de asociaciones. Recordé o creí reconocer, imprecisamente, una familiaridad. En un momento de ocio entre consultas volví al sobre y a su contenido, aguijoneada por la curiosidad. El texto estaba presentado en castellano e inglés, a dos columnas. No sin un par de interrupciones, me fui enterando de una trama dramática que me incluía. Allí figuraba yo como la Bruja o la Poseída (*the Witch*), en una escena del segundo acto: "En el consultorio de la Bruja" (*At the Witch's Office*). Por supuesto que en un primer momento pensé que la Bruja o Witch sería una adivina, curandera o médium, genérica digamos, de esas que suelen condimentar cualquier cuento al igual que las monjas, vírgenes, huérfanas, bastardas y demás personajes liminales. Poco a poco, sin embargo, las imágenes y circunstancias evocadas empezaron a producir en mí sensaciones de reconocimiento más concretas que las que suele generar la pura imaginación. No voy a describir la genealogía exacta de este proceso. Baste decir que hubo un momento en el que entendí que esta ficción no era tal (cosa realmente irrelevante y corroboración de algo ya bien sabido entre literatos, si bien aún es materia de disputa entre etnógrafos).

(O.) Lo interesante, entonces, es que descubrí que la realidad escondida en esta obra de ficción me contenía como referente y, más precisamente, como depositaria de la memoria y para mi espanto, de la Memoria del Poder. No sé si estará demás aclarar a los lectores (el hecho de que el escrito sea bilingüe me dificulta evaluar los conocimientos de la potencial audiencia) el peligro en el que me posiciona semejante irresponsabilidad por parte del autor o la autora o los autores. Indignada por esta falta de sensibilidad, ligereza, o manipulación deliberada, emprendí las investigaciones necesarias con el propósito de develar la identidad autoral e iniciar un juicio por daños y perjuicios que me limpiara de culpas, cargos y sospechas. Bien. Y así llegamos a cómo me aboqué a la tarea de rastrear uno por uno a los otros personajes de esta obra infame. Supuse que ellos también habrían corrido mi misma suerte. Para abreviar: no logré contactarlos en persona; conseguí hacerme de los escritos dejados por algunos de ellos en manos de parientes y amigos; jamás pud averiguar el nombre o identidad del autor o autora. Y así se inicia la historia de este libro que, aconsejada por mi abogada, me decidí a publicar como compilación.

(O.) Incluyo, entonces, la tangópera en su totalidad tal como llegó a mis manos, algunas notas del autor/a, y una selección de los escritos y documentos producidos por algunas de sus protagonistas. A saber: Elvira Díaz, etnógrafa; Manuela Malva, crítica de cine; y Angora Matta, poeta y filósofa. Agradezco a sus familiares y amistades su amable colaboración. Me ofrecieron algunos datos invalorables, en particular sobre la compleja identidad de las mencionadas, que con su permiso explícito paso a relatar. Según la información de la que dispongo, estas personas (al igual que la mayoría de los habitantes de este mundo) llevan una doble, sino una múltiple, vida. Sus identidades por lo tanto son complejas. En particular sus allegados estuvieron interesados en abordar lo que podríamos llamar sus identidades nocturnas que, en ciertos casos, coinciden con actividades ilícitas o simplemente poco aceptables. (Ver al respecto el trabajo de Elvira Díaz que incluyo en esta compilación.)

(O.) El lector podrá apreciar dichas complejidades existenciales al comparar las facetas que de algunos han quedado representadas en el libreto de la tangópera con los intereses que se hacen presentes a través de sus propios escritos. Es así cómo nos encontramos con una Elvira Díaz, que al mismo tiempo que es una milonguera empedernida, escribe sus observaciones antropológicas sobre esta actividad nocturna; con una Manuela Malva, dada a los tragos y el café, que sueña con ser cantante de tango pero que se gana la vida dignamente como crítica de cine extranjero; y con Angora, que a veces elige apellidarse Matta y a veces Kils (cosa que me hace sospechar que ninguno de estos nombres es el verdadero), de quien aprendimos bastante poco. Parece ser que Angora es una ex guerrillera urbana, que se habría exiliado en los años setenta tal vez en Europa o México, y que la vida la habría llevado a residir en Los Angeles donde ahora disfruta de una situación acomodada. El mentado libreto indicaría que se dedica al crimen por encargo. Los breves escritos, que he recuperado con gran esfuerzo y artimaña, me llevan a pensar que ésto tal vez sea cierto, dada su obsesión con un cuchillo, con la muerte y con el mal. Mariano Monteamor, otro con quien tenía gran interés en contactarme, sigue siendo una incógnita. No pude obtener información directa confiable ni documentación. Sólo me llegaron habladurías: que es un vivillo, que es amoroso, que es un vago, que es un pobre diablo, que es un buscavida y otras cosas por el estilo, bastante típicas del ambiente nocturno y tanguero. En lo que se refiere a los otros hombres, los poderosos (el Presidente, los Detectives, los Políticos), aclaro lo evidente: se hicieron negar reiteradamente o, personalmente, negaron toda relación entre la realidad y la ficción. Entre los muchos que contribuyeron a dilucidar este asunto, que llevó a quitarme el sueño, las milongueras y milongueros fueron los más prolíficos a pesar de la discreción que los caracteriza. Sigo en deuda con ellos y he ido retribuyéndoles en la medida de mis posibilidades con mis servicios profesionales.

(O.) Por último, quiero agradecer a mi agente literario y también abordar el problemático tema de mi motivación, para adelantarme a las especulaciones ingratas. Esta publicación no es el producto de ansias de dinero o fama sino un gesto, que algunos considerarán deleznable, de venganza. Paso a calificar esta pulsión para orientar a los proclives a la exageración analítica.

Creo tener derecho a contextualizar esta tangópera agregando la documentación que he considerado pertinente. Eso es todo. Considero que así como el autor/a se tomó la libertad de hacer de mí y de mi trabajo un simple objeto alrededor del cual enmarañar interpretaciones imaginarias, "creativas", sin mi conocimiento o aprobación, sin detenerse a ponderar los efectos potencialmente nefastos para mi reputación e incluso (y tiemblo de sólo pensarlo) para mi existencia, creo, repito, estar justificada al atreverme a responder con este acto que de ningún modo llega a la arrogancia encubierta del artista o académico en cuestión, quién no tuvo empacho en hacer de mí, y sospecho que de los otros protagonistas, una extraña parodia dramática de claros tintes ideológicos comprometidos. En pocas palabras, un panfleto exótico en el que, a pesar de mi breve intervención (para mayor precisión en la escena 13 del acto 2) llevo la voz cantante de una supuesta Memoria del Poder.

(O.) En síntesis, el mío es un intento de reapoderamiento de identidad, un ejercicio de mi propia libertad creativa, a la vez que un llamado de atención. ¿Qué entendemos por responsabilidad artística? Discutir este punto supone revisitar el tema del poder en conexión con esta obra anónima y, por supuesto, con mi propia reconfiguración de la misma. Entiendo que resultará un tanto enigmático, pero así mismo prosigo. Esta compilación asume un intento deliberado y por demás ambicioso. Busco, en una palabra, reapropiarme de mi destino. Para ello hago uso de una técnica de re-presentación y encuadre que, conservando el original (en este caso los textos mismos, sin intervención alguna de mi parte, cosa que considero sería una profanación), logra transfigurar el sentido y el *locus* de enunciación. La esencia, por lo tanto, se mantiene intacta, y sin embargo cambia como por obra de magia, al ubicarse uno que era tan sólo un personaje (un otro) como figura de autoridad, como voz y punto de vista. Como cuerpo coherente incuestionado. (Eso por lo menos en el momento de someterse el lector o espectador a experimentar la obra en cualquiera de sus formas: la compra de la entrada o el libro, el mero gesto de movilizarse a la biblioteca, librería o teatro, el abrir las páginas o ocupar una butaca en la sala oscura, etcétera, independientemente de la decisión ulterior de interrumpir o abandonar la lectura o el local con antelación al final establecido por el autor o director. Lo mismo cabe decir para las intenciones previas del sujeto receptor que, pongamos por ejemplo, ingresa en la experiencia de la obra de otro con sospechas o resistencias y, sin embargo, se entrega a las manos de este liderazgo, aunque más no sea para alimentar esas sospechas o ejercer la crítica mordaz.) Interrumpo ahora. Reconozco cierto desvarío en estas últimas reflexiones. Suele ser el síntoma que evidencia el inicio de una nueva oleada de trances, junto con el aflojamiento de la lengua.

Sería irresponsable si no confesara mi esfuerzo por atenerme a esta leve coherencia.

[(T.) Nota de la Libretista como Editora/Traductora: *He considerado cuidadosamente la inclusión del siguiente ensayo de XYa en este lugar, donde ella lo tenía planeado, es decir, como parte de su introducción al volumen. Sin duda puede leerse como pieza independiente, un género totalmente distinto, pero es informativo aquí en varios sentidos. (O.) En primer lugar, XYa estaba sin duda empecinada en diferenciarse del personaje de mi tangópera que, a su entender, distorsionaba peligrosamente sus intenciones, intereses, y hasta su propio ser. En la obra, como verán más adelante, la Bruja figura como una ideóloga influyente, historiadora a la vez que analista del poder, del ejercicio de la dominación y la explotación. Especulo que XYa escribió este borroneo de ensayo filosófico para desligarse de las posibles contaminaciones de tinte político y reafirmar su estatura de profesional seria, abocada a la investigación del tráfico de sustancias y potencias. En segundo lugar, y ya sin juzgar sus dobleces y manipulaciones, (T.) el ensayito muestra sus incursiones legas en profundos temas filosóficos que, aunque con cierta falta de rigor, reflejan su sincera preocupación por problemas antropológicos de antigua data. Aparentemente llevada por las exigencias de su práctica, y desgraciadamente sin contar con las herramientas necesarias, ella se dispone a trabajar en los enigmas o aporías que yacen encrucijados en lo que ella ha dado en llamar corporalidad y que, luego de burdas ruminaciones sobre los equívocos del concepto, se propone abordar a través de la transubstanciación. Es así como considera ventajoso, por lo que consigo deducir, concentrarse en un proceso (en sus palabras, una "mecánica") más que en una cosa. Su práctica de Bruja, en la que fundamentalmente emplea técnicas de médium afines a la posesión (frecuentemente hace referencia a las "visitas" que se apoderan de ella o que, por lo menos, crean confusión respecto a su identidad al instilarle otros puntos de vista, sensaciones, memorias . . . y es aquí precisamente cuando el cuestionamiento se desencadena: ¿dónde?, ¿será en su cuerpo?, ¿en su mente?, ¿en su conciencia?, ¿en su alma?) parecería poner su corporalidad y su identidad en peligro. (El tono de sus observaciones denota cierto temor.) Su profesión le impide hallar fácil refugio en las consabidas (y para ella, artificialmente establecidas) conexiones fisuradas entre mente, cuerpo, alma, conciencia, coporalidad, subjetividad, identidad, racionalidad y experiencia. Sus visitantes la transforman; nunca se apoderan totalmente de ella y nunca la dejan del todo. Sus escritos, complementados por las observaciones que pude hacer durante mi breve período como aprendiz, sugieren que es necesario un cambio de paradigma para dar cuenta de este tipo de fenómeno. Su meta sería captar lo que le ocurre no a cada cuerpo, alma, subjetividad o identidad por separado, por así decirlo, siguiendo sus procesos de entrada, permanencia y finalización de contacto con otro. Ese modelo atomístico no daría en el blanco.*

(T.) Según XYa, me parece, tenemos que tratar el contacto en sí mismo, el tráfico de sustancias en sus cantidades, calidades, velocidades, direccionalidades, y así sucesivamente. Le interesan las propiedades y comportamientos propios de la transubstanciación; no de las entidades involucradas. Las cosas y los seres se

conectan entre sí y con el otro, y en el proceso intercambian sustancias que afectan su propia transformación así como la de todo lo que los rodea. Una vez producido el contacto (y el consiguiente tráfico de sustancias y potencialidades) nada ni nadie continuaría siendo estrictamente lo mismo que antes. Diversos factores claves relativos al proceso no quedan claros y pasaré a mencionar sólo algunos. En mi opinión, "contacto" es un término mal ajustado al proceso que XYa intenta abordar. "Co-presencia", como ella misma propone en cierto momento, alude con mayor precisión a este aparentemente incesante e incontrolable tráfico que incluye lo real y lo imaginario, lo visible y lo invisible, sólidos y no sólidos, lo vivo y lo inerte, lo conciente, lo indiferente y lo alienado. (Entiendo, sin embargo, que "co-presencia" puede a su vez evocar una imagen más bien estática, donde el tráfico en sí correría el peligro de perderse.) A su discusión también le estaría faltando un tratamiento de la forma y configuración de los seres, cosas y fuerzas involucrados, antes, durante y después de pasar por este proceso. La relación crucial entre la forma y el contenido, y sus modos específicos de respuesta a la co-presencia, quedan velados. Por ejemplo me interesaría saber cómo tratar la acumulación de entidades (sociales e individuales, y ésto a nivel corpóreo y psicológico) que momentáneamente conforman una fuerte direccionalidad combinando diversas intencionalidades. Tengo en mente una revolución o un movimiento de resistencia, pero también el conformismo y la apatía generalizados. Siguiendo esta línea de pensamiento podría especular que los cuerpos físicamente discretos con conciencia de singularidad se juntan para configurar una masiva fuerza intencional que puede, o no, estar compartiendo el mismo espacio al mismo tiempo, y sin embargo conformar una corporalidad social (moral y política) que no obstante contiene diferentes facciones o grupos de intereses en un estado de negociación volátil o viscoso. Figuras prominentes de la filosofía política han discutido estos temas produciendo modelos explicativos y analíticos concernientes a la operatoria de este proceso (Antonio Gramsci 1971, Antonio Negri 1999, y Ernesto Laclau y Chantal Mouffe 1985, entre otros). Me pregunto si las especulaciones de XYa apuntan a lo que ocurre específicamente en ese momento del juntarse, poniendo digamos bajo la lupa no el entrecruzamiento de intereses sino de sentidos, término que permitiría contemplar tanto las inclinaciones irracionales como las elecciones racionales, las decisiones y las indecisiones, las intervenciones inesperadas (las memorias y los deseos, una tormenta repentina, un neumático pinchado, un dolor de muelas, un árbol caído en medio del camino), los aspectos tangibles e intangibles que intervienen en la constitución de los pensamientos y los sentimientos. Entiendo que los conceptos elegidos por XYa se ajustan a intereses muy distintos. Ella a todas luces se resiste a entrar en el terreno de la política. A ella le preocupa legitimar su práctica de médium, y distinguirla del sin sentido y la locura. Sus escritos (más que nuestros intercambios verbales) demuestran que sus formas de desarrollar conocimiento siguen trayectorias razonadas si bien no estrictamente lógicas.

(T.) XYa piensa que los pensamientos son tipos particulares de sentimientos (sabemos/ decimos que estamos pensando y no soñando porque sentimos la diferencia, dice ella; también decimos que recordamos y percibimos, diferenciándolos del pensar, porque distinguimos entre diferentes formas de codificar los sentimientos). Discutimos ligeramente la fenomenología, pero XYa se resiste un poco a la práctica de la epoge, esa técnica de despojamiento que aprendiera al visitarla una etnógrafa argentina, entrenada en la Universidad de Buenos Aires durante la dictadura de los años setenta. (La mencionada visita habría comentado que su profesor, un refugiado fascista italiano, aplicaba la fenomenología a sus estudios de mitología indígena entre poblaciones nativas cuyos integrantes insistían en contaminar su trabajo con información cotidiana, académicamente insignificante, sobre cuestiones de supervivencia material. El se proponía preservar sus culturas, no sus vidas.) Ella no se aventuraría en otras transubstanciaciones que la llevaran en esa dirección. (Cree que los libros, las palabras, el acto de leer participan en el tráfico de sustancias y de allí la así llamada afinidad, que otros abordan en términos estéticos, que interviene en nuestras opciones teóricas.) Cuando intenté presionarla para que estableciera algunas definiciones operativas sobre lo que a su entender serían los sentimientos, los pensamientos, las palabras y los conceptos (yo quería mapear un territorio compartido), XYa me eludió con el pretexto de sufrir estrés postrance. Pude, sin embargo, aislar, mover y reordenar algunas de sus ideas/sentimientos/creencias sobre estos temas.

(T.) A las argumentaciones semanticistas, con las que parece acordar, responde (comunicación personal, junio del 2000) con Hannah Arendt que "están absolutamente en lo cierto: en último análisis todos los problemas son problemas lingüísticos; simplemente no saben las implicancias de lo que están diciendo" (Arendt 1969: 49). (O.) Pienso que quería decir que, al menos en lo concerniente a su práctica, esto no es suficiente. Las palabras son cosas con propiedades sensoriales y emotivas, y repercusiones éticas. (T.) En este ensayo, en una nota incompleta, ella discute hasta cierto punto el tema en relación a la práctica de citar. Se vale de la introducción de Hannah Arendt a Illuminations de Walter Benjamin (1969). Lamentablemente no cosubstancializa con la obra de Jacques Derrida (1988), con la lectura de Derrida que hace Gayatri Spivak (1980), ni con la que Judith Butler hace de Derrida y su omisión de Spivak (1993). (Al respecto ver Jeff Tobin 1999.) Esas lecturas (y transubstanciaciones concomitantes) tal vez hubieran llevado a XYa a reflexiones interesantes. Por ejemplo, podría haberse extendido sobre las diferencias que suscita el considerar la citación desde el punto de vista de la reiteración, digamos desde la física de la repetición, o desde una preocupación como la suya que se centra en el intercambio de sustancias propio de dicha operación.

(T.) Tengo en mente su interés en la viscosidad, por ejemplo. (Ella lo trajo a colación precisamente como prueba de las desfiguraciones a las que se veía sujeta en la tangópera ya que, en la Escena 13, la Bruja hace uso de la viscosidad para analizar las operaciones del poder.) Me pregunto cómo esa propiedad de adherirse o pegotearse que las sustancias presentan en ciertos estados, ni sólidos ni líquidos, moviéndose a una velocidad relativamente baja, y generando una cierta reacción expectante y revulsiva (que podríamos aducir a un comportamiento aparentemente indeciso), ¿cómo interviene ese estado en el hacer y deshacer de las corporalidades, la formación

y deformación de las identidades, y la circulación de las palabras? (Al respecto XYa
podría haber conjurado a Jean Paul Sartre 1956, 1964, y a Mary Douglas 1984, así
como a Eduardo Savigliano, ingeniero nuclear quien a mi pedido hizo la siguiente
contribución desde el punto de vista de la física experimental: (O.) "En mecánica de
los fluidos, llámase viscosidad a la resistencia que tienen las moléculas del fluido a
desplazarse unas respecto de las otras. En realidad, todos los fluidos [gases y líquidos]
son, en mayor o menor grado, viscosos. Si aceptamos la teoría corpuscular de la
materia, en última instancia los sólidos también están constituidos por pequeñas
partículas separadas por enormes distancias (relativas a sus dimensiones) las unas de
las otras, por lo que, en definitiva, los sólidos tampoco son compactos. Un fluido con
viscosidad nula es una abstracción matemática y no existe en la realidad. Como
consecuencia de la viscosidad, cuando un fluido es agitado, el rozamiento entre las
moléculas que se desplazan a distintas velocidades origina calor y el fluido aumenta
su temperatura. Los sólidos se diferenciarían de los gases y líquidos por las fuerzas
intercorpusculares que se resisten a los desplazamientos relativos y originan su
relativa impenetrabilidad. [Bajo grandes presiones, por ejemplo en el caso de los
laminados en frío, se logra producir una cierta difusión de un sólido en otro]"
(comunicación personal, junio de 2000). Me estoy ocupando de aplicar estas
investigaciones a las comunicaciones, encuentros y desencuentros fríos y acalorados.
Esta viscosidad tan negada podría revolucionar nuestra comprensión de la subje-
tividad y de la corporalidad al enfatizar nuestras conexiones, nuestro verdadero
"pegoteo" al otro, a pesar de todos los esfuerzos invertidos en silenciar y desdeñar
estas tracciones. Podría transformar las conceptualizaciones de la subjetividad, del
sujeto centrado en sí mismo, que asume la discreta separación entre cuerpos, cuerpos
que coinciden con conciencias de ser. Podría alertarnos sobre los esfuerzos hechos en
crear la separación y la diferenciación; desafiar la idea de que la comunicación viene
después de la singularidad individual. Mostraría que, muy por el contrario, llegamos
a ser lo que somos viscosamente conectados con otros, y que somos ideológicamente
impulsados a cultivar un sentido de separación discreta, discriminada y discriminante,
posible de superar sólo forzándonos a la comunicación racional. La importancia ético-
política de estas reflexiones, potenciales controversias incluidas, es realmente
prometedora.)
(T.) Podría haber discutido cómo la citación y la reiteración conllevan, entonces, no sólo
la cosa citada sino también el hecho de la visitación, el tráfico de sustancias que hace
a la conexión. Esto a su vez le hubiera permitido, quizás, confrontar ideas contem-
poráneas sobre la identidad y la "performatividad", porque podría haber reen-
cauzado, o digamos que revitalizado, la preocupación por los procesos hoy en día
sanitarizados de la formación del sujeto y de la constitución de la identidad, al poner
el foco no sólo en la diferenciación sino también en cuán permeables son esas fron-
teras, constantemente cruzadas por sustancias que en diferentes estados, a distintas
velocidades, y con propiedades diversas, transitan entre seres y seres, seres y cosas, lo
real y lo imaginado, lo conciente y lo inconciente, y lo hacen amable o agresivamente,
envenenando y bendiciendo, con o sin intenciones e intereses, generando transfor-

maciones que no se detienen ante la disímil composición y estado de las cosas o seres involucrados en el contacto. *(Aquí, si nuestra relación estuviera en buenos términos, le sugeriría leer a Baruk Spinoza 1989, a Gilles Deleuze sobre Leibnitz y Spinoza 1988 y 1989, y a Macedonio Fernández 1990.)* Y cuando escribo "contacto" no me refiero exclusivamente al tacto, sino a la presencia. Y cuando escribo "presencia" no me refiero exclusivamente a la co-temporalidad y ni siquiera a la co-espacialidad. Este tráfico pavoroso, y una bruja con la experiencia de XYa podría explicarlo mejor que yo, se produce a largas distancias, entre tiempos presentes y pasados, y aún entre lo vivo y lo muerto.

(T.) Esto no atañe a la percepción ni a cómo o dónde o entre qué y qué se produce; tampoco es una cuestión de experiencia procesada o registrada en mentes o cuerpos. No se trata de la memoria de las cosas vividas directamente o a través de la empatía (como cuando se transmiten a través del aprendizaje o la tradición). Estoy de acuerdo con XYa en que aprendemos a sentir y a nombrar nuestros sentimientos. Ese no es el punto que pretendo debatir. Pero el punto en cuestión no es mío sino suyo, si bien ahora ya ha sido transubstanciado y, pegado a las dos, se estira entremedio a medida que nos transforma y se transforma. Y esta larga nota queda ahora inserta, injertada en el cuerpo de su texto y en la textura de su argumentación. Y cuando la traduzco, como le prometí que lo haría, ocurre otra transformación (destrucción y revitalización). Y algo gotea, cayendo entre rendijas, algo que se perderá y que en la caída transformará su estado y tal vez su naturaleza, ahora materia que se mueve por ahí o permanece estática sin palabras que se le adhieren. ¿Será ésto a lo que se refiere cuando escribe corporalidad? ¿O será lo que yo quiero decir, tratando de asirme a una palabra lo suficientemente sonora como para hacer lugar a la traducción como forma de vida?

(T.) Y aquí me refiero a la traducción no como el quehacer del traductor puesto a transmitir los sentidos que un otro ha puesto en palabras. El traductor que hace metódicos malabarismos con la literalidad lingüística y la intervención poética para captar la coreografía y los componentes específicos de una escritura ajena, que deberá conocer como si fuera la suya propia y, que no obstante, mantendrá a la distancia que habilita el respeto para con las opiniones, elecciones y posiciones de un otro. *(Para los interesados en este tipo de traducción sugiero consultar Idelber Avelar 1999, Gayatri Spivak 1993 y 1999, Walter Benjamin 1969, y Jacques Derrida 1985 y 1998.)* El o la traductora que tengo en mente quizás merezca otro nombre. Ella vive en traducción. Ella traduce constantemente a los otros y a sí misma, ida y vuelta entre dos lenguajes que pertenecen a universos culturales diferentes; y cuando escribe, ella anticipa la traducción que vendrá. *(O. T. O. T. O.)* Y el original puede hacer su aparición en cualquiera de las dos lenguas, y la traducción que le sigue, por ser producto del auto-traducirse y no de traducir a un otro ajeno (si bien puede ser que la traductora de su propio texto sea en cierto sentido una otra que se traduce, pero no tan otra como otros), se dispondrá a corregir, embellecer, cuestionar y hasta suplementar el original sin grandes contemplaciones. Y así la traducción se convierte en el original que, a su vez, está listo para ser traducido.

(O.) Esta traductora obsesiva, empedernida (y juro que estoy simplificando su quehacer) toma cuenta de que algo se pierde entre el vaivén de palabras, algo sustancial a su práctica que no es una cosa sino un movimiento tendente a conectar, transmitir, efectuar un tránsito, un tráfico de sustancias y energías. Quisiera poder escribir sobre esto sin necesidad de recurrir a los antropomorfismos, la metafísica, los modelos que nos prestan la física, e incluso las humanidades (ya sean humanísticos o anti-humanísticos). Pero lo que más me molesta es la clinicalización, el juicio clínico que persiste en invadirme. Temo que esto sea la locura.

(T.) Volvamos al ensayo de XYa sobre la corporalidad. Sus palabras (que precedieron a las mías), a continuación.]

(O.) Soy una estudiosa del cuerpo pero no una anatomista. Mi interés en la corporalidad me ha llevado a este tema que no es el alma en el sentido religioso, ni los espíritus de los ocultistas, ni la psique de los psicólogos y psicoanalistas. La corporalidad atañe a los cuerpos con cierta conciencia de sí (conciencia es un concepto por demás cargado por el uso y abuso filosófico, de allí que diga "cierta" conciencia) simultáneamente falsa y precisa (según se tomen en cuenta particulares articulaciones espacio-temporales—aquí y ahora, allá y entonces, etcétera—o dimensiones específicas aisladas de complejas relaciones—clase, género, raza, etcétera). La corporalidad es un sentido ubicuo que posiciona al sujeto y genera orientación, como una brújula. Las cosas y las vivencias (el sentido de realidad) se organizan a su alrededor. La corporalidad y la identidad son dos elaboraciones conceptuales que intentan explicar lo mismo sin lograrlo: esa sensación de unicidad (de lo único y unido) propia de la singularidad individual. Sabemos cuán importante es la intervención de los otros en la delimitación de ese contorno. Sabemos que hay un referente físico claro, a pesar de sus transformaciones sustanciales a lo largo de eso que llamamos vida. No sabemos las proporciones exactas de la participación del lenguaje y lo social, lo biológico y sensorial en esta combinatoria. Tampoco sabemos cómo se articulan específicamente para producir eso que soy yo u otro. Los malentendidos proliferan. (Que los otros son cuerpos que desarrollan su propia conciencia. Que no hay lenguaje sin la base biológica que permite su articulación. Que sin pensamiento [sin palabras] los cuerpos no saben que saben que son. Que sin socialidad no hay corporalidad, y sin lenguaje [es decir, pensamiento] no hay socialidad.)

(O.) El lenguaje es pensamiento socializado; del pensamiento sólo sabemos por el lenguaje que le da forma; si hay pensamiento previo o fuera del lenguaje habría que llamarlo emoción, sentimiento o afecto. (Eso sin definirlo con exactitud ya que al intentar su especificación recurrimos al lenguaje.) La corporalidad (el concepto) es entonces una maniobra recuperadora de lo que se escapa de las redes del lenguaje y que se resiste (en realidad, que algunos se interesan en hacer resistir) al nominalismo aceptado e incluso, en algunos casos, por establecer. Los empeñosos en deshacer la díada mente/

cuerpo tropiezan básicamente con estas dificultades, y caen en el idealismo o materialismo, en nociones como corporalidad e identidad, experiencia y discurso, para continuar en el camino especulativo o interpretativo. Esto lleva a algunos desilusionados (a veces desahuciados) a interrogar la validez de la tradición (analítica o crítica) intelectual. Cultores de lo espiritual, artistas, y hasta algunos científicos o pensadores humanistas que se adhieren a uno u otro tipo de pragmatismo, prefieren dejar de lado estas interrogaciones y apuntar sus miras en otras direcciones. Dicen no interesarse en este juego de espejos. Es sabido que algunos cortan amarras, siguen sus cursos, y viven más o menos felices. No es mi caso. Continúo.

(O.) La corporalidad que me interesa tampoco es esa conexión o cultivo del equilibrio mente-cuerpo que busca el yogui o la meditación trascendental (ejercicios generalmente combinados que, como un movimiento de pinzas, abordan a dos puntas el entrenamiento físico y el control mental para armonizar las energías en un todo universal). No me interesa develar misterios; no hay misterios. Sólo ignorancia. No creo en las ánimas; (T.) pienso que los seres adoptan diferentes estados sustanciales (diferentes propiedades químicas y físicas), totalmente compuestos de materia y de sus transformaciones.

(O.) ¿Qué concepto no cooptado entonces podré aplicar a esta tangibilidad (no quiero decir "realidad tangible" porque tampoco soy empirista) de lo inexplicado (que no considero inexplicable)? Me fascinan las trampas del lenguaje, y si bien tiendo a aceptar que las palabras nos acercan y alejan al mismo tiempo de las "cosas" (experiencias incluidas), no lo vivo así cotidianamente. (En la vida diaria y fuera del quehacer profesional, utilizo todos los enfoques que acabo de descartar.) ¿Por qué ese empeño puesto en la corporalidad, entonces, cuya realidad no cuestiono pero sí considero imposible de verbalizar, que implica también de pensar? No quiero refugiarme en ese concepto tapón que es la "experiencia" donde se mezclan el vitalismo pagano, la intencionalidad materialista, el idealismo aparentemente pragmático y el espiritismo herético. Me espanta la fenomenología. Me es imposible confiar en la metafísica como base de mi práctica profesional. He estudiado con cuidado la forma en que estos principios se yuxtaponen y encubren mutuamente. Sabemos que sin subjetividad no hay sentido de experiencia (las experiencias sueltas, sin sujetos a los que ligarse, son impensables) y que la subjetividad es la suma de actos de sujeción, de definiciones forzadas, de delimitaciones violentas. Si la insistencia en la corporalidad es un acto de protesta contra la racionalidad y sus limitaciones (es decir, un acto político-filosófico), ¿cómo discutir sus particularidades con argumentos coherentes? ¿Cómo reivindicar el cuerpo sin afianzar la división cuerpo/mente que lo sitúa en el lugar de la diferencia marginalizada? ¿Y cómo trabajar sobre la no diferencia (sin caer en la indiferencia)? Para una especialista en la manipulación de las incorporaciones, que rehúsa creer en los espíritus, estas cuestiones son cruciales y obsesivas.

(O.) De allí mi interés en la transubstanciación o transformación de sustancias, no en sentido alquimista, sino en el de préstamos, injertos, dislocaciones y trastocamientos espacio-temporales que comprometen a la corporalidad y sus sentidos, sus memorias culturales e históricas. Recuerde el lector que en este consultorio se practica lo que vulgarmente se ha dado en llamar "posesión", término que a mi entender distorsiona los hechos al introducir pesadamente un sesgo metafísico. Aquí lo que se produce cotidianamente es un tráfico de sustancias, de materialidades de distinta composición y características (pesos, densidades, temperaturas, etc.) con comportamientos de diferente naturaleza. Recomponemos, por así decirlo, corporalidades. No hemos podido establecer con exactitud en qué medida estos contactos comprometen el estado de los entes visitantes y visitados. Decididamente observamos las transformaciones, la fluidez o el rechazo con el que se desenvuelven los contactos, en fin, los efectos más o menos positivos o negativos. La duración (persistencia o fugacidad) de estas transubstanciaciones no nos es clara. Indiscutiblemente hay efectos residuales, síntomas de la "ocupación" que, insisto, no consiste en el simple reemplazo de la interioridad de un ser por la de otro. Esto, señores, no es meter en la cáscara vaciada de una nuez un fruto que le es ajeno. Tampoco es la metamorfosis folklórica del lobizón. Personalmente, me interesa la materialidad y no la lógica de estos procesos, pero sin esos pasos tímidos que caracterizan a la racionalidad (ese sistema fantasioso con el que creemos domesticar lo ignorado) no puedo trabajar. (Esto lo explican otros mucho mejor que yo.) ¿Cómo llego a esos principios físicos de por sí ya infestados por el lenguaje que los define y constriñe? Repito que no confío en la experiencia ni en la racionalidad. Cuando de explicitar algo se trata, oralmente o por escrito, ahí están las palabras con su tiranía. Me pregunto, entonces, si no habrá un resto (de sentido o sinsentido) que se escape entre las rendijas de un lenguaje y otro, que se cuele entre dos lenguas que intentan referirse o construir lo mismo. Traducción. ¿Servirá de algo pensar en la traducción? La traducción como transubstanciación de lugares emocionales, contorneados por palabras que se dicen ser pensamientos. Todo un juego de máscaras enmascaradas.

(O.) Se me hiela la sangre (o se me congela el pensamiento) al imaginar (y eso ¿qué es?) las reacciones espantadas y, peor aún, aburridas. . . . Por supuesto que otros han discutido estos temas antes que yo, y mucho mejor. Me han visitado algunos y hasta los he leído, y creo recordar algo de ellos en ésto . . . pero si vuelvo a esos recuerdos y textos ahora, a rastrear con esmero lo que he asimilado, tendré que meterme en sus pensamientos (esos fuertes y enigmáticos sentimientos) como lo hice en su momento, y ahora no quiero voluntariamente someterme a esa transubstanciación de la cita.

(O.) Nota de XYa: No puedo dejar de traicionarme. Me visita Walter Benjamin, a través
de Hannah Arendt, al respecto: (T.) "Las citas en mis trabajos son como los ladrones

que a la vera del camino asaltan armados y alivian al indolente de sus convicciones"
(Benjamin, en Arendt 1969: 38). (O.) Las citas (a las que me resisto) tendrían a su
entender la capacidad de despertar, de cortar el fluir de los argumentos al injertarse
con fuerza reconcentraday, en última instancia, destructiva. Para Benjamin el poder
de la cita (T.) "no es la fuerza de preservar sino de limpiar, de arrancar de contexto,
de destruir" (Arendt 1969: 39). (O.) Bibliómano vuelto coleccionista de citas, aspiraba
a escribir a pura cita. Su proyecto era revolucionario. Me interesa por lo complicado y
por la metodología tan opuesta a la mía, si bien ambas confluyen en una fe empe-
dernida en la materialidad poco convencional. Continúo.

(O.) *En Benjamin, y hasta cierto punto en la lectura magistral que le dedica Arendt, el*
poder destructivo de la cita operaría a dos puntas. (Para seguirlos aquí me valgo de
mi familiaridad con el tráfico corporal.) Por un lado, la cita envenena el cuerpo
discursivo en el que se inserta; por otro, tajea el contexto original o cuerpo del cual
se la erradica. La cita extrapolaría un aspecto concentrado y valioso de un cuerpo
pasado a un cuerpo presente. En este proceso de revitalización por destrucción, la cita
sería el agente del contacto entre el pasado y el presente. La tradición, entonces, se
reconfiguraría como memoria de un cuerpo extraño y a la vez propio. (Yo agregaría
aquí que a este aspecto diacrónico misterioso habría que sumarle el sincrónico de la
interculturalidad, de los avatares del contacto coetáneo de tradiciones diferentes y de
los estragos y potencialidades revolucionarias que marcan a los cuerpos sujetos a los
diversos tráficos de desterritorialización. Exiliados, migrantes, refugiados, turistas,
viajeros, cada uno metido en particulares y disímiles dinámicas de asimilación,
resguardo y recreación de memorias culturales; millones de destrucciones y revita-
lizaciones simultáneas que cambian de signo hasta en el transcurso de cada vida
singular. Pienso en el que se va y sueña con volver, en el que quiere irse y no puede,
en el que se fue y vuelve para no encontrarse, en el que va y vuelve como si nada.
Cuántos cuerpos extraños y a la vez propios, apropiados y rechazados con inten-
sidades tan distintas, con consecuencias tan dispares, incoherentes e inconsistentes,
destruyendo y destruyéndose afanosamente para mantenerse vivos. Los hago
presentes con esta cita.)

(O.) *Acá hago otro aparte para explicar que Benjamin no confiaba en la comunicación, y*
que el poder de la cita nada tenía que ver para él con las interpretaciones o explica-
ciones que suelen precederla o seguirla. Es la citación en sí misma, la mecánica que
hace de la cita lo que es, aquello que cuenta; pero también su calidad. Y en este
punto nos encontramos con el problema de la identificación de lo que vale la pena
citar, no en tren de comunicar sino de transmitir. ¿Cómo se detecta lo citable? ¿Y
cómo puede la cita transmitir a pesar de la destrucción que crea?

(O.) *Benjamin ofrece la verdad como guía; confía en la consistencia de la verdad. Una*
vez más (a mi entender) estamos en el dominio de las propiedades de las sustancias.
(T.) "La tradición transforma la verdad en sabiduría, y la sabiduría es la consistencia
de la verdad transmisible" (Arendt 1969: 41). (O.) Entiendo que muchos se hay an
detenido y aún se detengan a considerar el origen de esa verdad, su llegada al mundo

*humano y el consabido problema de la autoridad, pero aquí me interesa la cuestión
de la consistencia y del sujeto identificador de consistencias. ¿En qué consiste la
consistencia de la verdad? ¿Deberíamos buscar en la sustancia constituyentes de
la verdad o en sus propiedades y movimientos, como la transmisibilidad? A lo que
agrego, y pido disculpas a los lectores por sumar tanto interrogante, ¿quién y qué
es el o la que se propone la mencionada tarea de identificar la verdad?*

*(O.) Las respuestas, como era de prever, vuelven todas mezcladas. Arendt escribe que
Benjamin, como buen coleccionista, (T.) "se confiaba al azar como guía en sus viajes
intelectuales de exploración" (43). (O.) Este método de pensamiento, a su entender,
se condice con la proclividad de Benjamin a la* flanerie *(algunos la traducirían
irreverentemente al criollo como "franela"), actividad privilegiada de esos observa-
dores profesionales que se paseaban por las capitales del mundo sin otra responsabilidad que degustar intelectualmente las impresiones altas o bajas que sus con-
géneres socialmente aturdidos infligían sobre sus exquisitas sensibilidades. Esta
ocupación de desocupado privilegiado ya estaba perimida en tiempos de Benjamin,
quien añoraba practicarla en la agitada Europa de la primera mitad del siglo veinte.
Aparentemente y según Arendt, quien merece toda mi confianza y respeto, Benjamin
rehusaba sumarse al cuerpo de miembros útiles de la sociedad, y por ende a definir
su función como intelectual, método incluido. Sin embargo se le escapó por ahí que
le hubiera gustado ser (T.) "el verdadero crítico de la literatura alemana" (su amigo
Scholem lo deschava en una carta) y en la introducción a* Elective Affinities *(1924,
1925), su ensayo sobre Goethe, escribe que "la crítica se ocupa de la verdad conte-
nida en una obra de arte. . . . El crítico se hace la pregunta básica de toda crítica—a
saber, si el contenido de verdad que brilla en una obra se debe a su materia temática
o si la supervivencia de la materia temática se debe a su contenido de verdad. Porque
a medida que se separan en la obra, éstas deciden su inmortalidad. En este sentido la
historia de las obras de arte prepara su crítica, y por eso la distancia histórica
incrementa su fuerza" (en Arendt 1969: 4–5).*

*(O.) A este brillante desvarío (que evito editar aún más para mi conveniencia en haras
de retener el curioso movimiento exploratorio de Benjamin así como de practicar sus
enseñanzas concernientes a la cita—destruyo lo suyo, destruye lo mío—mediada en
este caso por mi traducción de otra traducción y, por ende, por una cadena de
transubstanciaciones, y todo esto sin que se pierda—¿no es increíble?—la materia
temática que nos ocupa a todos los involucrados que les recuerdo, por las dudas, es
"la verdad", agrego otro dato que hasta ahora escamoteé al citarlo. Me refiero a la
comparación entre el crítico y el comentarista, artilugio que le permite a Benjamin
decir lo que quiere sobre el papel que ambiciona para el crítico. (T.) Cito:*

> *Si, haciendo uso de un símil, uno ve la obra que crece como una pira funeraria,
> el comentarista podría asemejarse a un químico, su crítico a un alquimista.
> Mientras el primero se queda con leños y cenizas como los únicos objetos de
> su análisis, el segundo se ocupa solamente del enigma de la llama en sí misma:*

el enigma de estar vivo. Así, el crítico interroga la verdad cuya llama viva con-
tinúa quemando sobre los pesados leños del pasado y las ligeras cenizas de la
vida que pasó. (5)

Arendt (citadora citada) comenta y/o critica el pasaje de Benjamin así:

> *El crítico es un alquimista que practica el oscuro arte de transmutar los*
> *elementos fútiles de lo real en el brillante y duradero oro de la verdad, o mejor*
> *dicho que observa e interpreta el proceso histórico que provoca tal transfigu-*
> *ración mágica—sea lo que sea que pensemos de esta imagen, difícilmente*
> *se corresponda con lo que normalmente se nos ocurre al clasificar a un escritor*
> *como crítico literario. (5)*

(O.) Queda claro que el crítico, más alquimista que químico (y que no es exactamente
ninguno de los dos), es un transmutador y transmisor, y no uno que se las da de
entendido. (T.) Este crítico que identifica a la vez que transforma para poder trans-
mitir la verdad (todo ésto a través de la práctica de citar, a la que sumo la de tra-
ducir) "preservaría 'la intención de tales investigaciones' [los estudios citados] . . .
'bombeando las profundidades del lenguaje y el pensamiento . . . mediante la per-
foración más que la excavación' (Briefe I, 329), para no arruinar todo con explica-
ciones que buscan suministrar conexión causal o sistemática" (Benjamin, en Arendt
1969: 48). Benjamin (y Arendt lo cita al respecto pero yo me lo salteo) reconoce
cierta pedantería y oscurantismo en esta propuesta, pero los prefiere a la falsificación
interpretativa.

(O.) Admito que me atraen sobremanera este método y forma de vida (mi experiencia
con flaneurs es limitada, no así con sus parientes cercanos los etnógrafos quienes fre-
cuentemente vienen a mí ya sea conjurados o como clientes), pero dadas mis limita-
ciones (históricas, sociales y personales) yo tengo que trabajar para comer y franca-
mente vivo al día con lo que me reditúa esta práctica que es casi una vocación; y que
en esta época de estrechez económica y estampidas del desempleo se ve afectada no-
tablemente en el flujo de clientes que, vale aclarar, depende en gran medida de las re-
comendaciones boca a boca. En síntesis, mis circunstancias dictan reflexiones no
tanto prácticas como practicables y, en lo posible, efectivas.

(O.) Vuelvo, entonces, al tema de la consistencia habiendo dado al lector algunas armas
para evaluar mi preferencia por el camino de la transmisibilidad. La verdad, como la
pepa de oro o la acción preferida en la bolsa, toma su consistencia de su modalidad
de circulación o transmisibilidad. (T.) Benjamin, siguiendo la lectura de Arendt,
sostiene que la verdad es un fenómeno acústico y privilegia la palabra y, especial-
mente, la palabra citada (no la oración) como aquello que hace blanco en la verdad.
Las palabras, escritas o silenciosas como en los pensamientos, acarrean la consisten-
cia de la verdad, y a mi gusto (que es diferente al de Benjamin y al de Arendt) hacen
la verdad posible e imposible.]

1. (O.) Quiero hacer un pacto, sin embargo, que tranquilice a los preocupados por las convenciones académicas a las que someto voluntariamente este libro. Debo ser responsable ante alguien y ahora. Bien. Propongo que este texto se lea en su integridad como una larga sucesión de paráfrasis, y renuncio a esgrimir originalidad. No así la creación. (Véanse mis reflexiones al respecto más arriba, que insisto se asemejarán a otras, pasadas y futuras, mejores.)

2. (O.) Invito a todo aquel que lo desee a visitar mi voluminosa biblioteca y a revisar mis subrayados y notas al margen, complementados en textos más recientes con esas esquelitas adhesivas amarillas (invento genial) que admiten comentarios más elaborados. Admito que ésta es una solución poco pedagógica, en el sentido de que la circulación a distancia de esta información queda restringida al contacto personal, pero me refugio en las ventajas de la corporalidad. No quisiera declarar públicamente esta sospecha cosquilleante que emerge en mis momentos de indefensión, y que en verdad no sé si es mía o de la voz de autoridad internalizada. (Me refiero a la pereza y la indulgencia.) Pero habiendo finalmente nombrado estas debilidades vergonzantes quiero aclarar que no pido clemencia. La neurosis, en sus movimientos adaptativos y transgresores, me impide llegar al fondo de mis motivaciones con absoluta honestidad.

3. (O.) No es inusual que el poseso o la poseída profesionales aprendan a detectar estos cambios de ánimo que acompañan, literalmente, a la suplantación de un ánima por otra. Esta transubstanciación, contrariamente a la impresión generalizada, no es del todo azarosa.

4. (O.) Dado que mis lapsos de coherencia parecen abreviarse, he decidido retomar estas breves notas introductorias antes de estar plenamente en control del fluir de mis ideas. Experimento el agotamiento típico que precede al abandono del ente visitante.

5. (O.) Temo perder estos instantes preciosos en los que creo reconocer una voz propia releyendo las líneas previas. Decido avanzar con esta salvedad. El tiempo me obsesiona. La urgencia, y hasta un sentimiento de emer-

gencia, sostienen esta empresa. Creo recordar haber mencionado este impulso recurrente.

6. (T.):

"Y así vivieron entre tres imposibilidades . . . : la imposibilidad de no escribir" dado que sólo podían librarse de su inspiración escribiendo; "la imposibilidad de escribir en alemán"—Kafka consideraba el uso del idioma alemán como la "usurpación abierta o encubierta, o posiblemente el tormento auto-infligido de una propiedad ajena que no ha sido adquirida sino robada, y adoptada relativamente rápido, y que continúa siendo la posesión de otro aún cuando no se detecta ni siquiera un error lingüístico"; y por último, "la imposiblidad de escribir diferente", ya que no se dispone de ningún otro idioma. "Uno casi podría incluir una cuarta imposiblidad", dice Kafka en conclusión, "la imposibilidad de escribir, porque esta desesperanza no era algo que pudiera mitigarse con la escritura"—como sería usual entre los poetas, a quienes un dios les ha dado el decir lo que los hombres sufren y sobrellevan. La desesperanza en este caso se vuelve más bien "un enemigo de la vida y de la escritura; escribir era aquí sólo una moratoria, como lo es para el que escribe su último deseo y testamento justo antes de colgarse". (Hannah Arendt, introducción a *Illuminations* 1969: 31–32)

7. (O.) Hago entrega de la primera página de esta introducción (y por ende completo la transferencia de dicho escrito) en Buenos Aires, el 14 de mayo del 2000.

(T.) Nota Final de la Libretista como Editora/Traductora: *Finalmente creo haber dilucidado lo que XYa tenía en mente cuando me pidió que incluyera su bosquejo de introducción como sola condición para transferirme el derecho y la responsabilidad de publicar este volumen. Una razón obvia: implantar la duda. (A esta altura podrían bien estarse preguntando si todo este volumen, incluyendo el libreto de la tangópera y hasta yo misma no seremos todos productos de la imaginación industriosa de XYa.) Otra: como buena observadora de los hábitos de los lectores contemporáneos, ella contaba con que se saltearan gran parte del texto hasta llegar al final de esta introducción y, consecuentemente, con quedarse ella con la última (y verdadera) palabra. Finalmente tengo que decir que inclusive sospecho que XYa escribió estas elucubraciones para reírse de mí, de mis intentos de entenderla y de mis esfuerzos puestos en traducirla que, al final, han generado una obertura a este volumen lo suficientemente fastidiosa como para desalentar hasta al o la más paciente y mejor dispuesta lectora. (Los Angeles, 15/6/2000)]*

Part II

The Contested Object

Parte II

El Objeto en Disputa

Angora Matta: "Tangópera"-Thriller in Two Acts and Fourteen Scenes

by Marta E. Savigliano

Summary

Angora Matta is a tangópera in two acts and fourteen scenes that uses the renowned stereotype of the femme fatale (the dangerous woman who intelligently manipulates her sexual attraction, carrying fatalness to others and, in the end, to herself) to develop a thriller where the genres of tango, opera, film noir, and magic realism interlace. Angora Matta (Angora Kils) evokes through her name the sensual fluffiness of a feline and the sordid threat of death. She moves smoothly through the story, accomplishing her fatal task—to murder the President—with noiseless steps, calling lots of attention to herself but leaving no traces. She is a master of disguise. Her crime is political, but she will induce the other protagonists and the audience to believe that her target and motives are passional. We learn only in the second act of the opera that her target is the President rather than a lover (and so does the lover himself, convinced up to then of his victimization). The Secret Service Police, who are eager to identify the assassin, hire La Poseída (a medium possessed by the spirits of former military Dictators and their victims) to divine the motives for the crime. La Poseída, who keeps the Memory of Power, reviews the last twenty-five years of political history in Argentina.

The opera's dramatic and absurd atmosphere is conveyed through the vocabulary of the tango—a musical, poetic, and choreographic genre symbolically associated with melodrama, suspense, intrigue, conflict, danger, and sensual fascination. The central theme of the opera is the "Memory of Power," a musical composition that runs throughout the piece and moves from background to full intensity in the penultimate scene. This modernist tango is intercepted by some instrumental tangos that highlight important moments in the plot (such as the "Knife Under the Pillow," a tango that marks Angora's retrieval of the murder weapon and her readiness to attack). A series of traditional-style tangos (more accentuated and playful) as well as other Afro-Creole music and dance genres of the Southern Cone of Latin America (milonga, candombe, and murga) are featured, with original lyrics, in particular scenes. The songs describe the city of Buenos Aires, narrate successive events and characters' states of mind, and expose political ideologies and attitudes of particular social groups (exiles, survivors of the dictatorship, and young generations struggling to understand Argentine history). The transition between the first and second acts is marked choreographically through a milonga scene, in the tango dance club El Tugurio (The Dump). Although all characters move, sing, and play musical instruments following a paradigmatic tangoesque corporeality, this scene, in which the plot "twists" extensively, features tango dance and the rituals of *tanguidad*.

The tangópera has been conceived as an experimental multiart collaboration, with a strong educational component focused on intercultural creation and reception. Narrative, choreography, musical composition, scenography, and film genres (animation, documentary, and music video) are brought together to create a politically informed tango spectacle that generates the opportunity for critical reflections on exoticism and cultural appropriation.

Angora Matta will be presented in its original Spanish version with English subtitles.

Angora Matta: Tangópera-"Thriller" en Dos Actos y Catorce Escenas

por Marta E. Savigliano

Resumen

Angora Matta es una tangópera en dos actos y catorce escenas que toma el conocido estereotipo de la *femme fatale* (la mujer peligrosa que manipula inteligentemente su atracción sexual, acarreando fatalidad a quienes la rodean y, por último, cayendo ella misma en su propia trampa) para desarrollar un *thriller* en el que se entrelazan tango, la ópera, el film noir y el realismo mágico. Angora Matta evoca con su nombre la sensual voluptuosidad del felino y la sórdida amenaza de muerte. Se desliza tranquilamente a través de la historia, cumpliendo con su misión fatal—asesinar al Presidente—con pasos inaudibles, atrayendo las miradas de todos los testigos de sus andanzas pero sin dejar rastros. Angora es una artífice de la transfiguración. Su crimen es político, pero ella induce tanto a los demás protagonistas como a la audiencia a creer que su objetivo y sus motivos son pasionales. Sólo en el segundo acto de la ópera sabremos que su objeto es el Presidente y no su amante. (El amante, Mariano Monteamor, está convencido de su victimización hasta ese momento.) Los motivos del crimen son develados por una bruja poseída—una médium—consultada por los investigadores de los Detectives del Servicio Secreto, urgidos por identificar al asesino. La Poseída, quien es portadora de la Memoria del Poder, cae bajo el influjo de Dictadores militares y de sus víctimas. En sus trances ella recorre los últimos veinticinco años de la historia política de la Argentina.

La atmósfera dramática y absurda de la ópera se transmite a través del tango, un género musical, poético y coreográfico simbólicamente asociado con el me-lodrama, el suspenso, la intriga, el conflicto, el peligro y la fascinación sensual. El tema central de la ópera es la "Memoria del Poder", una composición musical que recorre la obra con distinta intensidad alcanzando el clímax en la penúltima escena. Este tango modernista es interceptado por tangos instrumentales que realzan situaciones claves del argumento (como, por ejemplo, "El Cuchillo Bajo la Almohada", que señala el momento en el que Angora expone el arma del delito y su decisión de perpetrar el crimen). Una serie de tangos de estilo tradicional así como otros géneros afro-criollos músicales y bailables del Cono Sur de Latinoamérica (milonga, candombe y murga) figuran en determinadas escenas con letras originales. Estos temas describen la ciudad de Buenos Aires, narran sucesivos hechos y estados de ánimo de los protagonistas, y expresan divesas ideologías políticas y actitudes de ciertos grupos sociales (exilados, sobrevivientes de la dictadura, jóvenes generaciones luchando por comprender la historia argentina). La transición entre el primer y el segundo acto será marcada coreográficamente a través de una escena en la milonga El Tugurio. Si bien todos los protagonistas se mueven, cantan y tocan instrumentos musicales siguiendo el estilo paradigmático de la corporalidad tanguera, esta escena en la que el argumento cambia abruptamente de curso se caracteriza por el tango baile y los rituales milongueros.

La tangópera ha sido concebida como una colaboración experimental multiarte, con un fuerte componente educativo centrado en la creación y recepción interculturales. Narración, coreografía, composición musical, escenografía y géneros fílmicos (animación, documental y video musical) intervienen en la creación de un espectáculo de tango con contenido político, generando la oportunidad de reflexionar críticamente sobre el exotismo y la apropiación cultural.

Angora Matta será presentada en su versión original en español con subtítulos en inglés.

Protagonistas

Personajes principales

Angora Matta, *mezzo/bailarina*
Elvira Díaz, *soprano*
Manuela Malva, *mezzo-soprano*
Mariano Monteamor, *tenor*
Bruja, *mezzo/bailarina (misma q' Angora)*
Presidente, *barítono*

Personajes secundarios

Hotelero, *actor*
Librero, *barítono (mismo q' Presidente)*
Maestro de Ceremonias, *actor*
Mozo, *actor (mismo q' Hotelero)*
Milongueras *(Elvira y Manuela; bailarinas)*
Milongueros, *tenor, barítono y bajo; bailarines*
Amigo de Mariano, *actor (mismo q' M. C.)*
Políticos, *tres (mismos q' Milongueros)*
Periodista, *actor (mismo q' M. C.)*
Detectives, *dos (mismos q' Milongueros)*

Personajes filmados

Tango-raperos *(video musical)*
Presidente, *barítono (pseudo documental)*

Otros

Orquesta Típica
Coro de Vestiditos *(mismo q' Milongueras)*
Bailarines de Tango, *cuatro fem., tres masc.,*
más figuras de cartón y mural
Perrito de Angora/Gato de Bruja, *bailarina*
Murgueros
Títeres de Sombra, estilo Balinés. Funcionan
como la proyección de un film animado entre
diversas escenas, esquematizando eventos.
Contribuyen a acelerar la dinámica del argu-
mento. *(Puede reemplazarse por dibujos anima-
dos.)* Los títeres—figuras de cartón en las que

Protagonistas

Main Characters

Angora Matta, *mezzo/dancer*
Elvira Díaz, *soprano*
Manuela Malva, *mezzo-soprano*
Mariano Monteamor, *tenor*
Witch, *mezzo/dancer (same as Angora)*
President, *baritone*

Secondary Characters

Hotel Clerk, *actor*
Bookseller, *baritone (same as President)*
Master of Ceremonies (M.C.), *actor*
Waiter, *actor (same as Hotel Clerk)*
Milongueras *(Elvira, Manuela; dancers)*
Milongueros, *tenor, baritone, bass; dancers*
Mariano's Friend, *actor (same as M.C.)*
Politicians, *three (same as Milongueros)*
Journalist, *actor (same as M.C.)*
Detectives, *two (same as Milongueros)*

Filmed Characters

Tango-Rappers *(music video)*
President, *baritone (mock documentary)*

Others

Tango Orchestra
Chorus of Disguises *(same as Milongueras)*
Tango Dancers, *four women, three men,*
plus cardboard figures and mural
Angora's Dog/Witch's Cat, *dancer*
Murga Dancers/Singers
Shadow Puppets, Balinese style. They work
like an animated film background projection
between scenes, schematizing events. They
contribute to accelerate the pace and dynamic of the plot. *(Could be replaced by
animation.)* The puppets—cardboard

57

se destacan las siluetas—poseerán características que los harán identificar con los personajes y actores que reemplazan.

Ambientación

Los Angeles, Buenos Aires, y Miami; fin del siglo veinte. Verano en EE.UU., invierno en Argentina. La historia se desenvuelve en el transcurso de una semana.

Todas las escenas se montarán con un mínimo de recursos escenográficos. Se destacan la simplicidad, los colores primarios. Todas se desarrollan en ambientes cerrados (salvo las que están a cargo de los títeres de sombra). Se destacan los letreros y puertas de acceso o umbrales que conectan las escenas entre sí (el dormitorio de Angora en Los Angeles; la salida del hotel Nuevo Sur en Buenos Aires; la Librería Pasado y Presente; el Café Los Emigrados; el Cuarto de Hotel de Angora; la milonga El Tugurio; el dormitorio de Mariano; el recinto gubernamental; el set del telenoticiero; el consultorio de la Bruja). La iluminación es fundamental en la creación de los ambientes.

Vestuario

Todos los personajes visten de negro (excepcionalmente de gris o blanco). Los sombreros y zapatos llaman la atención por sus formas y colores estrafalarios. Angora Matta lleva la misma cartera roja a lo largo de toda la obra.

Coreografía

El tango es un baile popular de parejas y los bailarines profesionales del género rara vez realizan coreografías grupales. La tangópera pro-

Setting

Los Angeles, Buenos Aires, and Miami; end of the twentieth century. Summer in the U.S., winter in Argentina. The story unfolds over the course of a week.

All scenes will be built with a minimun of scenographic resources. Simplicity and primary colors will be highlighted. All scenes take place in enclosed environments (except for the ones performed by shadow puppets). The focus is on billboards, entry doors, and thresholds that connect between scenes (Angora's bedroom in Los Angeles; entrance to Buenos Aires's Nuevo Sur hotel; the bookstore Pasado y Presente; the café Los Emigrados; Angora's hotel room; the tango dance hall El Tugurio; Mariano's bedroom; governmental office; news TV set; the Witch's office). The lighting is essential for creating the environments.

Costuming

All characters dress in black (exceptionally in gray or white). Hats and shoes focus attention through extravagant shapes and colors. Angora Matta carries the same red bag throughout the entire performance.

Choreography

Tango is a partnered social dance, and tango group choreographies are seldom pursued by professional tango dancers. The tangópera

pone una colaboración coreográfica donde los enfoques tradicionales y modernistas se mantienen en lugar de fusionarse, generando un tenso diálogo de movimientos. Otros géneros incluidos son murga, milonga, y vals milonguero.

Todos los personajes cultivarán un lenguaje corporal tanguero en el caminar, en el sentarse, en el modo de aproximarse unos a otros, de cantar, tocar instrumentos y, por supuesto, bailar. Siguiendo los principios coreográficos del tango, cada uno desarrollará un estilo único y propio. Los pasos de Angora (su modo de caminar) son particularmente característicos.

proposes a choreographic collaboration where traditional and modernist approaches to the vocabulary will be interspersed rather than mixed, generating a tense movement-based dialogue. Other genres used include murga, milonga, and waltzed milonga.

All characters cultivate a tangoesque body language in the ways in which they walk, sit, approach each other, sing, play musical instruments, and, obviously, dance. Following tango choreographic principles, each character will develop a unique and personal style. Angora's steps (her walk) are very particular.

Acto I/Act I

Preludio	**Prelude**
Parte 1	Part 1

La ópera comienza con un preludio musical a cargo de una orquesta típica. La orquesta introduce el tema "Memoria del Poder". Escenario a oscuras. Se proyecta un cartelón con explicaciones sucintas, como en el cine mudo, que lleva la siguiente leyenda:

Angora Matta, exiliada de la Dictadura de los años 70, reside en Beverly Hills, California. Un día del final de siglo Angora es abordada por un desconocido interesado en contratar sus servicios. Estos requerirán un viaje a Buenos Aires.

The opera begins with a musical prelude performed by a tango orchestra. The orchestra introduces the leitmotif "Memory of Power." Stage in the dark. Projection of the following framed text (reminiscent of silent movies):

Angora Matta, an exile of the Argentine dictatorship of the 1970s, lives in Beverly Hills, California. One day at the end of the century Angora is approached by a stranger interested in contracting her services. These will entail a trip to Buenos Aires.

Parte 2	Part 2

Títeres de sombra (estilo balinés, efecto de filmación proyectada): perspectiva de una calle de Beverly Hills. Se ven avanzar dos líneas verticales en paralelo (perfil de títeres de cartón), que al dar una curva toman cuerpo. Una de las figuras es Angora paseando su perro; la otra un automóvil lujoso, convertible. Baja una figura masculina del auto y se aproxima a Angora, parada en la vereda. Se enfrentan. El habla, Angora le da una tarjeta. El lee. Ella lanza una carcajada sonora.

Sonido: los pasos de Angora; automóvil a marcha lenta que se detiene; ladrido; carcajada de Angora.

Shadow puppets (Balinese style, animated-film effect): a frontal view of a street in Beverly Hills. Two vertical lines advance in parallel toward the audience (profile of shadow puppets); figures take full shape as they take a turn. One of them is Angora walking her dog; the other, a stranger in a luxury car. A male figure steps out of the car and approaches Angora, standing on the sidewalk. They face each other. He talks, Angora gives him a card. He reads. She laughs boldly out loud.

Sound: Angora's steps; car driving slowly and stopping; dog barking; Angora's laughter.

Apagón	Black-out

61

Angora en Beverly Hills / **Angora in Beverly Hills**

Angora diseñando sus disfraces / **Angora designing her disguises**

Escena 1: El Contrato

Escena con un actor y coro: Angora canta este tema en su dormitorio mientras prepara las valijas. Muchos espejos y ropa desordenada en el escenario. Elige sus atuendos cuidadosamente para ocultar su identidad tras diversos disfraces. (Las transformaciones de Angora a lo largo de la ópera se centran en cambios de zapatos y sombreros estrafalarios.) Un pequeño coro interviene oculto tras los atuendos, produciendo el efecto de un "vestuario que canta".

Música: "Angora Matta"—tango de aire jazzeado. Se inicia con solo de trompeta; se va transformando con percusión.

Angora Matta:

Se me acercó en la calle.
Le pasé mi tarjeta.
Leyó: "Angora Matta,
servicio vil de urgencia".

Preguntó a quemarropa:
¿"Opera al exterior"?
Respondí: "Yo me vendo
al mejor postor".

Le aclaré que mi fama
me viene desde lejos,
ajusto cuentas raras
y no sigo de nadie los consejos.

Sellamos el contrato.
Un fato ultra secreto.
Ignoro los detalles,
la víctima, el objeto.

Sé que voy
a un país condenado . . .
Que de noche curte tanguidad.
Y en algún bolichón decadente
bailaré los compases de mi fatalidad.

Scene 1: The Contract

Scene with one actor and chorus: Angora sings the theme in her bedroom while packing for the trip. Lots of mirrors and clothes in disarray all over the place. She carefully chooses her attire, planning to hide her identity in various disguises. (Angora's transformations throughout the opera focus on changes of extravagant hats and shoes.) A small chorus intervenes hidden behind the garments creating the effect of "singing clothes."

Music: "Angora Matta"—jazzy tango. Begins with a trumpet solo. Transforms with the addition of percussion.

Angora Matta:

He approached me in the street.
I gave him my card.
He read: "Angora Matta,
nasty emergency service."

He asked point blank:
"Do you operate abroad?"
I answered: "I go
for the highest bid."

I made it clear that my fame
is long-standing,
I settle strange accounts
and I accept no advice, from no one.

We sealed the contract.
An ultra secret affair.
I ignore the details,
the victim, the purpose.

I know that I'm going
to a condemned country . . .
Where at night they cultivate tangoness.
And in some decadent joint
I'll dance to the beat of my fatality.

Angora empacando sus disfraces / Angora packing her disguises

Coro:

Angora viaja a Buenos Aires,
una misión de intriga y mal.
Tras los disfraces de una extraña
ocultará la cruel maraña
de una conspiración letal.

De día recorrerá las calles
sin dejarse reconocer.
De noche, sola en la milonga,
ojos de gata entre las sombras,
bailará hasta el amanecer.

Angora:

Sé que voy
a un país condenado . . .
Que de noche
curte tanguidad.
Y en algún
bolichón decadente . . .

Coro:

Desvencijado, irreverente . . .

Angora:

Un tugurio . . .

Coro:

Mal augurio!

Angora:

Ejerceré mi especialidad
que es mezcla de caridad
y final fatal.

Coro:

Angora viaja a Buenos Aires.
Un plan siniestro, enigma cruel.
Aplicando estudiada saña
atrapa giles, los engaña.
Los seduce con su desdén.

Chorus:

Angora travels to Buenos Aires,
a nasty, intriguing mission.
Disguised, as a stranger
she will hide the cruel cobweb
of a lethal conspiracy.

During the day she'll walk the streets
avoiding being recognized.
At night, alone in the milongas,
cat eyes in the dark,
she'll dance until dawn.

Angora:

I know that I'm going
to a condemned country . . .
Where at night
they cultivate tangoness.
And in some
decadent joint . . .

Chorus:

Run down, irreverent . . .

Angora:

A dump . . .

Chorus:

Bad omen!

Angora:

I will apply my specialty
which is a mixture of charity
and in the end, fatality.

Chorus:

Angora is traveling to Buenos Aires.
A sinister plan, a cruel enigma.
Applying studied malice
she entraps gullible guys, deceives them.
She seduces them with disdain.

Tras los disfraces de una extraña
ocultará la cruel maraña . . .
conspiraciones del poder.

Angora:

Buenos Aires,
buena guita, un amor . . .
Invierno porteño, gris . . .
el crimen y se acabó.

¿Angora Matta? Angora Matta murió.
Hoy la voy de Angora Kils.
Las carcajadas retumban
en todo Beverly Hills.

*Al finalizar el tango, Angora se pone un abrigo
negro, anteojos de sol, y carga sus valijas
apurada.*

*Un fondo de títeres de sombra muestra su viaje
en taxi al aeropuerto; la fila de pasajeros frente
al mostrador de check-in y, finalmente, Angora
sentada en la butaca del avión.*

*Música: continúa "Angora Matta", instrumental,
percusión acentuada.*

Apagón

Escena 2: Callecitas de Buenos Aires

*Títeres de sombra y coro de murgueros (en
el escenario): durante el apagón comienza a
insinuarse el tema "Callecitas de Buenos Aires",
una murga. Este tema ubicará a la audiencia
en el paisaje social de Buenos Aires. Mientras se
escucha la murga, el fondo de títeres de sombra
muestra a Angora dormida en el avión, el
aterrizaje, su paso por inmigraciones, el retiro
de equipaje, y su viaje en taxi rumbo a la ciudad.
Se proyectan imágenes de Buenos Aires, close-
ups (primeros planos) y panorámicas,
yuxtaposición de murales y fotos. Idea de mucho
movimiento.*

Behind disguises, as a stranger
she will hide the cruel cobweb . . .
conspiracies of power.

Angora:

The ticket to Buenos Aires,
good bucks, some love . . .
Porteño winter, gray . . .
the crime and that's it.

Angora Matta? Angora Matta died.
Now I go by Angora Kils.
Laughter echoes
all over Beverly Hills.

*Toward the end of the tango, Angora
reaches for a black coat and her sunglasses,
and picks up her bags in haste.*

*A background of shadow puppets shows her
taxi drive to the airport; the check-in line of
passengers in front of the airline booth,
and, lastly, Angora sitting in the airplane.*

*Music: "Angora Matta" continues, instru-
mental, percussive.*

Black-out

Scene 2: Little Streets of Buenos Aires

*Shadow puppets and murga-like chorus (on-
stage): during the black-out the theme "Callecitas de Buenos Aires," a murga, begins to
build. This murga will situate the audience in
the social landscape of Buenos Aires. While
the murga is playing, the shadow puppets
show Angora sleeping in the airplane, the
landing, her passage through immigration,
retrieving her luggage, and taking a taxi
from the airport to the city. Projection of images of Buenos Aires, close-ups and pano-
ramic views, juxtaposition of murals and
photographs. A sense of intense movement.*

Angora llega a Buenos Aires / **Angora's arrival in Buenos Aires**

Música: "Callecitas de Buenos Aires"—murga, primero instrumental y luego se suman solista y coro.

Solista:

¿Qué le puedo vender
que haga feliz su estadía
en esta ciudad tan al sur
de la historia y la geografía?
Un puerto de lujo y lata
junto al Río de la Plata.
Un obelisco, al centro,
marca obscena del encuentro.
Diagonales bien trazadas.
Cortaditas malintencionadas.
Casas bajas, rascacielos,
frenesí y desconsuelo.
Parques, viejos y mocosos:
verde, gris, y globos rojos.
Una city atolondrada
mezcla sucia y espejada;
farra, ruidos y negocios,
desvarío y mil antojos.
Puro politiquerío,
ansiedad, miedo al vacío.
Ciudadanos atrevidos,
arribistas, malparidos,
malhumorados y arpías
empeñados en utopías.

Coro:

Unos dicen: ¡qué cultura!
Otros dicen: ¡qué barbarie!
Yo sé bien lo que tienen
las callecitas de Buenos Aires.

Que se parece a París . . .
Que le recuerda a Estambul . . .
Bienvenido, don turista,
a la gloria, a la joya, a la diva *(a tres voces)*
de la América del Sur.

Music: "Little Streets of Buenos Aires"— murga, first instrumentally and then with the soloist and chorus.

Soloist:

What can I offer you
to make your visit pleasant
to this city so far to the south
of history and maps?
A port of luxury and tin
by the River of Silver.
An obelisk at the center,
an obscene rendezvous marker.
Well-traced diagonals.
Dead ends with bad intentions.
Low houses, skyscrapers,
frenetic and sorrowful.
Parks, old people, and kids:
green, gray, and red balloons.
A city on the go
dirty and mirroring mix;
party, noises, and business,
madness and a thousand cravings.
Pure politics,
anxiety, fear of emptiness.
Bold citizens,
ambitious, competitive,
moody and mean-spirited
bent on utopias.

Chorus:

Some say: What a culture!
Others say: What barbarism!
I know well what
the little streets of Buenos Aires have.

(You think:) It looks like Paris . . .
It reminds you of Istanbul . . .
Welcome, Mr. Tourist,
to the glory, the jewel, the diva *(three singers)*
of South America.

Solista:

Aconsejo al visitante
subirse a un colectivo
para ingresar al ambiente
cotidiano del nativo.

Apreciará, apretujado,
olor a nafta, accidentes,
y entre uno y otro tumbo:

Coro a Tres Voces:

Miraditas, cachetadas, carteristas
a velocidad creciente.

Solista:

Bájese en la parada.
¡Mire qué gente fina!
Ellos lindos como flores,
ellas flacas y divinas.

Los porteños pasan raudos,
pasos largos, siempre al frente.
Prendidos del celular,
las finanzas en la mente.

Uno va paseando perros,
otro, repartiendo pizzas . . .
Estos tipos venden todo:

Coro a Tres Voces:

Choripanes, lapiceras, estampitas
y le ofrecen la precisa.

Solista:

Usted va lo mas campante
gozando la ciudad bella . . .
Las palomas se alboratan,
un tumulto lo atropella.

Ya se escuchan los reclamos
y se agitan las pancartas,
vienen de Plaza de Mayo:

Soloist:

I advise the visitor
to jump on a bus
to enter the daily world
of the native.

Squeezed, you'll appreciate
the smell of gas, accidents,
and between stumbles:

Chorus of Three Singers:

Seductive glances, blows, pickpockets
at increasing speed.

Soloist:

Get off at the bus stop.
Look at these folks, so refined!
Men beautiful like flowers,
women slim and divine.

The porteños pass by hastily
always at the forefront, long strides.
Stuck to their cellular phones,
finances on their minds.

One of them walks dogs,
another delivers pizzas . . .
These guys sell everything:

Chorus of Three Singers:

Sausages, pens, cards with holy saints
and they offer you the last tip.

Soloist:

You're minding your own business
enjoying the beautiful city . . .
The doves are restless,
a crowd runs you over.

The protests can be heard
and the signs are waved,
they're coming from Plaza de Mayo:

Coro a Tres Voces:

Los maestros, jubilados, los travestis . . .
porque el sistema los mata.
Unos dicen: ¡qué cultura!
Otros dicen: ¡qué barbarie!
Yo sé bien lo que tienen
las callecitas de Buenos Aires.

Solista:

¡Los contrastes son de locos!
Entérese, don turista,
que estas calles esconden:

Coro a Tres Voces:

Desempleados, pobretones, deshauciados,
tras Christian Diores y Visas.

Coro, *recita, protesta:*

Contáte algo positivo, che . . .
Los tangos, lo intelectual,
la luna, no sé, los besos . . .
Este tipo, ¿qué va a pensar?

Solista:

Que la historia nos jugó
crueles, malas pasadas:
injusticias, guerras, muertos.
¡Queremos más democracia!

(Pausa)

Solista y Coro, *a todo volumen:*

Y mientras . . . nos distraemos:
fútbol, tele, pasaporte . . .
Soñamos con parecernos:

a los ricos, poderosos, posmodernos . . .
los del hemisferio norte.

Chorus of Three Singers:

The teachers, retirees, transvestites . . .
because the establishment kills them.
Some say: What a culture!
Others say: What barbarism!
I know well what
the little streets of Buenos Aires have.

Soloist:

The contrasts are maddening!
Beware, Mr. Tourist,
that these streets hide:

Chorus of Three Singers:

Unemployed, paupers, wretched,
behind Christian Diors and Visa cards.

Chorus, *recites, protests:*

Hey! Say something positive . . .
about our tangos, our intellectuals,
the moon, whatever, our kisses . . .
What's the guy gonna think?

Soloist:

That history has played us
cruel, bad tricks:
injustices, wars, deaths.
We want more democracy!

(Pause)

Soloist and Chorus, *full volume:*

And meanwhile . . . we distract ourselves:
soccer, TV, passports . . .
We dream of becoming like:

The rich, powerful postmoderns . . .
of the northern hemisphere.

¡Ay! La rabia y la ironía,
y esta dignidad sin rumbo . . .
¿Dónde andará la manía
de desafiar al mundo?

El coro de murgueros sale del escenario bailando pasos tradicionales de murga. Un murguero rezagado toma el centro del escenario con pasos de murga espectaculares. El apagón se produce con el murguero en plena acción.

Apagón

Escena 3: Primera Instrucción (a la Salida del Hotel Nuevo Sur)

Escena con actores: Angora, vistiendo su primer disfraz, sale apurada de su Hotel en Buenos Aires. El Hotelero la intercepta con un mensaje que le entrega en un papel de color estridente. Angora lee el mensaje y sale a paso decidido hacia la calle.

Música: "Callecitas de Buenos Aires" se continúa en esta escena hasta que Angora lee el mensaje, en silencio. Al salir definitivamente del hotel se escucha el tema "Memoria del Poder" (instrumental) en ritmo de candombe. (El candombe se inicia con los pasos de Angora.)

Apagón

Escena 4: Segunda Instrucción (en la Librería Pasado y Presente)

Parte 1

Títeres de sombra: la figura de Angora camina por Buenos Aires a paso firme. Iniciada su marcha, comienza a seguirla una figura femenina a paso menos resuelto. Imágenes de la calle Corrientes; close-ups de letreros de librerías, kioscos, carteleras de teatros, casas de música. Angora ingresa en una librería.

Ah! The rage and the irony,
of this dignity without direction . . .
Where did that maniacal impulse
to challenge the world go?

Murga chorus exits the stage dancing traditional murga steps. One murguero is left behind. He takes center stage, performing spectacular murga steps. The black-out catches him in full action.

Black-out

Scene 3: The First Instruction (leaving the Nuevo Sur Hotel)

Scene with actors: Angora, wearing her first disguise, leaves the Nuevo Sur Hotel hastily. The Hotel Clerk intercepts her at the door with a message written on a slip of brightly colored paper. Angora reads the message and walks out.

Music: "Little Streets of Buenos Aires" continues throughout the scene until Angora reads the message, in silence. As she finally leaves the hotel, the "Memory of Power" theme plays in candombe rhythm. (The candombe starts with Angora's steps.)

Black-out

Scene 4: Second Instruction (at the Pasado y Presente Bookstore)

Part 1

Shadow puppets: the figure of Angora walks in Buenos Aires with steady steps. Soon a female figure starts following her more hesitantly. Images of Corrientes Avenue; close-ups on billboards for bookstores, kiosks, theaters, music shops. Angora enters a bookstore.

Angora a la salida del hotel recibiendo su primera instrucción / Angora, leaving the hotel, receives her first instruction

Elvira sigue a Angora por avenida Corrientes / **Elvira follows Angora on Corrientes Avenue**

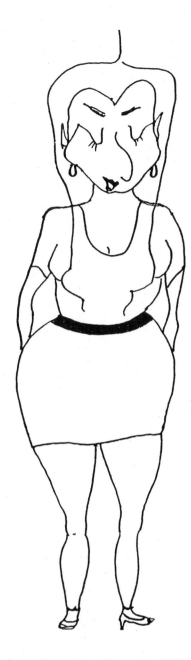

Retrato de Elvira Díaz / **Portrait of Elvira Díaz**

Angora y Elvira en la librería Pasado y Presente / Angora and Elvira at the Pasado
y Presente bookstore

Música: continúa el ritmo de candombe.

Apagón

Parte 2

Escena con tres actores ambientada en una librería de la calle Corrientes: Angora ingresa a la librería Pasado y Presente. Elvira Díaz, antigua compañera de militancia, ha creído reconocer a Angora por la calle y la sigue hasta la librería. Angora merodea entre los estantes, hojea libros distraída mientras Elvira canta "El Desencuentro". El librero las observa atentamente e interviene con un solo. Angora se siente provocada y decide hacerse oír (canta un solo y luego un dúo de mutuas acusaciones con Elvira). Finalmente Elvira sale de la librería con la última palabra.

Música: "El Desencuentro"—tango con dos ambientes: primera parte, íntimo; segunda parte, dúo de Elvira y Angora, con ruidos bulliciosos de la ciudad.

Elvira Díaz:

Buenos Aires es muy grande
pero, la pucha, que el mundo es chico.
La reconocí enseguida
por el caminar.

Iba por la calle Florida,
pegó la vuelta en Corrientes,
se metió en la librería,
preguntó por obras de Marx.

Elvira, *recita:*

La mirada distraída,
se paró en otros estantes,
sacó cuentos, poesía.
Las hojas parecían hablar.

Music: candombe rhythm continues.

Black-out

Part 2

Scene with three actors in a bookstore on Corrientes Avenue: Angora enters the Pasado y Presente bookstore. Elvira Díaz, an old friend through political alliances, believed she recognized Angora's particular way of walking. She follows her to the bookstore. Angora browses through the stacks, opens books distractedly while Elvira sings "El Desencuentro." The bookstore salesman observes attentively and intervenes with a solo. Angora feels provoked and decides to tell her side of the story (sings solo and then in duet, exchanging accusations with Elvira). In the end, Elvira exits the bookstore singing the last lines.

Music: "The Disencounter"—tango with two moods: first part, intimate; second part, Elvira and Angora duet, interspersed with street noise.

Elvira Díaz:

Buenos Aires is very big
but, jeez, the world is very small.
I recognized her right away
by the way she walks.

She was walking down Florida,
took a turn in Corrientes,
entered the bookstore,
asked for books by Marx.

Elvira, *recites:*

She glanced at the books distractedly,
stopped by other bookshelves,
picked up short stories, poetry.
The pages seemed to talk.

Tocaba las palabras como ciega,
me daba no sé qué interrumpirla.
"Angora", dije bajito
y ahora sé que hice mal.

Elvira, *canta:*

No quería darse vuelta,
se le notaba en la espalda.
El pasado en carne viva
desfilaba a su pesar.

Pero sonsa y egoísta
yo insistí en el encuentro,
pensando que de aflicciones
se podía conversar.

Acá, en el café, estos años
de estar quietos y a la fuerza,
nos fuimos acostumbrando
a discutir la impiedad.

Librero:

Quisimos convencernos que las palabras
gastarían lo terrible, lo ausente,
que de tan dicho se haría irrepetible,
que no volvería a hacernos frente.

La paradoja de cultivar el olvido
recordando el presente,
mezclando los tiempos y las cosas
con tal de escapar cuentas pendientes.

Angora:

Buenos Aires es muy grande
pero, la pucha, que el mundo es chico.
La reconocí enseguida . . .
Decidí disimular.

Sonsa, sonsa y egoísta
yo empeñada en ignorarla.
No quiero saber de nadie.
¡Déjenme vivir en paz!

She touched the words like a blind person,
I felt uneasy about interrupting her.
"Angora," I said in a low voice
and now I know it was wrong.

Elvira, *sings:*

She didn't want to turn around,
I could see it in her back.
The past, still an open wound,
paraded against her will.

But silly and egotistical
I insisted on our encounter,
thinking that afflictions
were a matter of conversation.

Here, in the cafés, these years,
forced to be quiet,
we got used to it,
to discuss impieties.

Bookseller:

We wanted to believe that words
would use up the terrible, the absent,
that such talk would preclude repetition,
that we wouldn't have to face it again.

The paradox of cultivating forgetfulness
remembering the present,
mixing times and things,
whatever to escape pending accounts.

Angora:

Buenos Aires is very big
but, jeez, the world is very small.
I recognized her right away . . .
I decided to fake it.

Silly, silly and egotistical
I was determined to ignore her.
I don't want to meet anybody.
Let me go my way!

Elvira:

"Disculpáme", dije apurada
pero esos ojos ya estaban clavados.
Me interrogaban con cierto desprecio,
acusadores, sin vueltas, traición.

Elvira y Angora:

Yo hubiera querido explicarle,
pero qué, si no se entiende,
si ni el inconsciente nos salva
*(el dúo continúa alternando líneas; tono
acusatorio)*
de habernos, de habernos vendido,
de apostar a la paz indecente,
de no querer armar lío,
de no chillar, de apretar los dientes,
de borrar las ganas de cambiar el mundo.

Angora:

De prohibirnos la revolución
de acomodarnos al curro, al curro,
matar los sueños y
comernos la corrupción, la corrupción.

Elvira:

Me fui, la dejé pagando,
apostando al desencuentro
de los sueños del pasado
y de un futuro signado, maldito,
por la falta de pasión.

*Angora intenta salir tras Elvira. El Librero le
sale al paso. Este le entrega un volumen
envuelto para regalo. Angora lo recibe con cierta
sorpresa. Se sobrepone rápidamente y sale de la
librería.*

Apagón

Elvira:

"I'm sorry," I said hastily
but those eyes were already piercing me.
They asked with some disdain,
accusingly, without hesitation, treason.

Elvira and Angora:

I would have liked to explain
but what? If there is no understanding,
if not even the unconscious will save us
*(duet continues alternating lines, accus-
ingly)*
from having, from having sold out,
from betting on an indecent peace,
from not wanting to raise havoc,
from not screaming, from gnashing teeth,
from erasing the will to change the world.

Angora:

From denying ourselves the revolution
from taking bribes, bribes
killing the dreams and
swallowing corruption, corruption.

Elvira:

I left, and left her hanging there
betting on the discounter
of past dreams
with a future marked, cursed,
by the lack of passion.

*Angora tries to leave after Elvira. The
Bookstore Salesman gets in her way. He
gives her a gift-wrapped book. Angora
takes it, somewhat surprised. She rapidly
recovers and exits the bookstore.*

Black-out

Manuela canta en el café Los Emigrados / Manuela singing in the Los Emigrados café

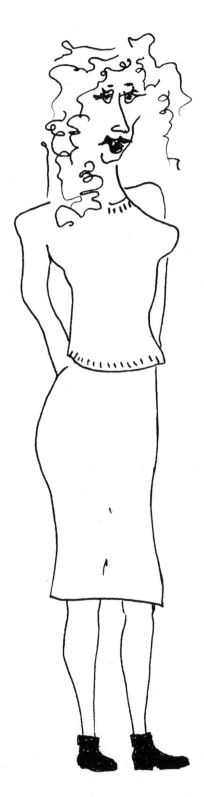

Retrato de Manuela Malva / **Portrait of Manuela Malva**

Escena 5: Tercera Instrucción
(en el Café Los Emigrados)

Parte 1

Títeres de sombra: la figura de Angora en la calle (pasan transeúntes y autos) rompe ansiosa el envoltorio y extrae un índice de papel estridente de entre las páginas del libro. Lo lee. Inicia rápidamente una corta marcha hacia un café situado en las inmediaciones. A la puerta del café (close-up sobre el letrero) finaliza esta escena.

Música: "Memoria del Poder" en ritmo de candombe. (El candombe sigue el ritmo de los pasos de Angora.)

Apagón

Parte 2

Escena con actores: Angora ingresa a un café lleno de gente ruidosa. Se sienta sola en una mesita incómoda, ubicada en un rincón. En un pequeño escenario se ubica un quinteto de tango y un maestro de ceremonias anuncia "La Noche de los Emigrados". A continuación presenta a la cantante, Manuela Malva, y la invita al micrófono. Manuela interpretará su nuevo tema, homenaje "a los que se fueron o están por irse, cualquiera sea la razón". Manuela se sube al pequeño escenario y canta.

Música: "La Emigrada"—tango rantifuso.

Manuela Malva:

Estoy podrida
del orden y parsimonia,
de tanta fobia,
de amabilidad tan fría,
del laburo obsesionante,
soledad y paz vacía,
de esta vida protegida
de oruga gris, embutida.

Scene 5: Third Instruction
(at the Los Emigrados Café)

Part 1

Shadow puppets: the figure of Angora in the street (people and cars pass by) anxiously unwrapping the book, taking out a colorful bookmark buried between pages. She reads the bookmark. She starts a short, fast walk toward a café located nearby. The scene ends at the door of the Los Emigrados café (close-up on the sign.)

Music: "Memory of Power," candombe rhythm. (The candombe follows Angora's steps.)

Black-out

Part 2

Scene with actors: Angora enters a café full of noisy customers. She sits down alone at a small, uncomfortable corner table. A tango quintet plays on a small stage. The M.C. announces "The Night of the Emigrés." He proceeds to introduce the singer, Manuela Malva, and invites her to the microphone. Manuela will sing her new song, an homage to "those who have left or are about to leave the country, for whatever reasons." Manuela takes the small stage and sings.

Music: "The Émigré"—ruffianesque tango.

Manuela Malva:

I'm fed up
with so much order and temperance,
with so much phobia,
with such cold niceties,
with obsessive work,
loneliness and empty peace,
with this sheltered life
like a gray, bottled worm.

Esto no es tango
ni tampoco poesía.
Esto es una porquería,
un ataque de nostalgia.
¡Pura queja de abundancia!
Duda loca, atravesada,
identidad complicada.
Lloriqueo de emigrada.

No me escuchés . . .
¡Ay! ¡Escucháme!
Decíme algo . . .
¡Salváme!
Distraéme, engañáme,
hacéme el verso adecuado . . .
Y ya que estás, pasáme un trago.

Mirá, no sé . . .
Ando harta y rabiosa,
desorientada, exaltada,
pesimista, acobardada . . .
¡Sacáme de la pavada!
Y ya que estás, llamála a mama.

No te sonrías,
¿no ves que sufro la historia?
Me atormenta la memoria
dislocada, dividida.
Quisiera hacer otra vida:
mate, siesta . . . y menos confusión.

*El tango de Manuela es recibido con fuertes
aplausos. Manuela deja el escenario y se dirige
decididamente hacia la mesa de Angora, como
si la conociera. Angora se pone de pie para
recibirla. Manuela la abraza y le murmulla algo
al oído mientras le coloca un papelito de color
estridente en el bolsillo. Otros miembros de la
audiencia rodean a Manuela para saludarla.
Angora aprovecha la confusión para salir del café
con disimulo.*

*Sonido: ruido de sillas, murmullos, risas,
excitación.*

Apagón

This is not a tango,
nor is it poetry.
This is trash,
a nostalgia attack.
Pure complaint out of abundance!
Crazy, stalled doubt,
complicated identity.
An émigré's whining.

Don't listen to me . . .
Ah! Do listen!
Tell me something . . .
Save me!
Distract me, trick me,
read me the appropriate script . . .
And in the meantime, give me a drink.

Look, I dunno . . .
I'm fed up and enraged,
disoriented, out of my self,
down, scared . . .
Get me out of this!
And in the meantime, call my mama.

Don't smile at me,
don't you see I suffer this story?
I'm tormented by memories,
dislocated, divided.
I'd like to live a different life:
mate, siesta . . . and less confusion.

*Manuela's tango is received with enthusi-
asm. She leaves the stage and walks straight
toward Angora's table—as if she knew her.
Angora stands up to welcome her. Manuela
hugs her and speaks into her ear while slip-
ping a piece of brightly colored paper into
Angora's pocket. Other audience members
surround Manuela. They want to congratu-
late her. Angora takes advantage of the confusion and exits the café unnoticed.*

*Sound: noises of chairs, murmurs, laughter,
excitement.*

Black-out

Angora frente al tango videoclip en el hotel / Angora watching a tango music video at the hotel

Escena 6: Videoclip de Tango en el Hotel

Parte 1

Títeres de sombras: la figura de Angora (en la calle) extrae el papel del bolsillo, lo lee, y camina decididamente hacia su hotel.

Música: "Memoria del Poder," ritmo de candombe (breve.)

Apagón

Parte 2

Escena con un actor: Angora, en su cuarto de hotel, se viste (otro disfraz) para ir a la milonga El Tugurio. Prende la televisión. Se sorprende con lo que ve y oye: un videoclip de tango. Una banda de Tango-raperos jóvenes interpreta el tema "Un Tango u Otra Cosa". (Videoclip proyectado en pantalla visible para la audiencia.)

Música: "Un Tango u Otra Cosa"—tango con trío de guitarras, estilo rap pero bien porteño. (Se destaca la similitud entre ambos géneros.)

Tango-raperos en Videoclip:

Me dijeron . . .
que entre el tango y yo
habia mil años
de disparate.
Cosa de viejos,
cuando era chico
crecí arruináo
entre el rock y los milicos.

Que las zapatillas
no van con la viruta.
Que primero hay que saber sufrir,

Scene 6: Tango Music Video in the Hotel

Part 1

Shadow puppets: the figure of Angora (in the street) draws the slip of paper out of her pocket, reads it, and walks determinedly toward the hotel.

Music: "Memory of Power," candombe rhythm (brief.)

Black-out

Part 2

Scene with one actor: Angora, in her hotel room, dresses up (another disguise) for her next incursion to the tango club El Tugurio. She turns on the TV. She is surprised with what she sees and hears: a tango music video. A Tango-Rappers band performs the theme "Un Tango u Otra Cosa" (A Tango or Something Else.) (Music video shown on a screen that the audience can see.)

Music: "A Tango or Something Else"—tango with guitar trio, rap style but clearly porteño. (Highlights the similarities between the genres.)

Tango-Rappers in Music Video:

I'm told . . .
A thousand years of madness
stand between
tango and me.
Already outdated,
when I was a kid
I grew up ruined
by rock and the military.

That sneakers
don't get along with dance floors.
That you've gotta know how to suffer,

andar sin pensamiento.
Y sobre todo amar
algo más que el vento.

Y que yo soy
de una generación quemada.
Esa . . .
¡que no siente nada!

Hasta acá
de drogones y anestesia.
Insolentes,
pero sin conciencia.

Me dijeron . . .
que no tenemos
barrio ni esquina;
criaos . . .
pa'l boliche y la oficina.
Administración
de empresas,
poca bola a Perón,
al Che y a la vieja.

Que nos da igual
Evita que Madonna,
la hamburguesa
que el bife de chorizo.
Que preferimos
el dólar verde
al pesito gastado,
desprolijo.

Que las mujeres
hacen lo que se les canta,
y a nosotros,
ni un nudo en la garganta.

Mirá, yo sé,
ando a los tumbos
y perdido.
No entiendo el mundo.
Quisiera esperanza.
Y sí . . .
Me importa la guita,
pero también
la confianza.

how to live without thinking.
And above all how to love
something more than money.

And that I belong
to a burnt-out generation.
The one . . .
that feels nothing!

Up to here
with druggies and anesthesia.
Insolent,
but without a clue.

I'm told . . .
that we belong
to no 'hood or corner;
reared . . .
for the dance club and the office.
Business
management,
no attention to Perón,
Che, or old mom.

Evita or Madonna,
what's the difference,
hamburger
or sirloin steak.
We prefer
green dollars
to the screwed-up
little peso.

That women
do whatever they want,
and we . . .
we don't even choke.

Look, I know,
I'm rambling
and lost.
I don't understand this world.
I'd like some hope.
That's right . . .
I care for money,
but also
for trust.

Quisiera hacer
un arte de mi vida.
Sé que, al final,
vos y yo nos entendemos . . .
Ese curro
de la globalización
no reparte amor
ni comprensión.

No sé si ésto es
un tango u otra cosa;
pero tu jubilación, viejo,
a mí me importa.
Y si salís a la calle
yo te sigo.
No me acusés
de andar mirándome el ombligo.
No me digás
que soy un caso perdido.
¡No me acusés!

Angora se sienta sobre la cama y mira el video-clip azorada. Al finalizar el videoclip, suspira, se levanta, y camina decidida hacia la puerta de su cuarto.

Apagón

I want to make
art out of my life.
In the end, I know,
you and I agree . . .
This scheme
about globalization
doesn't distribute love
or understanding.

I'm not sure if this is
a tango or something else;
but your pension, old man,
I care about that.
And if you take to the streets
I'll follow you.
Don't accuse me
of navel-gazing.
Don't tell me
that I'm a lost cause.
Don't accuse me!

Angora sits on her bed and watches the music video in disbelief. When it's over, she sighs, stands up and walks determinedly toward her bedroom door.

Black-out

Escena 7: Instrucción Final (en la Milonga El Tugurio)

Parte 1

Títeres de sombra y luego escena con actores y bailarines: una milonga del centro. Pista con parejas de baile; mesas ocupadas alrededor. Orquesta de tango sobre el escenario. Elvira Díaz y Manuela Malva llegan, independiente-mente, a El Tugurio. Se reconocen, se abrazan como amigas de viejos tiempos, se sientan juntas en una mesa.

La orquesta toca un breve fragmento de "Memoria del Poder" (tema que anuncia el final de las tandas). Las parejas de baile se desarman y

Scene 7: Final Instruction (at the El Tugurio Tango Club)

Part 1

Shadow puppets followed by a scene with actors and dancers: a downtown tango club. Dancers in couples at the dance floor; people sitting at tables located around it. Tango orchestra on a stage. Elvira Díaz and Manuela Malva arrive at the tango club independently. They recognize each other, hug like old friends, and sit down together at a table.

The orchestra plays a brief segment of the "Memory of Power" theme (which

Milongueras en El Tugurio / Milongueras at El Tugurio

Pista de baile en El Tugurio / El Tugurio's dance floor

dejan la pista camino a sus respectivas mesas.
Se preparan para el cambio de parejas. Las
milongueras esperan ansiosas que los galanes
las saquen a bailar. La orquesta inicia los acordes
de "Patrañas de Milonguera". Elvira, Manuela
y Angora Matta suman sus voces a las de otras
milongueras y a coro (desde sus respectivas
mesas) cantan el tema. Angora, quien ya se
encontraba en El Tugurio al inicio de la escena,
se hace notar cantando unas estrofas en
solo.

Música: "Patrañas de Milonguera"—valsecito
milonguero.

announces the end of each set). The danc-
ing couples split and walk toward their ta-
bles. They get ready to change partners.
The milongueras wait anxiously to be asked
to dance. The orchestra starts playing
"Patrañas de Milonguera" (Milonguera's
Tricks). Elvira, Manuela, and Angora
Matta join other milongueras singing this
song as a chorus (sitting at different tables).
Angora, who was present at El Tugurio
from the beginning of the scene, calls atten-
tion to herself by singing some lines solo.

Music: "Milonguera's Tricks"—waltzed
milonga.

Coro de Milongueras:

Estamos en El Tugurio
(antro desvencijado, de mal augurio).
Acá no se muestran los dientes;
bailamos bien, pero sin cortes indecentes.

Vienen viejos y salameros,
pobres, giles y mujeriegos.
A nosotras ¡qué nos importa!
Nos seduce el bailarín sentimental
que en la noche nos transporta.

Y cuando lo vea aburrido
ponga en su oreja un suspiro, suspiro,
pa' que dure un tango más.
Y cuando lo vea aburrido
ponga en su oreja un suspiro, suspiro
pa' que dure un tango más.

Angora:

Me hago la linda, la poco complicada;
la osa, la que no anda en nada.
Ni perdida, ni buscada,
ni tonta, ni alucinada.

Me siento por ahí y espero . . . y,
cuando me clavan la mirada,
respondo pero desganada.

Milongueras' Chorus:

We are at El Tugurio
(a dump, a bad-omen place).
Here teeth are not shown;
we dance well, but without indecent steps.

Old guys come and the sleazy,
poor, naive ones and womanizers.
To us, who cares!
We're seduced by the sentimental dancer
that at night transports us.

And when you see he's bored
a sigh, a sigh into his ear
so he lasts one tango more.
And when you see he's bored
a sigh, a sigh into his ear
so he lasts one tango more.

Angora:

I pretend to be sweet, not too difficult;
easygoing, someone up to nothing.
Neither lost, nor sought,
neither stupid, nor stoned.

I sit there and wait . . . and
when they pierce me with their look,
I respond but with low energy.

Dejo la silla sin ahínco,
voy al encuentro sin esmero,
me abrazo al fulano relajada,
no le prometo nada,
parezco ensismismada
(para mí, francamente, una pavada).

Y cuando lo veo aburrido
pongo en su oreja un suspiro, suspiro,
pa' que me dure un tango más.

Coro de Milongueras:

Y cuando lo vea aburrido
ponga en su oreja un suspiro, suspiro,
pa' que le dure un tango más.

Angora:

Y así la noche entera
hasta que me eche el ojo
el galán que desespera.

*Elvira y Manuela se sorprenden al ver a Angora
en la milonga. Intentan acercarse a su mesa,
pero Angora las ignora sistemáticamente. Las
confunde. Angora Matta baila con varios.
Escenas de sacar a bailar al estilo milonguero;
escenas de levante. Hacia el final de la escena,
Angora baila con Mariano Monteamor. Entre un
tango y otro, un mozo se acerca a la mesa de
Angora (está sentada sola toda la noche) y le
pasa un papel de color estridente. Angora se
levanta para irse. Mariano le sale al encuentro
para pedirle el teléfono. Angora se lo da apurada
y se va. Los juegos de iluminación durante esta
escena son muy importantes: los focos, erráticos
sobre distintas parejas, se centran en Angora en
los momentos claves. Foco sobre Mariano y
Angora; y la luz sigue a Angora hacia la salida
de El Tugurio.*

*Música: segmentos de tangos bailables
populares, interrumpidos por la "Memoria
del Poder" (el tema que señala el cambio*

I leave the chair without effort,
approach the encounter without caring,
embrace the guy relaxed,
not promising him anything,
seeming self-absorbed
(for me, frankly, a cinch).

And when I see he's bored
a sigh, a sigh into his ear
so he lasts one tango more.

Milongueras' Chorus:

And when you see he's bored
a sigh, a sigh into his ear
so he'll last for you one tango more.

Angora:

And this way all night long
until I catch the eye
of the desperate guy.

*Elvira and Manuela are surprised to see An-
gora at the tango club. They try to approach
her table but Angora ignores them systematically. They are confused by her behavior.
Angora Matta dances with several partners.
Several episodes of asking to dance tango-
style; episodes of picking up. Toward the end
of the scene, Angora dances with Mariano
Monteamor. Between tangos, a waiter approaches Angora's table (she sits by herself
all night) and leaves a colorful slip of paper.
Angora stands up, ready to leave. Mariano
steps in her way to ask for her phone number. Angora responds hastily, and leaves.
Lighting is crucial during this scene: erratic
spotlights on various couples, focusing now
and again on Angora in key moments. Focus
on Mariano and Angora; the spotlight follows Angora as she leaves El Tugurio.*

*Music: segments of popular "dancey" tan-
gos, interrupted by the "Memory of Power"*

de parejas y otros movimientos en la
milonga.)

(the theme that announces the end of a set,
the opportunity for changing dance couples
and other movements in the dance club).

Parte 2

*Escena con actores: en El Tugurio sigue la ac-
ción. El foco se concentra en el bar. Acodados sobre el mostrador tres Milongueros conversan sobre Angora Matta. Los Milongueros se turnan en
cantar las líneas, siguiendo el sentido de una
conversación. Mariano se les suma al final.*

Música: "Chismes de Milongueros"—milonga.

Milonguero 1:

¿Te fijaste en ésa, la nueva?

Milonguero 2:

¿La que camina sin ruido de pisadas?

Milonguero 3:

¿La que perturba el aire sin moverse?

Milonguero 2:

¿La que apenas se deja ver la cara?

Milonguero 3:

¿Esa de la voz de terciopelo?

Milonguero 2:

¿La que baila como de duelo?

Milonguero 1:

¿Será viuda?
Dicen que es medio rara,
que de día teje encrucijadas
que de noche las tiende,
redes enmarañadas, invisibles,
que no se sienten.

Part 2

*Scene with actors: action continues in El
Tugurio. Spotlight on the bar section. Three
Milongueros leaning on the bar gossip about
Angora Matta. The Milongueros take turns
singing the following lines as in a conversa-
tion. Mariano joins them toward the end.*

Music: "Milongueros' Gossip"—milonga.

Milonguero 1:

Did you notice that one, the new one?

Milonguero 2:

The one who walks with noiseless steps?

Milonguero 3:

That one who moves the air without moving?

Milonguero 2:

The one who hardly lets her face be seen?

Milonguero 3:

That one with the velvety voice?

Milonguero 2:

The one who dances as if in mourning?

Milonguero 1:

Could she be a widow?
They say she is kinda strange,
that by day she knits crossroads
that in the night she lays them out,
nets, enmeshed, invisible,
that nobody feels.

Milonguero 2:	Milonguero 2:
¿Será espía?	Could she be a spy?
Puede ser coleccionista.	She could be a collector.

Milonguero 3:	Milonguero 3:
¿Será bruja?	Could she be a witch?

Milonguero 1:	Milonguero 1:
¡Pará! Cortála . . .	Stop . . . Cut it out!
Entre las milongueras se chimenta	The milongueras gossip
que es una de esas mudas sin pasado,	that she's one of those mute ones
que no tiene nada que esconder;	without a past, nothing to hide;
sólo aires de poder.	only airs of power.

Milonguero 2:	Milonguero 2:
¡Pura envidia!	Pure envy!

Milonguero 3:	Milonguero 3:
¡Competencia!	Competition!

Milonguero 2:	Milonguero 2:
Yo la saco.	I'll ask her (for a dance).

Milonguero 3:	Milonguero 3:
Yo me borro.	I'm out of here.
Mejor observar de lejos.	Better to watch from afar.

Milonguero 1:	Milonguero 1:
Pero vamos, che, es una señora . . .	Hey, come on, she is a lady . . .
Sospecho que es escritora.	I suspect she is a writer.
Yo me juego, quién te dice, una changa,	I'll take the risk, who knows, a gig,
clases de tango, propaganda,	tango lessons, publicity,
actor de cine, estrellato . . .	movie actor, stardom . . .

Milonguero 2:	Milonguero 2:
Dejáme . . . Sí, seguro . . .	Yeah . . . Sure . . .
otra historia de contratos,	another of those stories of contracts,
de acá a Broadway,	from here to Broadway,
después Hollywood . . .	then Hollywood . . .

Mariano Monteamor:

Sigan delirando . . .
Yo les digo porque hice la experiencia:
es livianita en el baile pero espesa,
sabe de firuletes
pero prefiere lo simple,
la música, la acongoja
y para las marcas, es una diosa.

Apagón

Fin de Acto I

Mariano Monteamor:

Continue your delirium . . .
I tell you, 'cause I tried it:
she's a light but thick dancer,
she knows fancy steps
but prefers it simple,
the music, it gets her
and in following her partner she's a goddess.

Black-out

End of Act I

Milongueros en El Tugurio / **Milongueros at El Tugurio**

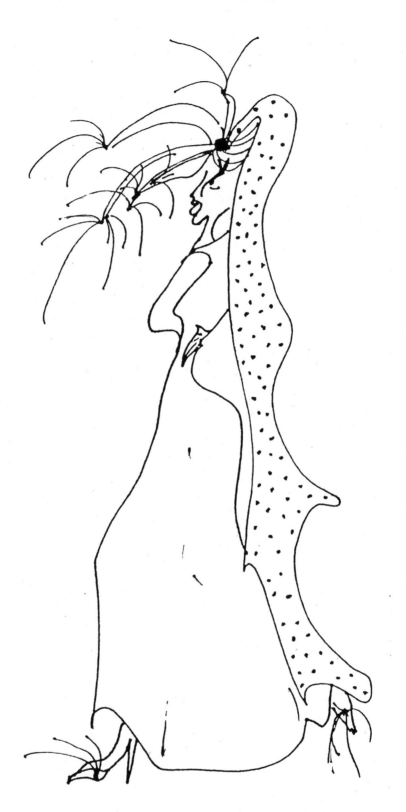

Angora a la salida de El Tugurio / **Angora leaving El Tugurio**

Retrato de Mariano Monteamor / *Portrait of Mariano Monteamor*

Acto II/Act II

Escena 8: Angora Sale a Matar

Escena con un actor: escenario a oscuras. Conversación telefónica entre Mariano Monteamor y Angora Matta. (Puede ser una grabación con ruidos de líneas, etcétera.)

Mariano Monteamor:

¿Qué hacés?

Angora Matta:

Ando apurada. *(Duda un instante.)* Voy al cine.

Mariano:

¿Solita?

Angora:

Mirá, ya estaba por salir.

Mariano:

¿Te acompaño?

Angora:

No. Me distraigo.

Mariano:

¿Te busco entonces?

Angora:

No. Voy a volver en tren.

Mariano:

(Se ríe) No te deja ni cerca . . .

Scene 8: Angora Gets Ready to Kill

Scene with one actor: stage in the dark. Telephone conversation between Mariano Monteamor and Angora Matta. (Can be a recording with phone line noises, etc.)

Mariano Monteamor:

What are you doing?

Angora Matta:

I'm in a hurry. *(Doubts for a second.)* I'm going to a movie.

Mariano:

All by yourself?

Angora:

Look, I'm about to leave.

Mariano:

Can I join you?

Angora:

No. I'll get distracted.

Mariano:

Then I'll pick you up?

Angora:

No. I'll take the train.

Mariano:

(Laughs) It doesn't go near your place . . .

Angora:

Bueno, el subte, lo que sea.

Mariano:

¿Qué te pasa?

Angora:

Te dije que no me llamés.
Corto ahora.

Mariano:

Pará. Explicáme.

Angora:

No tengo tiempo.
En otro momento; otro día.

Mariano:

No entiendo. Anoche parecía . . .
No sé qué decirte.
Me dejás helado. Me tenés loco.

Angora:

Te dije, Mariano. Olvidáme.
Me atrae la traición y la distancia.
La vida para mí es hipocresía.

Mariano:

¿Qué querés entonces?

Angora:

Mañana, con vos, en esta cama.

Foco sobre Angora que cuelga el teléfono impaciente. Está en su cuarto de hotel, en semipenumbra, terminando de vestirse con otro disfraz. Ya lista, se acerca a su cama y extrae el arma que había escondido debajo de la almohada. Pone el arma en la cartera. Parte apurada.

Angora:

Well, I'll take the subway then, whatever.

Mariano:

What's going on?

Angora:

I told you not to call me.
I'll hang up now.

Mariano:

Wait. Tell me what's going on.

Angora:

I have no time now.
Some other time; another day.

Mariano:

I don't get it. Last night, it seemed like . . .
I don't know what to say. You are driving me nuts.

Angora:

I told you, Mariano. Forget me.
I'm attracted to distance and betrayal.
Life for me is hypocrisy.

Mariano:

What do you want then?

Angora:

Tomorrow, you, in this bed.

Spotlight on Angora as she hangs up. She is in her dimly lit hotel room, getting into another costume. Once ready, she walks to her bed and retrieves the weapon she kept concealed under her pillow. She tucks it into her bag. She leaves in a hurry.

Música: "El Cuchillo Bajo la Almohada"—tango instrumental.

Music: "The Knife Under the Pillow"— instrumental tango.

Apagón

Black-out

Escena 9: El (Que Se Cree) Condenado

Scene 9: The (One Who Believes He Is) Condemned

Escena con actor: escenario poco iluminado. Foco sobre Mariano Monteamor en la intimidad de su cuarto (sencillo, prolijo). Mira el teléfono. Se sienta en una silla. Mariano se cree condenado por el amor fatal que le propone Angora. Se siente víctima de la pasión. Canta en tono de reflexión.

Scene with one actor: dim stage. Spotlight on Mariano Monteamor in the privacy of his bedroom (simple, tidy). He looks at the phone. He sits on a chair. Mariano believes he is condemned by Angora's fatal love. He feels he is a victim of passion. He sings in a reflective tone.

Música: "El Condenado"—tango ultra-dramático.

Music: "The Condemned"—ultra-dramatic tango.

Mariano:

No quisiera arruinar esta noche.
Las preguntas matan la intimidad.
Respeto el enigma de tu vida.
Presiento que esto va a acabar mal.

Entraste con aire de otro mundo.
Nadie te conoce por acá.
Insinuás sonrisas y miradas.
Más de dos palabras no largás.
Tomás en copas altas algo frío.
Bailás especulando la pasión.
¿Por qué, por qué jugás con lo nuestro?
¿Te tendrá mal un revés? ¿La ilusión?
Te tiembla todo el cuerpo . . .
Pero al final,
tus tangos me dejan muerto.

No sos mi primera pesadilla.
Anduve angustiado por amor.
Pero esta intriga, espanto, dolor . . .
Confusión pesada . . . Estupor.

Poción envenenada, violenta.
Callada y dulce, dulce maldición.
Quién sabe qué arma vertiginosa

Mariano:

I wouldn't want to ruin this night.
Questions kill intimacy.
I respect the enigma of your life.
I can tell this will end bad.

You came in with an otherworldly air.
Nobody knows you around here.
You feign a smile and stare.
You give away not more than two words.
You drink something cold in tall glasses.
You dance speculating on passion.
Why, why do you play with our relationship?
Are you nursing a backstroke? Illusion?
Your whole body trembles . . .
But in the end
your tangos leave me dead.

You are not my first nightmare.
I've been anguished because of love.
But this intrigue, scare, pain . . .
Heavy confusion . . . Stun.

Poisonous potion, violent.
Quiet and sweet, sweet curse . . .
Who knows what vertiginous weapon

Mariano en su departamento / **Mariano at his apartment**

habrás hundido en mi corazón.

Tomás en copas altas algo frío.

Bailás especulando la pasión.

¿Por qué, por qué jugás con lo nuestro?

¿Te tendrá mal un revés? ¿La ilusión?

Te tiembla todo el cuerpo . . .

Pero al final,

tus tangos me dejan muerto.

¡Fulmináme! Ya estoy entregado,

infeliz, atrapado en tu red.

No me dejés herido, marcado.

Me resigno: ¡matáme de una vez!

you sunk into my heart.

You drink something cold in tall glasses.

You dance speculating on passion.

Why, why do you play with our relationship?

Are you nursing a backstroke? Illusion?

Your whole body trembles . . .

But in the end,

your tangos leave me dead.

Finish me! I've given up,

unhappy, trapped in your net.

Don't leave me wounded, marked.

I'm resigned: Kill me once and for all!

Apagón

Black-out

Escena 10: Al Otro Día

Scene 10: The Next Day

Títeres de sombra: flash de Mariano Monteamor con un Amigo, sentados en el café de la esquina. Mariano (demacrado, desesperado) le cuenta lloroso sus desventuras amorosas. (No se entiende lo que dice; palabras sueltas entre sollozos.) El Amigo lo escucha distraído mientras lee el diario. Lo interrumpe repentinamente con la noticia de la muerte del Presidente.

Shadow puppets: flash of Mariano Monteamor with a Friend, sitting down at a corner café. Mariano (desperate, in bad shape) tells his friend in tears about his love mishaps. (Incomprehensible words while weeping.) His Friend listens distractedly while reading the newspaper. Suddenly he interrupts Mariano with the news of the President's death.

Amigo:

Está muerto.

Friend:

He's dead.

Mariano:

¿Quién?

Mariano:

Who?

Amigo:

El Presidente. Dicen que fue una mujer la asesina.

Friend:

The President. They say it's a woman, the assassin.

Mariano:

¿La detuvieron?

Mariano:
Did they arrest her?

Mariano se entera por su amigo que el Presidente ha sido asesinado / Mariano learns from his friend that the President has been killed

Amigo:	**Friend:**
No. La andan buscando.	No. They're looking for her.
Dicen que tienen pistas,	They say that they have clues,
que están investigando.	that they're investigating.
Música: "Memoria del Poder"—tango instrumental, arranca con aire de suspenso al finalizar el diálogo.	*Music: "Memory of Power"—instrumental tango, starts with suspenseful mood toward the end of the dialogue.*
Apagón	Black-out

Escena 11: Reunión de Gabinete / Scene 11: Cabinet Meeting

Escena con tres actores: ambiente de recinto gubernamental. (Cuadros de antiguos presidentes, la bandera, etcétera.) Tres Políticos sentados alrededor de una mesa ovalada, sostienen una reunión secreta, de emergencia.	*Scene with three actors: a governmental office. (Pictures of former presidents, the flag, etc.) Three politicians sitting around an oval table. They are holding a secret emergency meeting.*
Música: "Memoria del Poder" continúa, con tonos de intriga política.	*Music: "Memory of Power" continues, with "political intrigue."*
Político 1:	**Politician 1:**
Esto hay que presentarlo	This must be presented
como una locura, puro azar . . .	like a mad act, random . . .
Una mujer cualquiera . . .	A woman in no way special . . .
Político 2:	**Politician 2:**
¿Terrorista? ¿Subversión?	A terrorist? Subversion?
¿Influencias foráneas?	Foreign influences?
Político 3:	**Politician 3:**
Por ahora no. Digamos	Not for the time being. Let's say
que es casi una extranjera . . .	that she is almost a foreigner . . .
Político 2:	**Politician 2:**
¿Turista? ¿Inmigrante?	Tourist? Immigrant?
Político 1:	**Politician 1:**
Una desocupada,	Unemployed,
de esas que cruzan la frontera.	one of those who crosses the border.

Los Políticos sostienen una reunión de gabinete / The Politicians hold a cabinet meeting

Prácticamente una mendiga
recién llegada a la ciudad.
Buenos Aires la confundió,
los tangos, malos ratos,
la noche la contrarió.
Algún síntoma,
un odio reprimido.

Político 3:

La infancia o el amor,
alguna proyección,
una fijación,
desplazamientos, fetiches . . .
Los gualichos, un conjuro . . .
Redactemos la confesión.

Político 1:

Consultemos una bruja
para que guíe la investigación.

Los Políticos asienten unánimemente al plan.

Apagón

Escena 12: El Noticiero

Escena con un actor: un telereportero anuncia el boletín de noticias.

Música: un segmento de "Memoria del Poder" como cortina de noticiero.

Periodista:

Y ahora sí, como prometimos,
haciéndonos eco del duelo nacional,
el último discurso oficial
de nuestro querido Presidente.

Se extingue la iluminación sobre el Periodista. Baja una pantalla de TV gigante. Se proyecta el último discurso del Presidente, un corto

Practically a beggar
just arrived into town.
Buenos Aires confused her,
the tangos, some hard times,
the night double-crossed her.
Some kind of symptom,
a repressed hatred.

Politician 3:

Childhood or a love story,
some kind of projection,
a fixation,
displacements, fetishes . . .
Magic charms, incantations . . .
Let's draft the confession.

Politician 1:

Let's consult with a witch
so that she'll guide our investigation.

The Politicians agree unanimously to the plan.

Black-out

Scene 12: The News Report

Scene with one actor: a TV news reporter announces the news bulletin.

Music: A segment of "Memory of Power" plays like a news broadcast's background music.

Journalist:

And now, just as we promised,
echoing the nation's mourning,
the last public address
of our beloved President.

Lights on the Journalist go off. Gigantic TV screen. Projection of the President's last public address, a "documentary." Chorus

Retrato del Presidente / Portrait of the President

"documental". El coro (sobre el escenario) interrumpe con aplausos, murmullos, gritos, chiflidos, taconeos y otras expresiones de apoyo o crítica.

Música: "Palabras de Presidente"—milonga campera.

Presidente:

¡Ciudadanos!
Me dirijo a ustedes,
en este día democrático invernal
orgulloso y optimista
pero hay detalles que ajustar.

A pesar de nuestro esfuerzo
el país aún retiene
un perfil de republiqueta
llena de vivos e infieles;
mercachifles de cuarta,
ánimos desasosegados,
ambiciosos, corruptos,
gauchaje triste y desalmado.

(Como verán,
nos tienen bien junados.)

Coro:

Protesta con silbatina y taconeos.

Presidente:

La imagen hay que cambiar.
Esto no se discute:
seguimos las instrucciones
del FMI y ¡salúte!
Poco hay pa' negociar.
La ruta está trazada:
nos vamos pa'l Primer Mundo
y la vida globalizada.

Coro:

Gritos y aplausos.

(onstage) interrupts the speech with applause, murmurs, shouts, whistling, stomping, and other expressions of support or protest.

Music: "Words of the President"—rural milonga.

President:

Citizens!
I address you
on this democratic winter's day
proud and optimistic
but there are details we need to consider.

Despite our effort
the country still maintains
a mock-republic profile
full of smart-asses and infidels;
of lowly merchant types,
of disgruntled souls,
the ambitious and the corrupt,
a horde of sad and merciless gauchos.

(As you can see,
they know us very well.)

Chorus:

Stomping and whistling in protest.

President:

This image we must change.
No discussion about it:
we follow the instructions
of the IMF and that's it!
Little room for negotiation.
The road has been defined:
We are going toward the First World
and a globalized life.

Chorus:

Shouts and applause.

Presidente:

No me vengan con que ésto es
pura cosa de alienados.
Me mueven la lucidez,
los créditos y el contado.
El pesito valdrá igual
que el dólar tan apreciado.
Prometo estabilidad,
para eso me han votado.

Coro:

Gritos de aprobación.

Presidente:

Garantizo dignidad
seduciendo al mundo entero
con la belleza sin par
de nuestras rubias modelos.
Shopping center e internet,
guita dulce y desempleo.
Parece cosa de locos
pero seremos posmodernos.

Coro:

Bombos y saltos, gran excitación.

Presidente:

Olvidemos el pasado,
la violencia, utopías.
La prosperidad requiere
una mente clara y fría.
Que muertos y generales
no agiten el avispero.
Cada cosa en su lugar
por las buenas, recomiendo.

Coro:

Murmullos; inquietud.

President:

Don't tell me that this amounts
to pure alienation.
Lucidity guides me,
the loans and cash.
Humble pesos will be worth
as much as the priceless dollar.
I promise stability,
that's why you voted for me.

Chorus:

Shouts of approval.

President:

I guarantee dignity
seducing the entire world
with the unmatchable beauty
of our blond models.
Shopping centers and Internet,
easy money and unemployment.
Seems like a crazy thing
but that will make us postmodern.

Chorus:

Drums and jumping, great excitement.

President:

Let's forget the past,
the violence, utopias.
Prosperity requires
a clear and cold mind.
The dead and the generals
should be kept still.
Everything in its place
in good faith, I recommend this.

Chorus:

Murmurs; unrest.

Presidente:	President:
Espero haber sido claro.	I hope I've been clear.
Lo que importa acá es la guita.	What counts here are the bucks.
El nuevo orden mundial	The new world order
así lo indica.	establishes that.
Inversiones extranjeras	Foreign investments
pa' salir del retroceso,	to overcome backwardness,
privatizar hasta la madre	privatize even your mother
y todo eso.	and all that.

Coro:	Chorus:
Una columna se retira en desacuerdo.	*A row of citizens leaves in disagreement.*

Presidente:	President:
Ahora, si me disculpan,	Now, I beg your pardon,
me retiro a descansar.	I must take to rest.
Y Argentina, patria mía,	And Argentina, my dear fatherland,
si querés llorar, llorá.	if you want to cry, cry.

Coro:	Chorus:
Final frenético; delirio, confusión.	*Frantic finale; delirious confusion.*

Apagón

Black-out

Escena 13: La Consulta con la Bruja

Scene 13: The Session with the Witch

Parte 1

Part 1

Títeres de sombra: un automóvil veloz da una curva. Chirrían las ruedas. Frena abruptamente. Se escuchan dos portazos. Dos Detectives a cargo de investigar la muerte del Presidente llegan al consultorio de la Bruja.

Shadow puppets: a fast car takes a turn. Tires screech. Abrupt stop. Doors slam loudly. Two Detectives in charge of investigating the death of the President arrive at the Witch's office.

Sonido: Chirrido de ruedas, frenada, portazos. Sin música.

Sound: Tire screeching, car stopping, door slamming. No music.

Parte 2

Part 2

Escena con actores: en esta escena son fundamentales las coreografías de la Bruja en diferentes estados de trance y del coro que la acom-

Scene with actors: choreographies for Witch and Chorus while undergoing different states of possession are key in this scene.

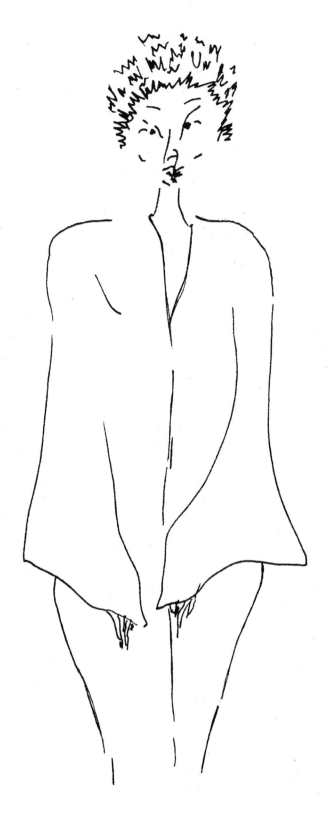

Retrato de la Bruja / Portrait of the Witch

Los Detectives / The Detectives

Los Detectives, Elvira, Manuela y Mariano en el consultorio de la Bruja / Detectives, Elvira, Manuela, and Mariano at the Witch's office

paña. La Bruja puede ser interpretada por distintos cantantes/bailarines a medida que se suceden los diversos episodios de posesión. Especial atención a los juegos de iluminación. La Bruja recibe a los Detectives en silencio, en un ambiente en semipenumbra (su consultorio). Sin hacer preguntas, entra en trance.

Detective 1:

Esta mujer delira.

Detective 2:

Parece poseída.

Detective 1:

Fijáte que alucina.

Detective 2:

Habla de un general.

Bruja:

Poseída por un General, camina como un militar borracho. Se lleva una mesita y una silla por delante. Pronuncia con voz grave y autoritaria:

"La confesión la hará fuerte.
La salvará de la muerte".

Detectives, asustados:

Ahora se viene . . . Te digo que da miedo.
Escuchá lo que dice. Es una historia pesada.
Parece que oyera voces . . .
Rumores . . . Está sacada.

La Bruja, poseída, empieza la confesión. Recita, junto con el coro, la "Memoria del Poder". Alternan estrofas en español e inglés.

The Witch could be played by several singers/dancers as various episodes of trance occur. Special attention to lighting. The Witch receives the Detectives in silence. A room with imperfect shadows (her office.) The Witch immediately enters a trance, without asking the detectives any questions.

Detective 1:

This woman is delirious.

Detective 2:

She seems possessed.

Detective 1:

Look, she's hallucinating.

Detective 2:

She speaks of a general.

Witch:

Possessed by a General, she walks like a drunken officer, runs into a small table and a chair, and recites in a grave, authoritarian voice:

"Confession makes you stronger.
It will keep you alive much longer."

Detectives, scared:

It's coming . . . I tell you, it's spooky.
Listen. It's a heavy story.
Seems like she hears voices . . .
Rumors . . . She is out of it.

The Witch, possessed, starts the confession. She recites, together with the chorus, the "Memory of Power." They alternate sections in Spanish and English.

*Música de fondo, progresivamente audible:
"Memoria del Poder"—tango apiazzolado a lo
largo de la escena.*

Bruja y Coro, *recitan:*

El poder es denso, pesado;
su naturaleza es viscosa . . . Es pegajoso.
Se esconde de sí mismo
como si estuviera siempre en otro lugar
y en manos de algún otro, atrapado,
listo para ser robado.

Tienta, fascina por su presencia ausente.
Constantemente rozado,
frotado a pelo y contrapelo,
imposible de agarrar . . .
Manotón.

El poder se cuela entre las manos.
Transporta con su olor animal.
Promete dar forma a los deseos impensables,
inconfesables al final.

El poder es un movimiento,
un desplazamiento como tal.
Cuando se lo piensa como una "cosa",
sólo se lo presiente
siguiendo sus rastros, su vida social.

No tiene punto claro de partida,
ni línea limpia, trayectoria,
ni fuerza constante, ni objetivo
a excepción de aumentar su propia gloria.

Apariencia majestuosa, de otro mundo.
Aferrado a la lucha terrenal,
el poder se mueve en un dominio
de pragmatismo total.

El poder pertenece a un universo
de intencionalidad absoluta:
desafía todo intento de representación
a excepción de la imagen de una "fuente" que,
paradójicamente,
consume recursos resistentes.

*Background music, progressively audible:
"Memory of Power"—Astor Piazzolla–style
tango throughout the scene.*

Witch and Chorus, *recite:*

Power is thick, dense, heavy;
its nature is viscous . . . sticky.
It hides from itself, as if it
were always somewhere else,
in someone else's hands,
ready to be taken.

Tempting, its absent presence fascinates.
Permanently fretted,
rubbed by and against it,
unable to take it . . .
A grasp.

Power melts when held in hands.
Transports with its animal scent.
Promises to shape
at last unspoken, unthought desires.

Power is a movement,
displacement as such.
When thought of as a "thing,"
it can only be sensed
by tracking its social life.

No clear point of departure,
no clean line, trajectory,
no constant thrust, or aim
except to augment its own glory.

Majestic appearance, otherworldly,
yet tied to grounded episodes of struggle,
power moves in a domain
of pure pragmatism.

Power belongs to a universe
of full intentionality:
It defies representation
except for the image of a "source"
paradoxically
pulling in resistant resources.

Sin definir su posición, pero
con gran don de ubicuidad,
el poder adopta rostros
y opera en un tiempo y en un espacio
que establece a voluntad.

Cortando moldes directamente
de texturas encarnadas,
hilvanando burocráticamente
piezas no coincidentes,
unas tras otras, con hilo invisible,
pisando el pedal incesantemente,
como una costurera loca y experta
que ambiciona crear modelos sin costuras,
el poder fabrica, crea locura.

Elvira Díaz y Manuela Malva llegan al consulto-
rio de la Bruja. Ella les abre la puerta anticipada-
mente. Sabe que, al igual que los Detectives,
vienen en busca de Angora. Les clava la mirada,
cae poseída y canta.

Bruja *en delirio, rodando por el piso, canta:*

Evoco al poder y sus pesadillas.
Confieso un crimen.
Esposada, me pudro en la oscuridad.
Me declaro culpable sin sentir ninguna culpa.
Convencida, es mi orgullo hacer el mal.
Al final, la justicia no ha sido justa conmigo,
¡jamás!

Un crimen perfecto,
nada que hacer al respecto.
Un poco de remordimiento,
pero nada de arrepentimiento.
Sin juicio, ni tribunales.
Mi culpabilidad es llana.
Confesar es irrelevante.
No confieso; no me da la gana.

Los dedos me señalaron.
La luz se hizo más fuerte.
El crimen nunca existió.
Le tengo miedo a la muerte.

Positionless and yet
ubiquitous,
power takes up faces
and operates in a time and space
it defines for itself.

Cutting off patterns directly
from embodied textures,
stitching bureaucratically
misfitting pieces,
one after another with invisible thread,
stepping relentlessly on a pedal
like a mad, expert seamstress
driven by ambitions of seamlessness,
power fabricates, creates madness.

Elvira Díaz and Manuela Malva arrive at
the Witch's office. The witch knows that,
like the Detectives, they are looking for An-
gora. She stares at them, falls into a trance,
and sings.

Witch, *delirious, rolling on the floor, sings:*

I evoke power and its nightmares.
I confess a crime.
Shackled, I rot in the dark.
I plead guilty without feeling any guilt.
Convinced, I'm proud of my wrongdoings.
After all, justice has never been just to me,
never!

A perfect crime,
nothing to do about it.
Some remorse,
but no regrets.
No trial, no courtrooms.
Plain confession.
Confessing is irrelevant.
I don't confess; I don't feel like it.

Fingers pointed at me.
The light grew stronger.
The crime never existed.
I am afraid of death.

Bruja *continúa, agitada, recita:*

Conversaciones como ésta
imponían los generales.

Coro:

1976.

Bruja:

Tenían inmensa confianza
en sus poderes mentales.
Conspiraciones creaban
y reprimían de un saque.

Coro:

1977.

Bruja:

Magos para gobernar,
los dictadores.

Coro:

1978.

Bruja:

Te hacen desaparecer
y ni se esconden.

Coro:

1979.

Bruja:

Sus subalternos operaban, obedientes.
Pero los muertos seguían presentes.
Los vivos exigíamos derechos humanos,
los generales se lavaban las manos.

Coro:

1982.

Witch *continues, agitated, recites:*

The generals imposed
conversations of this sort.

Chorus:

1976.

Witch:

They had great confidence
in their mental powers.
Conspiracies they created
and repressed in a single blow.

Chorus:

1977.

Witch:

They rule like magicians,
those dictators.

Chorus:

1978.

Witch:

They make you disappear
and don't even hide.

Chorus:

1979.

Witch:

Their subalterns acted obediently.
But the dead continued being present.
We, the living, demanded human rights,
the generals washed their hands.

Chorus:

1982.

Bruja:

Los días pasaban
culposos, pesados.
Miedo a todos y a todo,
gente y libros censurados.

*Mariano Monteamor llega al consultorio de
la Bruja. Manuela y un Detective lo dejan
entrar por indicación (gestual) de la Bruja.
Mariano ingresa confundido. La presencia de
los otros lo sorprende. La Bruja respira con
dificultad.*

Música: breve interrupción.

Parte 3

*La coreografía (mayormente minimalista) y los
juegos de iluminación son esenciales. El siguiente
texto corre a velocidad de lectura sobre una pantalla que ocupa un tercio del escenario.*

Música: "Memoria del Poder"—instrumental.

El general tenía tres caras
a la vez, y, cada tanto,
las cambiaba a todas juntas.
Siempre lo descubríamos,
a pesar de su astucia,
por el aspecto de su Ministro que
nunca lo dejaba solo.
Esas orejas extrañas . . .
siempre apuntando a Washington y
a los burócratas del FMI.
Exigía austeridad y sacrificio
a ese pueblo de ilusos arrogantes.
Al General le prometieron gloria
impopular pero histórica.

Solo y frecuentemente borracho, un día
el General tomó una decisión tajante.
Sospechaba el deshonor
de las guerras sucias.
Y la reina de Inglaterra, sorprendida,

Witch:

Days went by,
heavily, full of guilt.
Fear of everyone and everything,
people and books censored.

*Mariano Monteamor arrives at the Witch's
office. Manuela and one of the Detectives let
him in at the Witch's indication (a gesture).
Mariano looks confused. He is surprised by
the presence of the others. The Witch
breathes with difficulty.*

Music: brief interruption.

Part 3

*Choreography (mostly minimalist) and
plays of illumination are essential. The following text scrolls down a screen that takes
up a third of the stage (reading pace).*

Music: "Memory of Power"—instrumental.

The general had three faces
at a time, and every so often,
he would change them all at once.
We could always tell,
despite his cleverness,
by the looks of his Minister who
never left him alone.
Those strange ears . . .
always attuned to Washington and
to the bureaucrats of the IMF.
Sacrifice and austerity were demanded
from those arrogant, unrealistic people.
The General was promised
unpopular but historical glory.

Lonely and frequently drunk, one day
the General made a bold decision.
He suspected dirty wars
were dishonorable.
And the queen of England, surprised,

recibió la declaración:
"Las Malvinas son argentinas".
Duró una semana su sueño
de popularidad nacional.
Muchos jugaron
a las bombas y tiros,
y se rieron excitados
imaginando al príncipe Andrew batido
en el Atlántico Sur.

Al mundo le costaba creerlo:
Una colonia británica en aguas argentinas
estaba en disputa.
El Dictador se sumergió
en un delirio de sangre y fuego.
Ya no temía el infierno;
ahora era su creación.

Los jóvenes muertos se seguían apilando,
pero no se quedaban inertes.
Y descubrió que ni el infierno
está libre de traición.

"¡Ríndanse"! ordenó Washington.
"Han abusado de nuestra confianza
y buena voluntad".
Al Dictador le prometieron
una cómoda celda, y al pueblo,
la democracia.

*Mientras desaparece la pantalla la Bruja grita el
año, intentando sacarse de encima el peso de la
historia.*

Bruja:

1983.

*La Bruja cae desmayada. Elvira, Manuela y
Mariano se hacen cargo de continuar contando
la historia. La Bruja, cada tanto, recita los años
como en el medio de una pesadilla.*

*Música: "Memoria del Poder", efecto de "disco
rayado" (la melodía se atasca para acompañar a
los versos).*

received the notice:
"Las Malvinas son Argentinas."
His dreams of national popularity
lasted a week or so.
Many played
the bombing and bullets game
and laughed with excitement
imagining Prince Andrew defeated
in the South Atlantic.

The world could hardly believe it:
A British colony in Argentine waters
was being contested.
The General was immersed
in a delirium of blood and fire.
He needn't fear hell any longer;
he had created it on earth.

The young dead kept on piling up
but wouldn't remain inert.
And he found out that betrayal
occurs even in hell.

"Surrender!" ordered Washington.
"You have abused our trust
and goodwill."
The Dictator was promised
a comfortable cell, and the people
were promised democracy.

*As the screen disappears the Witch shouts
the year, attempting to get rid of the story's
weight.*

Witch:

1983.

*The Witch faints. Elvira, Manuela, and
Mariano take charge of the storytelling. The
Witch now and then mumbles the years as if
she were in the middle of a nightmare.*

*Music: "Memory of Power," "broken
record" effect (melody falls into ruts to follow the lines).*

Elvira Díaz, *canta:*

¡General! En tu juicio
leías frenéticamente la biblia
mientras los jóvenes muertos
desfilaban acusaciones:
torturas, asesinatos, violaciones.

Bruja, *recita:*

1984.

Manuela Malva, *canta:*

No te volví a ver hasta ese día
en que te paseabas con tu señora
por el lujoso shopping
recientemente inaugurado
donde, democráticamente,
limpias conciencias
se venden de liquidación.

Bruja, *recita:*

1990.

Mariano, *canta:*

Todo el mundo
pagando el precio de la deuda nacional
y el impuesto al perdón.
Sombras, exiliados, cadáveres.
Culpa, alivio, manía.
El camino a la reconversión.
Listas de candidatos electorales
¡encabezadas por ex-dictadores,
paramilitares!

Bruja, *recita:*

1993.

Elvira, Manuela y Mariano, *cantan:*

Hijos de los exterminados,
las vueltas que da la vida,

Elvira Díaz, *sings:*

General! At your trial
you frantically read the Bible
while the young dead
lined up accusations:
torture, rape, murder.

Witch, *recites:*

1984.

Manuela Malva, *sings:*

The next time I saw you,
you strolled with your wife
through the recently opened
shopping mall,
where, democratically,
clean consciences
were on sale.

Witch, *recites:*

1990.

Mariano, *sings:*

Everybody
paying the price of the national debt
and the pardon tax.
Shadows, exiles, corpses.
Guilt, relief, mania.
The road to reconversion.
Voting lists of candidates
headed by ex-dictators,
the paramilitary!

Witch, *recites:*

1993.

Elvira, Manuela, and Mariano, *sing:*

Children of the exterminated,
life takes such turns,

descubren que sus familias adoptivas
llevan las manos cubiertas de sangre.

Bruja, *recita:*

1998.

La música se interrumpe.

Coro, *canon a capella, tres voces lideradas
por Elvira, Manuela y Mariano:*

Maldiciones circulares . . .
La bruja conjura
el recuerdo de las impiedades.
La historia, ¿se repite? ¿Continúa?
¿Es así cómo el poder circula?
Un país de poder estancado,
encerrado bajo llave, arrestado. *(Pausa.)*

*Se reanuda la música mientras la Bruja sale de
su estupor.*

Bruja, *canta, saliendo de su estupor:*

Esta es una historia de brujería,
del poder sentenciado.
De deseos de muerte.
Los crímenes no han terminado.
Yo estoy enferma de memoria;
llevo las cuentas de lo ocurrido.
Me poseen los recuerdos;
me rehuye el olvido.

Detectives, *en tono impaciente, inter-
rumpen a la orquesta:*

¿Y el asesinato?

*Elvira, Manuela y Mariano se quedan helados
con la pregunta de los Detectives. Repentinamente establecen la conexión. Exclaman mirán-
dose unos a otros y luego dirigiéndose a la Bruja.*

discover that their adoptive families
carry blood on their hands.

Witch, *recites:*

1998.

Music stops.

Chorus, *canon a capella, led by
Elvira, Manuela, and Mariano:*

Circular curses . . .
The witch conjures
the memory of impieties.
History, repeats itself? Continues?
Is this how power circulates?
A country of stagnant power,
locked up, arrested. *(Pause.)*

*Music starts again while the Witch recovers
from her stupor.*

Witch, *sings, recovering from her stupor:*

This is a story of witchcraft,
of condemned power.
Of deadly desires.
The crimes have not ended.
I'm sick of memory;
possessed by remembrances.
I do the bookkeeping;
forgetfulness evades me.

Detectives, *impatient, interrupt the
orchestra:*

What about the murderer?

*Elvira, Manuela, and Mariano are stunned
by the Detectives' question. Suddenly they
realize the connection. They exclaim looking at each other and then addressing the
Witch.*

Mariano, *recita incrédulo y desesperado:*

¡¿Mi amor?!

Manuela y Elvira, *recitan lenta y temerosamente, como si el nombre se les escapara de la boca:*

¡ . . . Angora . . . !

Bruja, *recuperada y lúcida, responde, recita:*

Un trabajo a sueldo.
Una profesional del destino.
El arma del delito: la indiferencia;
instigadores: la secta de los ambiciosos;
el móvil, el propósito, la razón:
fortalecer las redes multinacionales
de la corrupción,
encubrir el terrorismo económico,
distraer al pueblo de la explotación.

Apagón

Escena 14: Epílogo

Parte 1

Títeres de sombra: la figura de Angora con las valijas subiendo al avión. El avión alza el vuelo.

Sonido: ruido de jet.

Parte 2

Escena con actor: foco sobre un rincón del escenario. Mariano Monteamor "lee" (canta) la carta de despedida enviada por Angora. La voz de Angora se suma a la de Mariano a medio camino, en un dúo. Hacia el final del tango, Mariano lee en silencio mientras se escucha la voz de Angora cantando las últimas líneas.

Mariano, *recites desperately and incredulously:*

My love?!

Manuela and Elvira, *recite, slowly and fearfully, as the name slips out of their mouths:*

Angora . . . !

Witch, *recovered and lucid, answers, recites:*

A hired killer.
A fated professional.
The murder weapon: indifference;
instigators: the sect of the ambitious;
the motive, the purpose, the reason:
to strengthen the multinational networks of corruption,
to cover up economic terrorism,
to distract people from exploitation.

Black-out

Scene 14: Epilogue

Part 1

Shadow puppets: figure of Angora with bags getting on the airplane. The plane climbs.

Sound: jet noise.

Part 2

Scene with one actor: lights on a corner of the stage. Mariano Monteamor "reads" (sings) a good-bye letter from Angora. Angora's voice joins Mariano's midway in a duet. Toward the tango's end, Mariano stands in silence, while Angora's voice is heard singing the final lines.

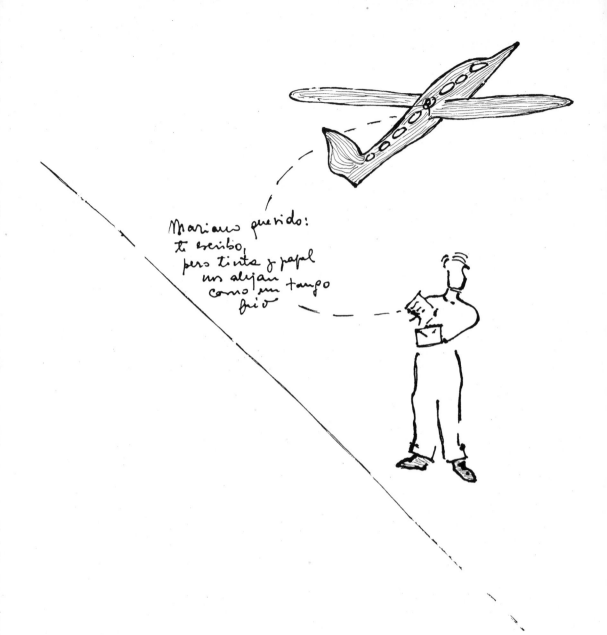

Mariano lee la carta de despedida de Angora / Mariano reading Angora's farewell letter

Música: "Sin Remitente"—tango.

Mariano, *canta leyendo carta en voz alta:*

Mariano querido:
Te escribo
pero tinta y papel nos alejan
como un tango frío.

Extraño . . .
tu mirada gris, acorralada;
tu voz
áspera de entrega y duda;
la risa esquiva, desconfiada;
los abrazos lentos de amargura.

Mariano y Angora:

Mariano, querido, te escribo no sé . . .
Para aclararte:
Esa que quisiste
no es, ni fue.
No digo que te fallen los instintos . . .
los sentimientos son laberintos . . .
Yo, así lo quiso la vida,
llevo puesta la mira
en mi profesión.

Angora, *solo:*

Nuestro encuentro . . . un mal momento.
Mi trabajo . . . no podía esperar.
El amor me asaltó en un descuido.
No entendí, te debo confesar.

Me voy, pero de vos no me escapo.
Tampoco vuelvo.
(No lo tomés como algo personal.)
No me olvidés, no ves que tengo miedo
de tu loco empeño en atraer el mal.

Mariano, querido, te escribo no sé . . .
Para aclararte:
esa que quisiste
no es, ni fue.
No digo que te fallen los instintos . . .

Music: *"No Return Address"—tango.*

Mariano, *sings reading the letter aloud:*

Mariano dear:
I write to you,
but ink and paper pull us apart
like a cold tango.

I miss . . .
your gray, besieged glances;
your voice,
roughed by doubt and surrender;
your laughter, crooked, mistrusting;
your slow, bitter embraces.

Mariano and Angora:

Mariano, dear, I'm writing, who knows?
To make it clear:
The one you loved
doesn't exist, and never did.
I'm not saying your instincts are wrong,
but feelings are labyrinths . . .
I, as life wanted it to be,
keep my sight set
on my profession.

Angora, *solo:*

Our encounter . . . bad timing.
My work . . . it couldn't wait.
Love assaulted me when I was off guard.
I didn't understand, I must confess.

I'm leaving, but it's not you I'm escaping.
I'm not coming back either.
(Don't you take this personally.)
Don't forget me, don't you see that I fear
your mad determination to attract evil.

Mariano, dear, I'm writing, who knows?
To make it clear:
The one you loved
doesn't exist, and never did.
I'm not saying your instincts are wrong,

los sentimientos son laberintos . . .
Te quiero más que nunca ahora.
Besos ardientes (sin remitente),
Angora.

Apagón

Parte 3

Escena con dos actores: foco sobre otro rincón del escenario. Una silla de escritorio confortable, de respaldo alto, de espaldas a la audiencia. (El que ocupa la silla no es visible.) Ruido de tipeo en el teclado de una computadora. Una pantalla gigante muestra los signos característicos de un programa de correo electrónico. Una a una aparecen las letras de un mensaje.

Leyenda del mensaje por correo electrónico:

"Plan saliendo a las mil maravillas.
Llegué a Miami sin valijas
pero con guita hasta la coronilla.
Angora cree que cumplió su cometido.
Pagále según lo convenido.
De las elecciones ni me cuentes.
Estoy hasta acá de ser Presidente".

Música: "Rumbango"—rumba; tarareada por el Presidente al compás de una radiotransmisión de grandes hits de la temporada.

Presidente, *acompañando radio:*

Un precipicio,
la cuerda floja,
bombea la sangre
vertiginosa.

Piel de gallina,
gritos ahogados,
colgao de un hilo,
desesperado.

but feelings are labyrinths . . .
I love you more than ever now.
Ardent kisses (no return address),
Angora.

Black-out

Part 3

Scene with two actors: lights on another corner of the stage. A comfortable desk chair, with a tall back facing the audience. (The one sitting on it is not visible to the audience.) Noises of clicking on a computer keyboard. A big screen appears with typical icons of an electronic mail program. One by one the letters of a message appear on the screen.

Text of the message sent by e-mail:

"The plan is working out marvelously.
I've arrived in Miami without luggage
but with money coming out my ears.
Angora believes she did her job.
Pay her as we agreed.
Don't even mention the elections.
I'm up to here with being the President."

Music: "Rumbango"—rumba; sung by the President following a radio broadcast of the season's greatest hits.

President, *following radio:*

A precipice,
a slack high-wire,
blood pumps
vertiginously.

Goose bumps,
muffled screams,
held by a string,
desperate.

Caída libre,
salto al vacío,
ojos cerrados
al desafío.
Todo o nada,
la vida al filo,
sangre de hielo,
ritmo de abismo.

Rumba furiosa,
tango fatal,
este rumbango
me tiene mal.

Tango caliente,
rumba que llora,
los bandoneones,
las tumbadoras.

Corte y quebrada
tumba el rezongo,
baile de herejes
compadre y congo.

Rumbango viene
tangumba va.
¡Ay que mareo!
¡Pará o me muero!

En respuesta al ruido de una puerta que se abre seguido de pasos en tacos altos, la silla de escritorio gira hacia la audiencia. El Presidente, atónito y pegado a la silla, ve entrar a Angora. Ella abre la cartera con tranquilidad y extrae el cuchillo mortal.

Sonido: ruidos de una puerta que se abre (goznes) y de pasos en tacos altos se superponen a los de la conexión de módem.

Música: "Rumbango" continúa como música de fondo acompañando el ritmo de los pasos de Angora.

Presidente, *recita aterrorizado:*

¡Angora! ¿Qué hacés acá?

Free fall,
jump in a vacuum,
eyes closed
to challenge.
All or nothing,
life on edge,
frozen blood,
abysmal rhythm.

Furious rumba,
fatal tango,
this rumbango
drives me mad.

Hot tango,
weeping rumba,
the bandoneons,
the tumbadoras.

Halts and bends
drumming complaints,
heretic dance
compadre and congo.

Rumbango comes
tangumba goes.
Dizziness!
Stop! I'm dying!

In response to the sound of an opening door followed by high-heeled steps, the desk chair turns toward the audience. The President, paralyzed and stuck to the chair, watches in disbelief as Angora enters. She calmly opens her bag and pulls out the deadly knife.

Sound: noises of an opening door (hinges) followed by high-heeled steps over the modem connection.

Music: "Rumbango" keeps playing in the background, matching the rhythm of Angora's steps.

President, *recites in horror:*

Angora! What are you doing here?

Angora, *responde tranquila:*

Siempre cumplo con los encargos pagos.

Música: Pulsaciones de una bordona, clima de desenlace.

El Presidente se abalanza desesperado sobre el cajón de su escritorio.

Apagón

(la pantalla de computadora continúa titilando en la oscuridad)

Sonido: Ruidos de conmoción en la oscuridad, seguidos de un breve silencio.

Parte 4

Escena con varios actores: Angora establece diálogos imaginarios con los Políticos, Elvira, Manuela y Mariano, quienes aparecen en escena como figuras fantasmales. (Ver detalles más adelante.) Mientras se oye a Angora cantar el "Rumbango", la página principal (home page) del Banque de Crédit Suisse aparece en la pantalla. (Resto del escenario permanece oscuro.) Se activa una transferencia de fondos a nombre de Angora Kils. Simultáneamente se oyen ruidos de marcar un número telefónico y de señal de llamada.

Música: la orquesta reanuda "Rumbango", esta vez cantado por Angora en el oscuro.

Sonido: Ruidos de tipéo y de conexión telefónica (marcado de un número y llamada).

Angora duda a quién llamar. Los Políticos, Elvira, Manuela y Mariano aparecen iluminados, uno a uno, en distintos puntos del escenario. El efecto buscado es de diálogos imaginarios, que se suceden dentro de la cabeza de Angora. Angora permanece iluminada en el centro del escenario. Los otros son iluminados sólo mientras cantan. Luz

Angora, *responds calmly:*

I always give customers what they pay for.

Music: Pulsations of a bass string announcing the climax.

The President desperately reaches into his desk drawer.

Black-out

(the computer screen continues to flicker in the dark)

Sound: Noises of a commotion in the dark followed by a brief silence.

Part 4

Scene with several actors: Angora establishes imaginary dialogues with the Politicians, Elvira, Manuela, and Mariano. They appear on stage as ghostly figures. (See details below.) Angora's singing ("Rumbango") is heard while the home page of the Banque de Crédit Suisse appears on the screen. (Rest of the stage remains dark.) Funds are transferred into an account in the name of Angora Kils. Simultaneously, dialing and ringing noises are heard.

Music: orchestra restarts "Rumbango," now sung by Angora in the dark.

Sound: Noises of typing on a keyboard and of a phone connection (dialing and ringing).

Angora wonders whom to call. The Politicians, Elvira, Manuela, and Mariano appear, one by one, under spotlights at different places on stage. Overall effect of imaginary dialogues that take place in Angora's head. Angora remains under a spotlight, center stage. Spotlights on the others

sobre Los Políticos (dos), como si estuvieran atendiendo la llamada de Angora.

Los Políticos *(juntos, salvo otra
indicación):*

Sabemos, perfectamente,
por donde andás . . .
Seguimos todos tus pasos.
No nos despistás.

Angora *(respondiéndoles):*

No me engaño, tengo miedo.

Político 2:

De estas changas no hay salida . . .

Angora:

Los presagios, la ironía . . .

Político 1:

Tu contrato es de por vida.

Angora:

¡Guárdense las amenazas!

Político 2:

Nadie abandona este tren.

Angora:

El sucio juego se acabó.

Políticos:

¡Dejá de hacerte la estrella!

Angora:

Rompí el pacto macabro.
Gané y decido yo.

only as they sing. **Lights on Politicians
(two) as if they were picking up a call from
Angora.**

Politicians *(together unless indicated
otherwise):*

We know, perfectly,
your whereabouts . . .
We follow your steps.
You can't sidetrack us.

Angora *(in response):*

I know that, I'm scared.

Politician 2:

There's no way out of these gigs.

Angora:

The bad omens, the irony . . .

Politician 1:

Yours is a lifetime contract.

Angora:

Keep your threats!

Politician 2:

No one steps out of this train.

Angora:

The dirty game is over.

Politicians:

Stop behaving like a star!

Angora:

I broke the macabre pact.
I have won and now I decide.

Políticos:

Nosotros pagamos bien.

Angora:

Ustedes tendrán poder . . .
¡No pienso serles fiel!

Políticos:

No tenés opción.
Fin de la cuestión.

Angora:

No me engaño . . . ¡Tengo miedo!

Políticos:

De estas changas no hay salida.

Angora:

Desperté. ¡Nada es igual!
A ver si entienden:
soy Angora, la femme fatale.

*La luz sobre los Políticos se extingue. Más ruidos
de conexión telefónica mientras aparece Mariano
iluminado.*

Mariano y Angora *(luz sobre Mariano,
como atendiendo la llamada de Angora. Dúo
en el que se yuxtaponen las palabras de
Mariano y la respuesta de Angora. La
melodía de Angora es la misma del tema
"Angora Matta" [escena 1] que se inicia con
"Sé que voy a un país condenado"):*

Mariano:

Caída en picada.
Araño y resisto.

Politicians:

We pay you well.

Angora:

You might hold the power . . .
I won't be faithful to you!

Politicians:

You have no choice.
End of the matter.

Angora:

I know that . . . I'm scared!

Politicians:

There's no way out of these gigs.

Angora:

I woke up. All has changed!
Let's see if you understand:
I am Angora, the femme fatale.

*Lights on Politicians fade out. Phone con-
nection noises continue while Mariano appears under a spotlight.*

Mariano and Angora *(light on Mariano
as if he were picking up Angora's phone
call. Duet follows in which Mariano's
words and Angora's responses are juxtaposed. Angora's melody is the same as
the "Angora Matta" theme [scene 1]
starting with the line "I know I'm going
to a condemned country."):*

Mariano:

Falling, a dive.
Clawing the air, I resist.

Mariano: / **Angora:** / **Mariano:** / **Angora:**

Mariano (español)	Angora (español)	Mariano (English)	Angora (English)
	Mal de amor, revés que arde en tu ausencia.		Lovesick, this wrong turn burns in your absence.
Tu daga al fondo. Infierno de frío.		Your dagger at the bottom. Cold hell.	
	Los estragos . . . Obra de mi ambición.		All mishaps . . . Outcomes of my ambition.
Bomba de tiempo . . . Yo acá, un infeliz . . .		Time bomb . . . Here I am, a poor fool . . .	
	No hubo tiempo . . . Y me falta la paciencia . . .		There was no time . . . And I lack the patience . . .
Te extraño sin pensar. Te pienso y es sufrir.		I miss you absentminded. I think about you and I suffer.	
	Yo quiero todo: justicia, plata y vos.		I want everything: Justice, money, and you.
La angustia no afloja. Se anuda el destino.		The anguish doesn't let go. Fate knots up.	
	¿Te acordás? Vos verás . . .		Remember? See what you think . . .
Hablamos de una isla . . .		We talked about an island . . .	
	Las nubes cargadas, se abre el abismo.		Heavy clouds, the abyss opens up.
¡Dejáme vivir! ¿Te acordás? Vos verás . . .		Let me live! Remember? See what you think . . .	
	Ya lo sé . . . ¡Soy asesina!		I know . . . I am an assassin!
Te fuiste . . . Volaste. ¡Qué ciego! Qué necio . . .		You left . . . Flew away. So blind! So dense . . .	
	Ya sé . . . ¡Soy asesina!		I know . . . I am an assassin!
Negador, embelesado, obsesionado . . . ensimismado . . . ¡Un gil!		In denial, dazzled, obsessed . . . self-centered . . . A fool!	
	No entendió . . . No entendió nada, ¡nada!		He didn't understand . . . Didn't understand anything, nothing at all!
No entendí nada y te perdí.		I didn't understand anything and I lost you.	

Se extingue la luz sobre Mariano. Angora se pasea nerviosa con su andar característico, el teléfono en la mano. Empieza a discar, cuelga. La luz sobre Elvira se va intensificando. Al diálogo imaginario entre Elvira y Angora se suma Manuela, compitiendo con Elvira por la atención de Angora. Todo se sucede rápidamente, con efecto caótico.

Elvira *(como respondiendo a la llamada de Angora)*:

¡Angora! ¿Sos vos?
¡La vengadora!
¡Cambiaste la historia!

¡Qué bien estuviste!
¡Vení! ¡Celebremos!
Ya pasó lo peor . . .

Angora *(respondiendo a Elvira, impaciente)*:

No me mueven la venganza,
la nostalgia o el despecho.
Lo que me tiene atacada
son las ínfulas taradas
y el desdén, desalmado,
que nos carcomen el seso.

Luz sobre Manuela, quien busca intervenir en la conversación. Más ruidos de conexiones telefónicas de fondo.

Manuela *(irrumpiendo)*:

¿Angora? ¡Borráte!
¡No hay vuelta atrás!
Ya hiciste tu parte . . .
Ahora . . . . disfrutá!

Manuela *(recita)* y Elvira *(canta)*:

Cortáte sola.
¿Qué vas a hacer?
¡No seas loca!
Ni pienses en volver . . .

Lights on Mariano fade out. Angora paces nervously with her characteristic walk, phone still held in her hand. Starts to dial, hangs up. Light on Elvira starts intensifying. Manuela joins the imaginary dialogue between Elvira and Angora, competing with Elvira over Angora's attention. Everything happens rapidly, with a chaotic effect.

Elvira *(as if she were answering Angora's call)*:

Angora! Is it you?
The avenger!
You've changed history!

You've done it so well!
Come back! Let's celebrate!
The worst part is over . . .

Angora *(responding to Elvira, impatient)*:

This is not about vengeance,
nostalgia or resentment.
What prompted me to act
were the arrogant stupidity
and the soulless lack of care
that eat up our brains.

Lights on Manuela, who attempts to intervene in the conversation. More phone connection noises in the background.

Manuela *(interrupting)*:

Angora? Flee!
There's no way back!
You've done your part . . .
Now . . . enjoy!

Manuela *(recites)* and Elvira *(sings)*:

Cut loose!
Whatcha gonna do?
Don't be crazy!
Don't even think about coming back!

Elvira *(recita)* y Manuela *(canta):*

¡Sos la esperanza!
¡Volvé, por favor . . . !

Angora *(confundida):*

¿Lo habré matado?
¿Robé la plata?
¿Cambié la historia?
¿Quién me lo aclara?

Manuela y Elvira *(luchando por hacerse oír):*

Manuela:

¡Hola! Hola . . . ¿Me oís?
Mala conexión . . .

Elvira:

¡Veníte ya mismo!
¡No nos podés fallar!

Manuela:

¿¡Líneas intervenidas!?
¡Ni aparezcas por acá!

Angora *(respondiendo a ambas):*

¿Soy la heroína
sin pagar las culpas?
¿La que triunfa al final?
¿Soy la femme fatale?

¿Qué hice de mi vida?

Elvira:

Cruel filosofía . . .

Manuela:

Un tango . . . ¡Un tango!

Elvira *(recites)* and Manuela *(sings):*

You are our hope!
Please . . . come back!

Angora *(confused):*

Have I killed him?
Did I steal the money?
Did I change history?
Who can tell me?

Manuela and Elvira *(struggling to make themselves heard):*

Manuela:

Hello! Hello . . . Can you hear me?
Bad connection . . .

Elvira:

Come back right now!
You can't let us down!

Manuela:

The lines are tapped?!
Don't come even close to here!

Angora *(responding to both):*

Am I the heroine who
doesn't pay for her faults?
The one who wins in the end?
Am I the femme fatale?

What have I done with my life?

Elvira:

Cruel philosophy . . .

Manuela:

A tango . . . A tango!

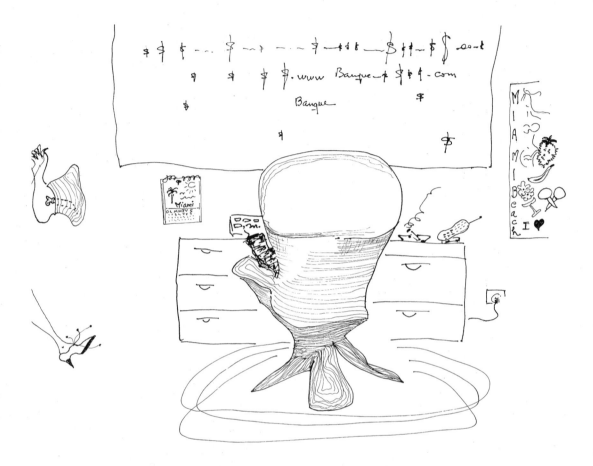

Encuentro final de Angora con el Presidente / Angora's final encounter with the President

Angora, Manuela y Elvira:

Una ópera . . .

Angora decide finalmente con quién comunicarse. Sacudiéndose los fantasmas de estos diálogos imaginarios, enfrenta a la audiencia. Luces sobre los Políticos, Elvira, Manuela y Mariano. Todos atienden sus teléfonos simultáneamente, en diferentes tonos de voz.

Políticos, Elvira, Manuela y Mariano, *atendiendo sus teléfonos:*

¿Hola? !Hola!

Angora, *del otro lado de la línea:*

Soy yo. Mirá . . .

El volumen creciente de la música torna el resto de sus palabras inaudible.

Apagón Total

Música: "Memoria del Poder", introduciendo percusión hasta llegar al final.

Angora, Manuela, and Elvira:

An opera . . .

Angora finally decides whom to call. Shaking off the ghosts of these imaginary dialogues, she faces the audience. Lights on the Politicians, Elvira, Manuela, and Mariano. They all pick up their ringing phones, simultaneously, and answer in different tones of voice.

Politicians, Elvira, Manuela, and Mariano, *answering their phones:*

Hello? Hello!

Angora, *on the other end of the line:*

It's me. Listen . . .

The music's increasing volume renders the rest of her words inaudible.

Total black-out

Music: "Memory of Power," introducing percussion, until the finale is reached.

FIN

Part III

The Controversial Evidence

Part III

Las Evidencias Controvertidas

Exhibit A
Writings Attributed to Elvira Díaz

Prueba A
Escritos Atribuidos a Elvira Díaz

Librettist's Note

XYa (the Witch) attributed the following writings to Elvira Díaz, one of the main characters in my libretto. As an author—if we are to believe the Witch's claims—Elvira adopts the positions of a feminist ethnographer and a wannabe milonguera. She is interested in bodies in movement and in performative writing, and she is troubled by ethnographic practices of representation that tend to flatten the complex identities and undertakings of those under study. The Witch submitted these writings as proof of Elvira's existence. As far as I know, I created this character as an old friend of Angora Matta who, in the 1970s, shared revolutionary political ideals and perhaps militant activities with her. I am quite certain I wrote these hybrid essays (a mixture of autoethnography and critical fiction) on the tango world of Buenos Aires in an attempt to develop Elvira's personality as a character. I have to admit, however, that my own interests are also multifold: these same essays have been presented at various international scholarly meetings and dance festivals. I will explain no more.

Nocturnal Ethnographies

Following Cortázar in the Milongas of Buenos Aires

An Anomalous Project

How to write an ethnography and a critique of the ethnographic predicament at the same time? How to create ethnographies, the descriptions and interpretations of something exotic brought into the familiar or of something familiar turned into the exotic, while simultaneously addressing the ideological traps and the political stakes of the ethnographic enterprise? How to deliver an ethnographic product that retains the tension of the ethnographic encounter, the romance and the fallings-out, the fascination and the disgust, the wealth and the poverty of ethnographic knowledge—and the differences for its participating subjects and objects? An enumeration of some approaches to ethnographic writing might help to clarify what I am struggling to get at. I do not mean, for example, the inclusion of a critical perspective within an ethnography—as in, "For starters, be aware, dear readers, that I know ethnographies are problematic intellectual exercises." And then, after a self-reflexive statement (more or less elaborate, more or less incisive, more or less honest and devastating), a switching into the ethnographic mode, framed by a mixture of resigned resentment and vindictive nostalgia—as in, "After all, I have spent all these years perfecting the arts of representing others, identifying and analyzing their otherness, and there is an audience out there made up of academics, amateurs, and even some of those very others whom I am representing ready to consume my ethnoproduct, so here it is." Nor I am making reference to an ethnography that in incorporating critical statements would promise to deliver a new ethnography, as if ethnography could run against itself (its premises and practices) and still claim an ethnographic status—as in getting away with ethnographic murder, if not in actual practice at least in intention. My list of neithers and nors also accommodates the possible critiques of ethnography of "other" ethnographers and their writings, dealing at a distance with the past history of ethnographic enterprises and/or ethnographic futurology. Innovative recipes without the actual experimentation—as in, "Here are the problems," followed by some examples, and then, "Here are some possible solutions; now you try it out"—would also be ruled out.

I do not wish to condemn any of these approaches to ethnographic writing or its critiques, nor to judge what they have to offer to either the reproduction, the revolution, or the death of ethnography. Such an assessment would require engaging with a moral ground and a technical investigation that would take me away from the questions posed in the beginning of this essay. How do you identify and represent otherness while conducting a resilient study of ethnographic representation, its uses of fiction and its scientific pretensions? Is it possible to make an ethnography that works against ethnographic authority? Can an ethnography retain its seductive powers if its Eurocentrically defined organizational concepts (alterity, orality, timelessness, and unreflexivity) are persistently exposed? My purpose here is to generate an ethnographic anomaly. The topic and the setting of my fieldwork, the milongas of Buenos Aires, as well as my nightmarish ways of engaging with them have led me into what I will call a nocturnal ethnography. Imagine an ethnographic ghost haunting daytime ethnographies when the world turns dark—an ethnography that occupies the same space as traditional ethnographies and yet transforms that space by taking place later, much later. This ethnography will then move almost blindly in the ethnographic night, a time when strange things happen or at least when stories about strange things are told. (For a footnote: See "Story Time," in de Certeau 1984: 77–90.) Nocturnal story times could produce ethnographic accounts in which the critique of ethnographic doings would be as vivid and present as the seductive narrative, so integrated into the story as to make it incomprehensible without its very questioning. The ethnographic object, othered, (a)temporalized, and (over)spatialized, would return reciprocating ethnographic gestures. (For a footnote: Fabian 1983; Thomas 1996: 1–17, 117–127; de Certeau 1988: 209–244). The ethnographer now situated in a slightly recognizable place, after hours, will stumble; the ethnographic writing will stutter, the ethnographic project will lose ground and coherence. An ethnography finally othered, at least for the night? A nocturnal ethnographic anomaly?

Writing at night—the ethnographer thought and wrote—might bring these writings closer to what they are supposed to do. At midnight. Right before sleep starts to sink in and after a day of futile overwork and frustration has kept her awake long enough for her to fantasize about another life. Not the afterlife, but a parallel one out there in the dark, one that starts happening when the inhabitants of the everyday retire and seclude. Curiosity. An other life, nocturnal, stirs up the hopes for wonders pushing you out of boredom. You drop the chance for promising dreams and choose to join the restless, out there, in that obscure reality. You are on your feet. Freshened up, you get ready to meet not the dead but the not quite alive either, who now populate the city at their own risk. . . . This failed experiment—no point in concealing the result here, she thought and wrote—requires an adequate environment and a loyal accomplice for the attempt, if not the outcome, to be successful. The nights of Buenos Aires will be the place to start; my co-perpetrator, Dr. Marcelo Hardoy. I was the one who thought of this nocturnal adventure, but Dr. Hardoy, I must admit, had initiated similar activities, as far as I know, in the early 1950s. In delimiting the scope and thus intensifying the depth of our potential insights, we happened to coincide in our choice of research terrain. (I would also soon discover that although our objects of inquiry pretty much overlapped, our manifest interests were rather different.) The milongas of Buenos Aires—the nature and culture of which will occupy the rest of these writings—attracted both of us. He declared that in his case this was mostly because of boredom and curiosity. In my case, the reasons have already been exposed. (For a note card on methodology: Dr. Hardoy was more of a witness than an accomplice. He was dead by the time I (we?) began the work.) (Insert another note in invisible ink explaining that these notes that resist footnoting are Cortázar/Dr. Hardoy's idea. I follow them.)

An Elusive Field

Milongas, in the current tango lexicon, are the tango joints—a space and a time when and where tango bodies get together to produce *tanguidad* (tanguity, tangoness). They are the physical site of the corporeal, temporary encounter of the practitioners of the tango dance. The milongas of Buenos Aires are a slippery landscape. They are invisible to eyes untrained in tango and elusive to those who do not keep up with current milonga tips. Every time I go back—Elvira Díaz reflected and jotted down—usually once a year, I find that some milongas have folded, others have moved, and new ones have opened. The next time, old ones have reopened, new ones have disappeared, and established ones are there but with a different clientele. Milongas go through persistent transformations in terms of where they are located, what they look like, who attends them, and how they operate.

There is no generic milonga except for the fact that in order for there to be a milonga, a gathering of tango dancers of some sort has to occur. Milongueros and milongueras (milonga habitués) actually make the milongas wherever they go and settle for a while. The physical requirements for the locale (the location in the city, the material conditions of the building, the size of the dance floor, the quality of the music equipment, etc.) are very elastic. What matters is who goes there and how often. The crucial figures are the milonga's organizer and the disc jockey, who have the power of convoking the milonguera clientele, a rather small and capricious crowd. A milonga—Elvira struggled to specify—can be a year-long, seasonal, weekly, daily, frequent, sporadic or one-time occurrence in a dance hall, a nightclub, a social club, a private house, a patio in a tenement house, a park, or the streets. It can be loosely or well organized. The decor can be run-down, kitsch, luxurious, or insipid. The ambience can be decadent, pretentious, or cool. The purpose, however—Elvira analyzed—is clear: tango will be danced (not just played or watched as in a tango show), and the participants will perform to the best of their abilities. In the milongas the participants are, simultaneously, the performers and the audience of the tango spectacle.

Milongas are definitely social events—Elvira clarified and classified—although the opportunities for socializing are rather restricted. Tango is not strictly a social or ballroom dance. (From a note card: Check the lengthy discussions on this topic on the e-mail tango listserv, May 1996.) People do not attend milongas for the purpose of getting to know anyone, really. They are a site of performance, of watching tango and being watched dancing tango and all the rituals that go with it, including the careful construction of paradigmatic tango characters—milongueros and milongueras of different types. Milongas are usually not a recreational or entertaining activity either, given that a fair proportion of the dancers take them as the most serious things in their lives. (For a footnote: See Harris 1992: 147–174 for an account of leisure studies in the British context, and especially his discussion of Chris Rojek's figurational sociology. Rojek asserts that the disciplining of emotions and regulations of spontaneity "help deny that leisure is 'free time' at all." The activities in question "express an historically specific affect economy of balances and restraints" (Harris 1992: 164). Also, see Barthes 1977: 83 for an analysis of what constitutes the boundaries between work and pleasure. In his discussion of Fourier, Barthes addresses the ambition to transform work into pleasure (and not to suspend work for the sake of leisure time). Milongueros seem to be invested in the opposite. They transform leisure into work, and thus attain pleasure—the pleasure of doing at least in that other life of the night a pleasurable work by working at what gives them pleasure.) Performing at the milongas requires dedication, effort, preparation, and hard training. If we were to locate milongas on the leisurely, as opposed to the laboring, side of everyday (or everynight) life—Elvira pondered—then the trying work involved in the pursuit of pleasure must be emphasized. Milongas are clearly an "escapist" activity, but the tango-laboring body—and not the relaxed, disengaged body of the one seeking relief from efforts and preoccupations—is at the center of the milongas' economy and politics of pleasure. (For a footnote: Cf. Dyer 1992a.) At the milongas the tango bodies are monitored and evaluated in terms of weight, strength, responsiveness, flexibility, focus, dancing style and choreographic skills. The measuring sticks are gender specific, and I will address these issues later—Elvira pointed out and restrained herself from running down a tangent. My point here is that the milongas demand the presence and circulation of tango bodies ready to sweat their way into the milongas' political economy of pleasure, an economy that pivots on the use value of tango bodies only occasionally associated with monetary exchange. (From a quick note scribbled on the margin: On prostitution and drugs. To be addressed in a lengthier report? Also cheap entrance fee, cheap drinks, overall little circulation of money.) The rewards of tangoing at the milongas are very tangible to its participants, but they are not easily attainable. The milonga delivers its pleasures only with the investment of time and bodily work.

What characterizes the milongas, then—Elvira summarized—is the presence of devoted milongueros and milongueras, tango music, and open floor space for dancing the best possible tango. *Prácticas* (practice sessions) and tango lessons do not count as milongas. The milongas are a site of tango dancing as performance, a public exhibition of tango dancing skills. Training and practicing take place somewhere else (not necessarily in some other space, but if in the same space, at a different time, where and when either the presence of money in payment for classes or the absence of risk entailed in the prácticas changes the nature of the dancing event).

If you stride across the Buenos Aires milonga scene, from the point of view of an onlooker, difference is what will strike you, and not just among milongas. The eclecticism is also to be found within: the ages and social classes as well as the nationalities of the habitués defy all classificatory rigors. And yet, all milongas are identified as such for their combination of intensely technical and transcendentally mystical investments in the tango dance tradition. They make up a parallel world devoted to the reproduction of tango skills and the cultivation of its affects. Milongueros and milongueras easily switch between materialistic and metaphysical discourses in order to account for their experiences at the milongas. Thus, at times milongas evoke images of small, labor-intensive tango factories crowded with male and female workers striving to produce the best possible tango bodies, and at other times they recall isolated shrines peopled by local worshipers and by foreign pilgrims of the tango cult. To its participants, milongas are a source of mixed pleasures and displeasures, a complex politics linked to the disciplining of the tango body and to the rewards that the trained tango body is capable of delivering. (For a footnote: See Mercer 1983; Jameson 1983.) When looked at from the point of view of its displeasures, milongas emerge as a rough, shady world, highly competitive and hierarchical, codified in terms of selfish interests, male dominance, and even moral corruption. Milongas, as sites of pleasure, are regarded as democratic, even revolutionary experiments that allow age and class differences to blur, male and female differences to explode and yet seductively combine, and self-interests to cede to the higher common purpose of keeping tango alive, reasserting the capacity to produce a local cultural form in the midst of bombarding foreign influences, of providing a non-monetary-based source of leisure and even an elusive, yet very real, experience of passion. As sites of both pleasure and displeasure, milongas' outlooks change as the events of the night develop for the participants, meeting or defying their expectations.

Romantic and harsh views of the milonga pervade the night, and the habitués cherish their moody and inconsistent judgments. (From an underlined note on the margin: Check with "informants" whether they would like to be mentioned by their real names or would prefer to choose pseudonyms.) This is especially true when in the presence of interested outsiders, whose beliefs will be systematically tested, contested, and unsettled. Milongueros and milongueras seek to prove the complexity of the milonga world and its impermeability to the analytical eye. Milongas are to be judged by the irresistible seduction they are capable of exerting beyond, and because, of its risks. They cannot be contained by logical interpretations. Proving oneself at the milonga—risking not being recognized as a worthy dancer— is what ultimately constitutes the pleasure. To the milongueros, an outsider who settles for a seduction-resistant interpretation of the tango world is sure to miss the best of it, namely the pros and cons that engender the formation of the milonga's pleasures.

A Questionable Source

In 1951 Julio Cortázar—Elvira wrote under a new, tentative headline— published a poignant description of a trashy milonga of the 1940s in downtown Buenos Aires. (Insert footnote on Julio Cortázar, an Argentine novelist, etc., born in 1914 in Brussels to Argentine parents, raised in the Province of Buenos Aires and educated at the Universidad de Buenos Aires, moved to Paris in 1951, the same year *Bestiario*—the collection that includes "Las puertas del cielo"—was published, died in 1984, etc.) His story "Las puertas del cielo" (The Gates of Heaven) (Cortázar 1993) presents the ambivalences to which an outsider is drawn in trying to deal with the milonga world. Cortázar's story offers the opportunity to look at a quasi-ethnographer at work, fascinated and scandalized by an underworld that escapes his judgments as it conforms to his categories of analysis. I will follow the descriptions/ interpretations of his fictive milonga as a pseudo-milonguera (an aspiring milonguera, partially saved from the milonga's harsh judgments of tango skills because of my anthropological interests and yet questioned, at least by some —including myself—because I live the milonga in order to write about it). I will undo his analysis with my own judgments and by updating what he "saw" in the 1940s with what I have seen and heard in the milongas of the 1990s. (From a Post-It note attached to a scratch pad: Include references to anthropological uses of fiction writings, fiction as anthropological documents, anthropological representations as fictive (including Cortázar!) in García Canclini 1968; Appadurai 1991: 202–205; Archetti 1994: 16–21; Tobin 1998.)

Dr. Marcelo Hardoy, a practicing lawyer and collector of social curiosities, is Cortázar's chosen narrator. He is introduced into the milonga scene by two former clients, Mauro and Celina. They belong to a different Buenos Aires world, marked by a lower class and cheaper tastes than his. Celina, whose wake opens the story, was a dancer and hostess at a slummy bar. Mauro had rescued her from prostitution. Mauro is presented as a modest working-class guy who trades produce at the central market (El Abasto). Dr. Hardoy, a decadent professional disenchanted with the life of his own class, introduces himself as "one who watches from aside their hard, hot happiness" (120). (For a footnote: All quotes are my translation.) Like an ethnographer, he struggles with his voyeuristic and vicarious doings: "I leaned on them to be witness of what they themselves were never conscious of." Mauro and Celina, his key informants, lived that life, while Dr. Hardoy confesses, in a self-reflective and self-pitiful mood, that "it made me sick to my gut to think like that—for other people it's enough to feel that way, I have to think it." And he apologetically continues, knowing that his is a rather questionable anthropological experiment: "Mauro and Celina have not been my guinea pigs, no. I loved them. I still love them, a lot. Only I could never enter their simplicity, only I saw myself forced to feed myself on the reflection of their blood. . . . I know that my curiosity lies behind all this, notes that fill my files a bit at a time" (Cortázar 1993, 120–121). Dr. Hardoy dives into the often unaddressed practices of othering—identifying otherness only to rush into collecting it, characteristic of the ethnographic enterprise: "They came a little closer to me, but I was as far from them as ever." Dr. Hardoy, the ethnographer qua seducer, entered into their lives in order to watch them live. ("We went to the dances together and I watched them live.") Finally, in a torturous, honesty-driven declaration he addresses the thorny issue of ethnographic writerly appropriations: "It was an ugly thing to realize, but what I was doing, really, was collecting and reordering my data on Celina; they'd never been written out but I had it all in my head" (122). He is referring to the field-work experience of collecting headnotes that eventually will enter the composition of the ethnographic text (for a footnote: See Sanjek 1990); to the anguish entailed in the reporting and in the interpretation of the other; to the piracy, the appropriation for dubious scientific purposes bordering self-interest and narcissism; to the multiple betrayals at stake in the written representation; and to the imposition of an insurmountable interpretive distance after a temporary, sought-after immersion as a participant in the experiential world of the ethnographic other.

Dr. Hardoy's self-reflections are triggered by the traumatic event of Celina's death. It is as if her ghost would lead him into the fatality of both the self-analysis of his ethnographic motives and the ethnographic reporting in itself. In an attempt to console Mauro for his irremediable loss,

Dr. Hardoy drags Mauro (and you and me)—Elvira noted—into the world of the milonga: the Santa Fe Palace. Eventually we, the readers, will get a glimpse of what at least for the Celinas and Mauros are the gates of heaven —but like Dr. Hardoy, as outsiders, we will only observe with difficulty the politics of pleasure rather than live pleasure in itself.

> In my note cards I have a good description of the Santa Fe Palace, whose name is not Santa Fe nor is it located on that street, but on one nearby. A shame that none of that can really be described, not the modest facade with the promising posters and the sign falling apart, even less those hangers-on killing time at the entrance and who check everyone out from hat to shoes. What follows is even worse, not that it is bad because in those places there's nothing that's precise; but rather the chaos, the confusion rearranging itself in a false order: hell and its circles. (127)

Cortázar's narrator, with the care of an ethnographer concerned with protecting the privacy of his research subjects, names and unnames, locates and displaces the Santa Fe Palace. We, the readers, follow his Dante-esque steps from the outside to the core of the milonga: a hellish chaos. And from then on, we will be walked through an eerie experience, where the detailed observations noted on his cards try to undo the fascinating mystery of the milonga (a mystery that he also builds up for us). Dr. Hardoy, like an ethnographer, aggressively pierces the scene: he analyzes, interprets, judges the milonga and its strange population. He fights the convictions and the ease with which the milonga's fauna moves in the territory, now his "field." His mistrust, his skeptical detachment, and his disgust struggle against the insider's trust in tango's power to transport them to the realm of pleasure (their heaven, his hell). And we, the readers, are left to decide whom to follow—Elvira reads and writes, swinging undecidedly between positions: the gifted outside observer (who, after all, opens up this world to us) or the enraptured participants (that manage to betray the writer's efforts to contain them, even when we get to know about them only through his manipulative text.) (For a footnote: See Bakhtin 1981: 301–331.) Like the readers of any ethnographic text, here we are, situated at the "entrance," the threshold between two worlds, a threshold to which we will be continuously returned if we manage to read between the lines. The "hangers-on" at the milonga's entrance are measuring him (and us) "from hat to shoes."

At this point in Cortázar's story we (or they) are literally situated at the door of the milonga, paying our entrance fee—a different one according to our gender—to a slummish-looking hell that is also heaven:

> A hell of an amusement park for a two fifty entrance fee and ladies zero fifty. Badly isolated compartments, sort of successive covered

patios where in the first a *típica* [tango] band, in the second a *carac-terística* [all-purpose] band, and in the third a *norteña* [folkloric] band with singers and *malambo* [gaucho dance]. Located in an inter-mediate hall (I, Virgil) [for an asterisk: Dr. Hardoy's reference to Virgil the poet or to Virgil, the poet who appears in Dante's *Divine Comedy*, also divided into three circular domains?] we could hear the three musics and we could see the three circles dancing; then you could choose your favorite, or your could go from one dance to the other, from one gin to another, looking for tables and women. . . .

I took him by an arm and set him on the way to a table because he was still distracted and looked at the balcony where the *típica* played, the singer holding the microphone with both hands and shaking it slowly. . . . The table was right by the dance floor, on the other side there were chairs against a long wall and a bunch of women renewed itself with that absent air of the milongueras when at work or at play. There was not much talking, we could hear the *típica* very well, overflowing with *bandoneones* [concertinas] and playing with heart. (127–128)

I will interrupt Cortázar's Hardoy here, as a dancer responds to a *corte*, an abrupt halt in the tango trajectory—Elvira mimetically choreographed her written partnering—and take the opportunity to tell you, readers of my readings of Cortázar's fictive milonga of the 1940s, that in the 1990s milongas with these characteristics are not to be found in Buenos Aires—Elvira, back down to earth, from evocation to realism. Live bands and singers have been replaced by disc jockeys, very few locales have more than one dance floor, and tango rarely shares the same space with other music genres (and when it does, it is usually with "tropical" music, jazz, or rock and roll). But the rest of the setting is still pretty accurate—Elvira checked her fieldnotes, 1996, vol. 2—tables bordering a central dance floor, chairs against the surrounding walls, and, crucial to my own ethnographic pierc-ings intruding into the contemporary milongas in counterpoint to Cortá-zar's Dr. Hardoy, the gender dynamics. The difference is established from the beginning by the admission fees. Then, men wander like opportunistic hunters "looking for tables and women," women sitting in oblivion, "with that absent air," like enticing prey. And "there was not much talking," a deliberately rare occurrence among *argentinos*, those people renowned for their love of talk for talk's sake. Following the rules of the milonga, how-ever, I will allow Dr. Hardoy, my male ethnographic tango partner—Elvira, repeat offender, flew again into tango evocations—to declare his own interests and make his seductive steps before producing my own ana-lytical counters.

Alter-Time and Its Monsters

> At this point I believe it is good for me to say that I went to this milonga because of the monsters, and that I don't know of any other where so many can be found together. They show up by eleven at night, come down from vague regions of the city, poised and secure in ones or twos. (129)

Dr. Marcelo Hardoy arrives early at his chosen milonga with his working-class acquaintance Mauro. It is early enough to watch the "monsters" marching in, "poised and secure," in contrast to the state of anxiety that invades outside observers such as himself, prompting headnotes that will fill note cards, that will deliver written stories, that will keep a breathing space open between those monstrous others and himself—keeping his own monsters at bay? What makes them monstrous—Elvira confronted her self-appointed dance partner and ethnographic accomplice—what gives them appalling monstrosity, is their gathering. At night, after eleven, they come "together." The light of day, tired of safely running order, relaxes. The darkness, then, fills in the emptiness with chaos and its monsters, who were being kept isolated, in their daytime places, under control.

Milongas are nocturnal and not evening events. They are not a continuation of the day or even the end of the daily routines; they are *la noche*, the life of the night (for a footnote: see Ferrer 1995; Arlt 1993), a life that passes not only at a different time but in a different dimension from the daily one. When milongueros and milongueras enter the milonga, they enter a different world. If one were to locate it somewhere in reference to the world of everyday routines, milongas would be placed on the dark, smoky side of things. Under. Milongas are a permanent site of symbolic inversion. Unlike Carnivals or other seasonal festivals where normal life is interrupted and the status quo reversed for a set amount of time, milongas occur continuously and in parallel through the year. Milongueros and milongueras step in and out of the milongas, these places where a slice of life happens following a different time. (From the back of a note card: Might be useful to include a reference to de Certeau's (1984) concepts of "stratified places" and "casual time" regarding the "ubiquity" of places and the gaps of time observed in everyday life. On stratified places: "This place, on its surface, seems to be a collage. In reality it is ubiquitous. A piling up of heterogenous places. Each one . . . refers to a different mode of territory unity, of socioeconomic distribution, of political conflicts and of identifying symbolism" (201). On casual time: "Casual time appears only as the darkness that causes an 'accident' and a lacuna in production. It is a lapse in the system and its diabolic adversary" (202).) It is a time with a different rhythm, not only slower but also productively unproductive, a time that stretches through the night connecting the present with the past rather than with the future. In this sense, the milongas are "conservative" reservoirs of the practices of everynight life. They are sites of enduring microhistory, composed of anecdotes rather than events, that run underneath grand, fast-paced history. Milongas preserve *porteño* cultural resources, traditions, the old and their wisdom. (For a footnote or two: Here I have been following Braudel 1981 and Foucault 1972. Commenting on Foucault's conceptualization of history, according to which history would be the result of an accumulation of sedimentary strata rather than a single-layered process, Angela Dalle Vacche observes: "The traditional document belongs to the realm of fast-moving surface events. Ironically, it is the movement of the dancers themselves that . . . inhabits the level of the 'apparently immobile.' Dancers can represent layers that move slowly and thus tell a history of looks, gestures and movements, situating these elements on the edge between truth and fiction, writing and living, acting and being. Movement, however, has been rarely considered an acceptable historical document" (Dalle Vacche 1992: 282). Specifically on tango's relation to time and history, Castilla asserts that "tango has fulfilled its mission in a highly satisfactory manner. I say 'has fullfilled' and yet I do not mean that it is dead, although it is not quite alive either. Tango is enduring, like so many other things, because it is deeply rooted in the *porteña* soul and because much is done so that it will last and even revive" (1969: 438).) Milongas run against the hectic pace of productivity and even against what milongueros recognize as the "real world," a world ruled by parameters of success that they can rarely reach. Everyday alienations are confronted with the milongas' everynight possibilities of revindication.

The time at which one enters a milonga is crucial. (Dr. Hardoy calls attention to this fact. I will elaborate with the aid of my scratch notes.) At the beginning of the night (which is rarely before midnight), the milonga is pure anxiety, expectation. It is a time of great visibility, and not everyone wishes to be noticed right away. An early arrival has its advantages. There is less competition both for asking and for being asked to dance. In addition, the dance floor will be less crowded, allowing for more comfortable dancing and requiring lesser skills at navigating the dance floor. Access to a good location (from which to monitor good dancing partners) is easier. All these advantages, however, can be a sign of a milonguero's insecurity. If you are important enough, a table will be reserved for you, or else those at a well-located table will accommodate you when you arrive, or else you need no special location because you will be detected and sought after anyway. An early arrival entails the anxiety of being able to break with the day, to contribute from the start to create "the night." Usually the most accomplished tango dancers (and the ones in the prime of their milonga life) choose to slip into the night, when things are already flowing, happening.

The milonga environment has been built up. The competition for partners and space on the dance floor is at its peak. You sense this and show that you know you can do it—Elvira fell back into her memories of participant-observation. Leaving the milonga is another difficult decision-making process. The whole thing combined (when you arrive, where you locate yourself, how much you choose to or can dance and with whom, and when you leave) makes up your style, along with how relaxed or anxious you are during the whole process. Talking, drinking, smoking, and especially consuming drugs will be read as signs of lack of interest or commitment to what really counts in the milonga: dancing tango. These activities are present at the milonga, but they should be interrupted whenever the opportunity for dancing arises. What you do and what you look like at the milongas becomes spectacularized. To an outsider like Dr. Hardoy—Elvira distanced herself from her ethnographic and dancing partner—the inhabitants of the milonga are gendered, racially marked, nocturnal monsters; the presence of the night fetishizes their monstrosity.

> [T]he women almost dwarfs and mestizo-looking, the guys like javanese or *mocovíes* [native South Americans], bound into tight checkered or black suits, hard hair plastered down with fatigue, drips of brilliantine catching blue and pink reflections, the women with enormous, tall hairdos that make them look even shorter, laborious hairdos of which they retain the tiredness and the pride. The guys nowadays have a thing for loose hair and high in the middle, enormous and effeminate bangs that have nothing to do with the brutal faces below them, the wry faces of aggression ready and awaiting their hour, the efficient torsos set on thin waists (129).

Dr. Hardoy, coming from a different (class and race) world, is fascinated. He will tell us—Elvira flexed her knees before jumping at her partner's throat—his allied readers gathered on the nonmonstrous side of things, what these monsters look like: their hairdos, their style of dress, their dimensions and proportions, their racial and ethnic resemblances, their cross-gendered features, so that we can answer the question haunting monstrosity. (For a note card: Cortázar/Hardoy's insistence on marking racial differences associated with class could be making reference to the "invasion" of *cabecitas negras* (mostly mestizo-ancestry or mestizo-looking people from the less-developed interior provinces of the country) that took place during the years of Peronist government (1946–1955). The wave of migration from the impoverished rural areas into the city and suburbs of Buenos Aires was prompted by the expansion of the labor market created by the government's investments in industrialization and import substitutions. In the city, this working-class population became visible as outsiders to well-established *porteños* like Hardoy.) For what is the opposite of a monster? And how can we tell one from another without even a formal name for the non-monstrous condition? Know your monsters, especially as they dangerously gather, and you will know yourself. Cortázar's Dr. Hardoy takes us to the milonga "because of the monsters"—a most sincere declaration of the ethnographic predicament. But once declared, all responsibility vanishes in that "because," as if the monsters were there calling for his curiosity to awaken, waiting to be written about in order to exist. And how interesting—Elvira shook and threw them both off balance—that the "monsters" rarely see the Dr. Hardoys or the ethnographers as monsters. Oddities, different animals, even coveted prey, yes, but not monsters.

Cortázar's Dr. Hardoy introduces the milonga's monsters by proving that monstrosity resides on the surface, in the milonguero's and milonguera's bodies and their looks, as if monstrosity were an issue of aesthetics rather than of ethics, or as if the ethics of monstrosity would be embedded in monstrous aesthetics—Elvira, on all fours, proceeded to bite Dr. Hardoy's calves. He presents the bodies as definitely grotesque—an elaborated production of mismatches where, contrary to Bakhtinian teachings, the emphasis is placed on overdoing the upper body parts, especially the hair. (For a footnote: See Stallybrass and White 1986.) What seems to follow the politics of the carnivalesque smoothly, however, is the presence of symbolic inversions deployed over the monsters' bodies: they wear the wrong outfits, the wrong make-up, the wrong hairdos for their class and its racial associations. Their grotesque looks are the result of the appropriation of démodé or misinterpreted high-class ("classy") trademarks by low-class (déclassé) looking bodies. The aesthetic result provokes distaste in those who recognize the distorted appropriation that stands out as a tension between the two symbolic registers of distinction, high and low. Milonga aesthetics, like camp and *rascuachismo* (Latino/Chicano kitsch), challenge the status quo in that it shows that low bodies, despite their deprived social conditions, can display excess by putting it on.

From this point of view—Elvira, back on her feet, recomposed her hairdo and attire—the milongas I attended in Buenos Aires in 1996 do show the presence of "monsters," but they are referred to as milongueros and milongueras. Those terms are marked enough to denote the eye-catching aesthetics and also the ethics that characterize this core group within the tango world. The aesthetics, however, are different nowadays, although the impact for an intruder like Dr. Hardoy remains roughly the same. More than elaborate hairdo, what calls the attention (of both the milongueros and the outsiders) is the women's use of body-revealing attire: see-through and/or cropped blouses, very short miniskirts, or, more rarely, full-length tight skirts or slacks slit almost to the waist or made of transparent fabrics. Next, and also in contrast to what women wear in everyday life, come the ankle-strap shoes with the three-inch-plus heels. Female haircuts, rather than

complicated hairdos, reveal a preference for short lengths in disproportionate numbers compared to what one can see any day in the streets. And
make-up, in contemporary milongas, is not particularly striking. When
asked about these aesthetics choices, both milongueros and milongueras
stress that although this attire responds to trends in fashion, what matters
is that it is comfortable to dance in: the skirt does not get in the way of and
entangle in the legs along the tango walks and during the *figuras*; the high
heels facilitate pivoting on the ball of the foot so that the body can promptly
switch directions, and they also help to tilt the axis of the woman's body toward the partner in the tight tango milonguero (*tango de apile*); short hair
does not interfere with the milongueros' sight, given that their heads are
held in contact (cheek to cheek either facing the same or opposite directions), thus helping to prevent collisions with other couples on the dance
floor. The see-through materials or skin-tight cuts, as well as the cropped
blouses and even the extreme shortness of some skirts, are considered a current milonga fashion that has adopted some of the most sensual looks of the
mainstream trends (some of them reminiscent of a pre-*Evita* Madonna).

What makes them "monstrous"—Elvira hesitated on whether to question the milongueros' uncritical objectification of the female body or to continue pressing Dr. Hardoy's neck (where she located his prejudices); she
opted for the latter—to use Cortázar/Dr. Hardoy's term, is that these fashion indices in the milonga are redundant—too many women wear them at the
same time in the same place, as in Cortázar/Hardoy's monstrous gathering of
monsters—and that they are worn by mature women, women who are past
their miniskirted, cropped, see-through look prime in most public spaces
except the milonga. The mismatch is to be found in this age transgression,
where the appropriate age fit between the attire and the body that wears it
is being transgressed. As a result, the display of mature women's bodies
(women in their forties and up to their late sixties) is what calls the intruder's attention—Elvira pushed Dr. Hardoy off the dance floor. The milonga environment is thus charged with a female sensuality that is beyond
the parameters of everyday life, and the women who practice it enjoy it. It is
a practice of pleasure. In the milonga, not only can they choose to publicly
expose their body shape in an aesthetic that defies otherwise accepted age
parameters of old and young and their corresponding ethical (mis)judg-
ments (as in "only whores dress like that"), but this practice also asserts
their ability to compete with younger milongueras' strategies of visual seduction. In the milongas, mature women are still in the running. Plump,
bony, or out-of-shape female bodies are not to be concealed because what
(really) matters is the confidence with which the milonguera moves her body
on the dance floor. Thus, in the milonga, an otherwise grotesque body becomes beautiful by the way it engages with the tango dance. She must be
light but she should be fully "present" by investing effort in her arms and

thrust in her legs; she is expected to be focused, quick in responding to the *marcas*, and to give her weight to her partner and yet not fall off balance. The decisive moment for the judgment of the milonguera's beauty resides in movement, not in the still pose, as with pin-ups and models.

Milongueros also cultivate this age transgression by wearing toupées, dying their white hair, and even, occasionally, penciling in their thinning moustaches—Elvira wrote on a napkin and reflected on the feminization of macho hypermasculinity. Their appeal, however, is more related to their ostensible efforts in dressing up for the milonga. Casual attire (jeans, T-shirts, athletic shoes, and the like) are ill regarded in most milongas (with the exception of a couple of *milongas de jóvenes* [young people's milongas]). Milonga etiquette requires well-pressed jackets, ties, dressy pants, and shiny lace-up shoes with leather soles. In the milongas, male attire asserts the value of tradition and a concern with good manners (care as opposed to sloppiness) and with class. A milonguero's wardrobe is a noticeable monetary investment. As a matter of fact, many milongueros are blue-collar workers, small shopkeepers, salesmen, or white-collar workers in low positions, and a good number of them are retired or unemployed. Their jobs rarely require them to wear ties and jackets. This is an investment they make for the purposes of the milonga. Hair neatly combed back or to the side, rather short; clean-shaven faces; and gold jewelry (pinky rings and chains) are also milonguero traits. The availability of cash to buy drinks, take taxis, and, in general, look good contributes to the milonguero's appeal—Elvira took a drink, compared her headnotes, and decided that in the milongas femininity is assessed by focusing on the female body in movement, while masculinity resides in a combination of financial exhibitionism and ability to strategize the couple's displacements on the dance floor. Milongueros' body features are rarely at issue. Their ability to move on the dance floor and to relate politely to their female partners is what counts. And here, an important observation about the milonga tango style must be made. A milonguero is appreciated for his ability to navigate on often crowded dance floors, protecting his female partner—who walks backward and thus cannot monitor the movement of the couples ahead—from bumps and collisions. This ability to monitor the scene while performing improvised movements in unison with others is the key to a milonguero's success with the milongueras.

These men, who often are unable to exercise much real control over their lives—think of their fragile employment situations—do excel at controlling their bodies and those of their partners in the milonga. The "monstrosity" in this—Elvira rushed on to the dance floor with someone else—if one were to follow Cortázar's Dr. Hardoy some fifty-plus years later, is the time and effort that milongueros devote to this "unproductive" dancing skill, which often draws them to overlook their working responsibilities.

(Milongueros are known for fleeing their jobs during working hours in order to attend prácticas; they stay up late almost every night *milongueando* and skip work or arrive late.) This situation is more frequent among milongueros than milongueras because it is said that men require constant practice at doing the tango in order to maintain a high level of performance, while women need to devote less time and effort to maintain comparable levels of achievement. (Women are not required to navigate the dance floor or *marcar* (to prompt or "mark") the *figuras*. Their responsibilities during the dance, often referred to as "following the marks," are considered less demanding.) In sum—Elvira took a break—to contemporary outsiders, milongueros stand out not so much for their appearance or aesthetics, but rather because of their strange (work) ethic. In addition, there is a strong sense of grotesque mismatching in the milonga in the way the dancing couples are formed that strikes the outsider's eye once milongueros and milongueras step onto the dance floor in twos. But I will follow, once again, Cortázar/Dr. Hardoy's *marca*, showing his proposed steps into this terrain before responding with my own—Elvira consented to dance with him once again; she could not resist this tango.

Let us recall that we were already taught that milongueras and milongueros at the Santa Fe Palace carry two distinctive attitudes before stepping into the dance floor: the women, an "absent air" as they sit on chairs by a long wall; the men, with "wry faces of aggression," erect over alert torsos ready to move on "thin [and thus well-trained] waists." Milongueros wander around the dance hall studying the terrain; milongueras wait passively to be discovered. I have to say that this is pretty much the case today, at least as a first impression (and by this I do not mean a wrong one). A closer look—Elvira sat down at a table with other milongueras; she turned her back to Dr. Hardoy to avoid being disturbed—assisted by conversations with the milonga habitués on the subject suggests a more complex gender dynamic. Milongueras' apparent absentmindness is really a watchful attitude. They observe the movements and gestures of their potential male dancing partners in order to actively ignore those given out by men with whom they are not interested in dancing. At the same time, milongueras are busy not missing the inviting winks of the milongueros they like and sending encouraging looks toward them. Milongueras even report that they can keep male dancers hostage in the milonga by nailing them song after song with their eyes alone and thus preventing that milonguero from asking anyone else to dance. It is not in good taste to ask someone to dance verbally. Approaching a chosen partner with words and/or physical presence (as in walking to someone's table or chair) is an often unwelcome move, at best a sign of "unprofessional" behavior left to milonga newcomers—those who do not know how to read the glances. Physical or verbal impositions break the magic, the freedom of choice based solely on the appetite for dancing with someone. That freedom is compromised when a physical approach, noticed by the ones surrounding the potential couple, puts one of them at risk of being publicly shamed by a rejection. Only dancers unsure of their merits press their chosen partners into that uncomfortable situation. Under those circumstances, the dance is usually accepted, and if the milonguera dislikes her partner, she will excuse herself after the second or third tango (before the set is complete). The milonguera signals her intention to abandon the dance floor with a squalid "Thank you." Some milongueras call this a "sitting him down" move, alluding playfully (and vindictively?) to the reversal of gender roles—Elvira and her female companions in conversation exchange noisy chuckles.

Cortázar/Dr. Hardoy establishes a contrast between the milongueras' apparent absentmindness and the milongueros' faces, wry and ready with aggressive intentions. Male faces, at the milongas I attended, show more grave brows and sometimes scornful mouths than aggression. They seem to imply that they are serious at this business of dancing tango and, simultaneously, that they challenge women into taking the risk of embracing, tightly, and following the *marcas* of a male stranger. In addition, some milongueros point out—Elvira, situated at the milonga's bar interrogates some milongueros on what she perceived as hostile yet inviting male posturing—that many of the women who attend the milongas would be absolutely unavailable to them in other contexts because of the class and/or age difference between them. In the milonga, invitations to dance and acceptances can also be transgressions of everyday social barriers, a matching of (socially) odd parts. The milongas and their danced tangos are, from this point of view, a revolutionary experience—Elvira, surprised, jotted down the milonguero's use of the term "revolutionary."

Unreliable Words, Incongruent Bodies

I could not avoid anticipating Dr. Hardoy's questions here, but guessing one's partner's next step is one of the milonguera's required tango skills—Elvira shared another tango with Hardoy, tempted by the memory of prior pleasurable dances.

> They recognize and admire each other in silence without giving away understanding, it is their dance and their encounter, the night of color. (For a note card: Where do they come from, what professions hide them during the day, what obscure servitudes isolate and disguise them?) That's what they go for, the monsters lace into each other with grave discipline, song after song they gyrate, spaced out, without talking, many with their eyes closed, finally enjoying parity, the completion. (129–130)

Cortazar's Dr. Hardoy lets us know that, finally, he is captivated by the dancing. The monsters slip together into motion. They look enraptured, as if in a state of "completion." But it is "their dance" not ours, and we should avoid falling for the trance by thinking on the note cards, focusing on possible clues to this enigmatic effect. Like an ethnographer, he struggles, trying to keep his mind clear and his inquiries sound. I will follow those milongueros' "closed eyes" and speculate on that state of "completion"— Elvira excused herself from dancing with Hardoy by saying that her feet were aching. This is the state sought in and through the dance, when two bodies communicate perfectly (and look perfectly and beautifully matched, overcoming mismatching heights, weights, energy levels, thrusts, and mistrusts). Milongueros and milongueras describe it nowadays as fluid, calm, comforting: as when things finally fall into place, difficulties are left behind, and the reward is a transporting corporeal serenity. Absentmindedly, embracing tightly, they tilt their torsos toward each other in a delicate balance, their legs tracing sinuous paths on the dance floor, muscles fully alert to the doing and undoing of mutually provoked entanglements. Their improvised steps surprise each other, and yet the music (the rhythm and the melody, they insist) holds them together, prompting the smooth continuity of the conversation between these distinctly gendered bodies. Dr. Hardoy notices these gyrations "without talking," and so do the milonga habitués. The lack of verbal exchange is considered a tango trademark.

Tango is, or should be, a corporeal dialogue. It is a dialogue that in order to be perfect proscribes words, avoids the verbal pollution of the event, the awakening of intellectual sources that inevitably reproduce miscommunication. So the particularity of the tango resides in the purely chemical mix of bodily physicalities, and words are a matter of a different kind. Verbalizations are products of the mind and as such amount to either intrusive accelerators or breakers of the tango chemistry. Words irrupt the nature and speed of tango bodies' exchange of sweat (bodily fluids), of heat (bodily temperatures), of weight and balance (bodily gravities), of tensions (bodily strengths and efforts), of aesthetic intentions (bodily shapes and trajectories). Words are mistrusted in the milonga, but not so much because they lie while the bodies "speak" the truth. Rather, the problem resides in words' competitive effect vis-à-vis bodily conversations; as a matter of fact, words retain authority over truth-telling and carry the capacity to disrupt the lesser truths of the bodies, of those tango bodies whose radical physicality constitutes the matter, the surface without immaterial depth, that allows milongueros and milongueras to truly live their fantasies. It is as if words would tell too much unwanted, not untrue, information, information powerful enough to break the ignorance that the fantastic communication among tango bodies is intended to build. Words tell the truth about class differences, age mismatches, ethnic conflicts, and ideological incompatibilities, not necessarily in stronger terms than the bodies do but rather in more precise terms.

The bodies "speak" a lesser language, equally codified but more diffuse; the bodily surfaces tell in a way that invites misrecognition because the body is easily subjected to fragmentation, each body part or accessory telling a different story. The leg of a mature milonguera might indicate youth by its strength and aggressive projection, while her hairdo may points toward an old-fashioned, now lower-class taste, and the length of her dress or her jewelry could provoke mixed reactions as well. In addition, a milonguero's heaviness, noticeable dye job, or flashy pinky ring might provoke class and generational associations, appealing to some and distasteful to others, but agile feet and a firm gait while dancing will erase most misgivings and set aside most misapprehensions. Not only are the tango bodies, both male and female, perceived in a less seamless or fragmented way than that allowed by speech (which regardless of the presence of contradictions must retain some coherency in order to (mis)communicate), but also, milongueros and milongueras are particularly attracted to bodily contrasts and incongruencies. The milonga environment rewards transgression when it comes to bodies out of place and bodies doing the unexpected. Words become uninteresting because they speak too clearly and always about something else. However, this amounts not to a totally speechless situation but to a highly codified conversational system usually restricted to the moments in between dances. At those times, short phrases are exchanged, frequently geared toward commenting on the pleasure or displeasure of the dance and on the dancers' abilities. Sometimes they include flirtatious connotations, testing the availability of the dance partners for romance or sex. Whether welcome or unwelcome, rarely do the words outweigh the pleasure of having danced well and the promise of attaining that pleasure once again. In the milongas, words are not the site of creativity, of that which is being judged through what the bodies accomplish together on the dance floor. As a matter of fact, citation of tango verses, folkloric refrains, and clichés pervade the milonga's linguistic economy of scarcity—brief, bold remarks, with a history of telling tales that say almost nothing about the sayer, and whose lack of effect on the listener is taken almost for granted. In the milonga, words are a wild try. Milongueros and milongueros focus on and work with the body. (From my fieldnote booklet III, 1996: 31, 33, 44–46, 52, 61, 79.)

Addictive Enigmas

They recuperate during the intervals, at the tables. . . . In addition, there's the smell, the monsters can't be thought of without that smell of wet powder against their skin. . . . He watched the dance floor just like me. . . . Many were sweating, a *china* [*mestiza*] about the height of my jacket's second button passed by the table and I saw the water pouring out of the roots of her hair and running down the nape where a roll of fat made a whiter channel. There was smoke coming in from the room nearby where they ate *parrilladas* [charcoal-broiled meats] and danced *rancheras*; the *asado* [barbecue] and the cigarettes laid a low cloud that distorted the faces and the cheap paintings on the opposite wall. . . . It seemed as though a moment of immense happiness had descended upon the dance floor, I took a deep breath as if to participate in it and I believe I heard Mauro doing the same thing. (130–135)

In the milongas of contemporary Buenos Aires, tango is referred to as a drug, and the practice of tango as an addiction. (For a long footnote or integrate into the text: Drugs have always been present in the tango world. Lyrics, plays, memoirs, literary texts, and gossip mention their use among milongueros/as and musicians as well as the presence of drug traffickers in the milonga scene. See, for example, the plays *Los Dopados* ([1922] 1968), by Alberto T. Weisback and Raúl Doblasand; *Nobleza de Arrabal* ([1919] 1968), by Juan A. Caruso; and the poem *El violín del diablo, Maipú Pigall* ([1926] 1967), by Enrique González Tuñon. I wish to focus, however, on a different tango-drug connection, one unmediated by the consumption of substances. And this is also a connection that has a long history. René Briand, for example, in his account of early tango times, writes:

This time she fastened herself to his body, completely abandoned in his arms but obeying all of his dancerly orders. He made her knit a labyrinth of footwork, commanded by his right arm connected to the blonde's waist. The two swung in ecstasy, as if they were drugged by those perforating sounds that resembled syringes filled up with heroin-injecting, innocent bodies. The youngsters' contortions attracted the attention of other dancers, who looked at them with envy. (1972: 84)

In *Psicopatología del tango*, Roberto Puertas Cruse writes: "That is why a woman listens to tango with that dynamic ravishment of the dance, or with the psychic giddiness that it provokes, given that it works on her dearest emotions as a narcotic" (1959: 17). In "Elogio del Gotán," Last Reason (a pseudonym for Máximo Sanz) ([1926] 1968) writes: "Tango is the boss. Tango has intoxicated the couples with a strong poison of suffocated desire, and when the music stops, his eyes and hers, they are still wandering in the somber world of sensual ecstasy" (Lara and de Panti 1969: 323).) Tango, however, does not fall into the category of intoxicating products, the simple consumption of which generates an altered state of consciousness. Access to the tango ecstasy (Cortázar/Dr. Hardoy's "immense happiness") requires much preparation and much practice; it is a carefully crafted road that involves highly developed skills on the part of its practitioners. The tango "high" (and this is a rather bad choice of words, for reasons I will soon explicate) comes and takes hold of the tango dancers somewhat like a trance, a state of possession achieved only with much effort and usually not at all. The tango "trance" is thus a promise, nurtured by the milongueros' and milongueras' memory of past experiences or by the memories passed down to them by other, more experienced tango dancers.

This interpretation of tango, which lures practitioners and critics into the fascinating terrain of the occult, is, of course, strangely generative—Elvira, back at her desk (in body and soul) got carried away with her readings of Spinoza (1989) and of Deleuze's readings of Spinoza (1988)—in the sense that it provides a mysterious explanation for tango's addictive powers that shapes the awaited effects. After being hooked up, obsessed, irresistibly drawn to cross, again and again, the border from the everyday world into the tango world, risking family ties, breaking friendships, failing work engagements, ignoring coups d'etat and other social and moral obligations, the milongueros and milongueras feel compelled to explain, to identify a cause and invest it with insurmountable power. Their tango doings thus become passive undertakings compelled by the force of an intoxicating agent. Paradoxically, this force is not an external substance, as the tango-drug association would lead us to believe. The drug is the tango itself, that is an activity that requires the dancers' involvement in order to exist; the tango dancers produce the drug and their addiction to it simultaneously by dancing tangos. The flaw of the metaphor is precisely what creates the enigmatic nature of the tango endeavor.

For lack of a better word, this special tango "state" is referred to as passion. And I emphasize the imprecise nature of the word and concept of "passion" as ascribed to the tango in an attempt to echo that moment of hesitation, that searching of the mind's archives and of the taste of words in the mouth that takes place whenever I ask tango dancers to explain what is it that they are looking for, night after night, in the milongas. Passion, they repeat—Elvira moved, secretly, from citing milongueros to interpreting them; marked-up books on her shelves suggest she had been consulting Lebrun 1987; Heller 1979; Greimas and Fontanille 1993; Baudrillard 1984; Trías 1991; and Savigliano 1995, among others—taking hold of something somewhat recognizable, open, and ambiguous enough to accommodate a wealth of feelings, both positive and negative regarding what it takes to get there, to live with it, and to survive the consequences. For, let me remind you, tango dancers pursue passion, the sparkle of the passionate event in their lives, like addicts, as if against their will, as if they could not help but search for it. Performing tango steps, they cultivate passion, passionately. The passion is already there in the attempt, and yet it is displaced to that fortuitous moment of condensation, consecration—that moment at which a particular stabilized experience of passion is achieved. That moment, that event, is what I improperly termed the tango "high"—improperly because it is not euphoric, bubbly, happy, supernaturally transcendent, or otherworldly. The tango bodies are the site of the tango high.

The tango high is a paradoxical state of abandonment and full control— Elvira flipped through her fieldnotes (vol. 1), trying to elucidate whether these remarks were based on milongueros' actual verbal statements, on tango literary sources, on her own experiences at the milonga, or on her interpretive imagination—of bodily awareness and mental disengagement. The feet seem to be making all the necessary decisions. Bodies propose and respond to each other, without words and even without eye contact, as if the intellectual capacities would be channeled from the usual brain-language and soul-eyes connections into other organs and senses articulated on the skin's surfaces of different body parts with coordinated minds of their own. Tango bodies practice a corporeal sociality. Milongueros and milongueras undoubtedly construct their version of the body, just like everybody else. Their conceptualization of the tango bodies conforms to a strange philosophy, where ultraphysicality leads into a metaphysics of the corporeal. A belief in transcendental corporeality? Elvira slipped back into Spinozist musings. But regardless of its constructivism, tango practitioners dance their bodies with these corporeal concepts, physical investments, and metaphysical purposes not in their minds but somewhere else, wherever the body seems to be intelligent at the time. Seeking for "naturalness" in the tango dance amounts not to leaving the bodies to themselves, but to recognizing and thus reallocating intelligence to them, crossing over the mind-body divide, not avoiding the tension but rather attaining its comfortable manipulation. This is not an innate ability, but rather a skill painfully gained through experience—experience in dancing tango, experience in the tango world, experience in the world at large: street wisdom. It is a very ambitious state, no doubt, given the precarious material and emotional conditions under which most Argentine tango practitioners live. Which takes us back to Dr. Hardoy's note cards: "Where do they come from, what professions hide them during the day, what obscure servitudes isolate and disguise them?" (130). Milongueros and milongueras cultivate the enigma.

The smoke was so thick that the faces on the other half of the floor were blurred, so much so that the area of the chairs for those who were sitting it out could not be seen, what with the bodies in between and the haze. . . . Celina, who was on the right side of the floor, moving out of the smoke and whirling obediently to the lead of her partner, stopped for a moment in profile . . . I say: Celina; but it was a vision, a knowledge without understanding it . . . Celina there without being there . . . drinking in the tango. . . . [H]appiness transfigured her face in a hideous way. . . . There was nothing to stop her now in her heaven, her own heaven, she gave herself with all of her flesh to that joy. . . . It was her hard-won heaven, her tango played once more for her alone and for her equals. (135–137)

There is something otherworldly about the milongas, and they also join the porteño underworld. In the milongas you encounter faces, bodies, attitudes, behaviors, and existential plateaus that do not pertain to everyday, busy Buenos Aires. Cortázar's Dr. Hardoy goes to the extreme of bringing Celina back from the dead and into the dense atmosphere of the Santa Fe Palace in order to convey the milonga's uncanny (to him and to us) version of heaven and its fleshly joys. But I wish to call attention to Celina "moving out of the smoke" in a tango. Dr. Hardoy explains with difficulty that Celina, at that moment, is "there without being there." She is "a vision." The milonga is represented as a place and a time in between the real and the unreal. In "Las puertas del cielo," the fact of Celina's death dramatically asserts the power tango exerts over certain bodies—enough to transport the dead and the living into a common ground of nocturnal collapse. (From a note card: Cortázar/Hardoy's approach to the milongas' enigmatic pleasures seems to follow the utopian principles of a Barthes reading Fourier: "Pleasure overcomes Death (pleasures will be sensual in the afterlife). . . . [Pleasure is] what operates the solidarity of the living and the dead (the happiness of the defunct will begin only with that of the living, they having in a way to await the others: no happy dead as long as on earth the living are not happy)" (Barthes 1977: 83).) Dr. Hardoy stresses the tango connection between the living and the dead, and the milonga as a space where and when this strange encounter is likely to occur. The presence of an otherwise absent Celina, conjured by the tango into taking possession of a body in movement on the dance floor (not just anybody, for the bodies she takes hold of are of a certain gender, class, and have certain racial and ethnic features), signals the existence of a dimension outside daytime. *La noche* is central to this occurrence and to Cortázar/Hardoy's project, situated at the periphery of the day and of social order. (For a quote: "[Tango] calls attention to the things that die every day and that still come back, generating the enigma of being alive" (Ferrer 1995: 13).) But the knowledge that Celina is dead also distracts us—Elvira thought and wrote—from further analyzing what makes the living milongueros and milongueras, "her equals," capable of transporting and transforming themselves when at the milonga. "Where do they come from?" reads Dr. Hardoy's note card. Like an experienced ethnographer, Dr. Hardoy thinks of jotting down questions that, in surrounding descriptively what he really wants to know, eventually will deliver the awaited response to the question "Who are they?"

My own nocturnal incursions into the milongas of Buenos Aires as an aspiring milonguera and an anthropologist (although milongueros insisted on interpreting my work as philosophy) kept me trying to understand how tango dancers go about constructing these spaces and states of alterity for themselves. Even the milonga habitués often reflect on this matter. "Where are these people during the day?" they ask, as they pan over the dance hall's interiors, amazed at the collection of milonguero and milonguera characters of which they are a part. Everybody seems to be playing a part for everybody else. Some unusual looks are cultivated, but what magnifies the artificiality of the scene is that all participants are conceitedly on display, willingly offered for visual inspection. Everybody is ready for a close-up shot that will not amount to a revealing look. Milongueras and milongueros pursue close-ups that remain locked on their surfaces. (For a footnote: See Deleuze's discussion of the affect-image and the use of close-ups in cinema (1991a).) The visual scrutinies should not break into disbelief, but rather render a sparkling object suited to a fantasy that, upon the detection of the object, immediately wraps around it. In the milonga, seeing and knowing are never collapsed. The point is to believe. And yet, skepticism is keenly cultivated. Everybody wants to be a fetish, an object of somebody else's desiring fantasy, and a fetishist, a desiring subject that controls and contains his or her object of desire in an auto-generated fantasy. So, embedded in this control and containment lies the suspicion that the fetish is unreal and that the whole thing is a game. (For a footnote: See Apter and Pietz 1993.) Nevertheless, the skeptical fetishist finds pleasure in the game itself, because although the fetish and the game are just that— fabrications—the pleasure attained is real. To put it in other words, it works. Like a successful experiment, it delivers what is expected: in this case, a pleasurable *tanguidad* beyond ordinary reach.

(From a note card indicating "For an introduction, a conclusion, a quote, or a footnote": "[T]ango may not be important; its only importance is what we attribute to it. This is not unjust, but it applies equally to everything under the sun. . . . Tango can be discussed and we discuss it but it hides, like all truths, a secret. . . . It might be said that without the sunsets and the nights of Buenos Aires no tango can be made, and that a platonic idea of the tango, its form universal . . . , awaits us argentinos in heaven, and that this thriving species, however humble, has its place in the world" (Borges 1984: 147–148).)—Elvira modified the translation a bit and went to bed at dawn.

Habitual Elucidations

Several months later, on a bright and sunny afternoon in southern California, Elvira struggles to conclude her ethnographic account. She becomes aware of her own educated compulsion to shed light on the milonga scene by connecting tango nocturnality to everyday life in Buenos Aires in 1996. She shuffles through note cards and mental notes: "the milonga as sacred space/time: communitas, liminality, reaggregation (Turner 1987)"; "similarities between milongas and carnival: resistance or accommodation? (Da Matta 1991, Scheper-Hughes 1992: 480–504)"; "José Limón on Mexican dancing as manual laborer's joyous assertion of victory over capitalist claims on all their energy (1994: 165)." Elvira writes an illuminating conclusion, reciting the last twenty-five years of Argentine history in two or three sentences: the "dirty" war and state terrorism, redemocratization, neoliberal policies and privatization, political corruption, unemployment. . . . For whom is she writing? Elvira recalls a Dutch tango-tourist she interviewed in a milonga in Buenos Aires. "I dance tango because it is dark and my soul is dark." She remembers the Australian journalist who interviewed her in a tango club, encouraging Elvira to link—in fifteen seconds or less—the tango revival in Buenos Aires to mourning for the *desaparecidos*. Elvira imagines that some European readers—who are, after all, more informed than most *norteamericanos*—will read a connection between Celina's apparition in the Santa Fe Palace and the demand of the Madres de Plaza de Mayo for *reaparición con vida* (reappearance with life). She thinks of those milongueros and milongueras who proudly declare themselves apolitical, of those who consider milongas the only truly democratic space they have ever known, of those others who live the milongas as cultural bastions of an endangered national identity, and of those who value tango as a nomadic art and tango practitioners as an adventurous species proving transcendental beliefs in an art form that transcends national borders. She shudders. She sighs. She submits her paper.

Gambling Femininity

Wallflowers and Femme Fatales

Tango often evokes fatal men and women caught in a somewhat dangerous dance, where obscure desires (forbidden liaisons, provocation, transgression, betrayal, revenge, and jealousy) become spectacularly stylized. Depictions of tangos in narrative cinema, tango choreographies conceived for the stage, tango portrayals and tango metaphors in advertisement and literary fiction, and to some extent tango lyrics have contributed to this cliché, by now well established worldwide. As an ethnographer of the milongas and as an aspiring milonguera, I became increasingly puzzled by the presence of wallflowers and the absence of femmes fatales in the everynight tango scene of Buenos Aires.[1] This essay, then, situates wallflowers and more precisely the act of wallflowering at the center rather than at the outskirts of the milongas.[2] I am proposing the idea that a full tango experience is impossible without the presence of wallflowers and without the threat of

1. I have been attending milongas in Buenos Aires since 1989. I formally assumed a conflictive "insider/outsider" position ("Am I here to dance or am I doing research?") between 1994 and 1997, when I decided to undertake "fieldwork" in order to write an ethnography of the contemporary milonga scene. Since then, as some of the milongueros have pointed out to me, I have not really been a milonguera. My investments as a full dancing participant have been compromised by my "interests in living things in the milonga in order to write about them" (Eduardito, informal conversation, August 1996).

2. Readers should be aware of the maneuvering I am exerting here by setting the wallflower into motion, that is, into wallflowering. The story starts with the limits of translation. In the milongas, women wallflower (*planchar* is the slang Argentino-Spanish for this activity.) There is no corresponding noun to this verb that is applicable to the milonga setting. (*Planchadora*, as the one who *plancha*, would immediately bring to mind someone who presses or irons clothes for a living. It is a profession of sorts but has no relation to the dancing/nondancing economy I am addressing here. *Planchar*—and this is a wild guess—has been assigned to this active "waiting to be asked to dance," perhaps as an association with the unintended "ironing" of the garment on which the aspiring dancer sits for extended time.) Therefore, while *wallflower* (in English) ascribes a rather set identity to those who do not dance—meaning they probably never will because of who

wallflowering as the potential dancers enter the tango club. And I wish to clarify that wallflowering is a traumatic, intense, trying, unpleasant process to go through. Since all women in the milonga scene wallflower to a certain extent, wallflowering is both despised and admired, for reasons I will soon explicate.

Given that milongueras often wallflower more than they get to dance at tango clubs, and that they (we) endure rather than enjoy this rather humiliating position, I have wondered why and how they undertake this act of passivity, and what is at stake. Why do women attend the milongas night after night, persistently undergoing this enhanced state of anxiety that compromises their self-esteem? Unwilling to settle for a facile explanation in terms of heterosexual sado-masochistic dynamics (as in, "Women enjoy submission; they like to suffer"), I will entertain the idea that milongueras are irredeemable gamblers of their own femininity.[3]

---

they are—*planchar* (Spanish for "wallflowering") designates a (lack of) activity—not-dancing—into which some aspiring dancers happen to have fallen under certain circumstances. *La que plancha* (the one who wallflowers) is not as stuck in the character as "the wallflower": one wallflowers, the other *is* a wallflower. This picture does not include those who, either inside or outside the dance club or dancing situation, choose systematically or circumstantially not to dance. The lack of desire to dance immediately situates them outside the rules of the game (the economy).

3. Psychoanalysis has been explicitly and implicitly used (and more and less rigorously) to explicate women's participation in the running of patriarchal social settings. Often these explanations assume that the constitution of women's identity as sexed subjects conditions (overdetermines) their pathological behaviors. Clinical models of analysis seem to be the obvious and most appropriate choices for tackling women's contradictory, paradoxical, and thus pathological ("self-destructive," "masochistic," "narcissistic," "schizophrenic"—the list goes on) practices. Sigmund Freud's discussions of female sexuality (1962) and Jacques Lacan's rereadings of Freud's findings (1985) have been vastly cited, applied, used against the grain, and contested by feminist theorists. Psychoanalytic feminist approaches can be crassly divided into those that maintain that Freud's and Lacan's works portray male-female relations as they are (meaning not as they should be); those that consider Lacan's interpretations of Freudian findings to be theoretically enabling because of their constructivist (nonessentialist), semiotic (arbitrary and ambiguous), critical (theoretically concerned and revisionist), and provocative (he pokes fun at phallocentrism) discursive take on Woman and women's pleasures; and finally, those who insist in finding alternative theoretico-poetic spaces—usually by resourcing to "corporeal" language and *écriture*—to account for women's own representations and interpretations of pleasure. It is beyond the scope of this paper to review these arguments for and against the espousing of psychoanalysis's takes on women's or Woman-sexed identities or for explicating women's submission to the phallic order, to men, or to both. The field is rich and complex, and I invoke its conundrums in order to situate my efforts at and the impossibility of stepping aside. (For a fuller treatment of these debates, see Elizabeth Grosz 1990).

Zoning in on the tango "world," sexed identities and sexual matters are un-

Before discussing this idea, however, I wish to back track to the wallflowers so that you know more precisely who these tango characters are that have become my obsession and specifically what is it that they do. Along the way you will notice their invaluable contribution to rethinking the role of the dance scholar, and in particular, to the ethnographic technique of participant-observation. *[Warning: My references to wallflowers and wallflowering frequently shift from the position of the observing wallflower (the ethnographer) to that of the wallflowers being observed (the milongueras); and the wallflowering ethnographer here evoked is a self-reflexive type. My goal in so doing is to capture the state of confussion that characterizes participant-observation, 'native' ethnography, and auto-ethnography, on their own and combined.]*

---

avoidable. Pleasure and its sexual and sensual intricacies (tango practitioners insist on this enigmatic differentiation) motivate its producers and consumers and mark the form—tango as practice and representation. Thus scholars, artists (choreographers, filmmakers, dancers, writers), and, to a certain degree, practitioners, with and without feminist preoccupations, have faced the "woman's question" in tango. More frequently than not, women's participation in the tango scene, and, curiously, despite differences in terms of historico-cultural background or setting (not to mention ideological, economic, or political positions)—is explained in terms of (universal) sado-masochism. "Explain" here is a euphemism for "labeling and stopping" reflection, placing a familiar plug into the subject (and subjects) under scrutiny. Women who participate in the tango scene are tempted to accept these clinical views of themselves. They recognize their subservient position in most things they undertake in life. A certain discomfort, however, is enhanced when tango is at stake, because they participate in the milongas at their will and for the purposes of pleasure. (Alternatively, I could claim an "active," phallic-like, powerful masochistic role for milongueras following Gilles Deleuze's decoupling of the Freudian sado-masochistic dynamic (1991b, 1996). However, Deleuze's analysis vindicates the masochist as a man who produces and controls his (male or female) figures of infliction. This would apply to the milongueros if their portrayal as femmes fatales (which I advance toward the end of this paper) were accepted.) Culturalist explanations rush in: This is Latinamerica . . . so the answer lies in machismo. (I have undertaken an analysis of machismo and its politico-cultural dimensions elsewhere (1995).) How do you step away from sado-masochism and its shadows? Are there any ways to address heterosocial and heterosexual women's pleasures that do not immediately prompt interpretations in terms of victimization? I am trying to go beyond the comforts of compulsive repetition ("women are especially adept at it"; "women don't know any better"). I am especially concerned about the application of pathological explanations interwoven with culturalism. When women's presence in the tango world is explained (away) through *machista* sado-masochism (a specifically "Latin" and more resistant strain of the universal patriarchal virus), the often female and feminist researchers provide the diagnosis once they are safely back in their home laboratories (or, to put it in other words, once fieldwork is completed and they are back at their academic or creative desks). There is little contemplation of the intelligence of those other women, the "genuine" ones such as the milongueras, who continue enduring and enjoying that world under study that has been taken as a source of insightful inspiration.

The Ethnographer as Wallflower

[Warning: Readers less interested in ethnography than in wallflowers should skip to the next section.]

The following sections have the double purpose of introducing some paradigmatic tango *figuras* (movement sequences) while generating reflection on some paradigmatic ethnographic techniques. The tango embrace, hooks, spins, and so forth are described in order to call attention to the practice of description in itself. The result is a counter-transparent effect in that the dance ethnographer is caught in the work of ethnographizing, recurrently introjecting observations and interpretations. The dilemma of ethnographic participant-observation—of assuming alternately active passivity and passive activity—is thus highlighted in terms of a "problem" that is impossible to solve, given that it condenses the very possibility of the production of anthropological knowledge. What is at stake, then, in the denial of anthropology's intrinsic madness? What are those principles to which anthropology tries unsuccessfully to conform? And what would it mean for anthropology to give up the quest for the truthful representation of others and to recognize its fabrication of othered worlds?

The ethnographer, in this case a dance ethnographer, will be presented attempting to capture the signs and the signification of ephemeral choreographed movements. She is both an intruder in the dance scene and a necessary presence for the dance to actually occur. She is a troubled observer obsessively preoccupied by her desire to participate in the dance, while that desire strongly informs her renderings of the dance. The dancers' own

---

Benevolent expressions of concern and desires to salvage other female victims of culturally "residual," backward patriarchies are also rather suspicious. There seems to be no legitimate space in which to place those women uninterested in or unresponsive to accusations of victimization. It is assumed, by default, that they are stuck paddling in the deep waters of (self-selected?) victimization. These interpretations in fact show little "intercultural" gynosociality at play. There is little investment in learning from other "native" women the secrets of the worlds in which they live, including their survival tactics and their concepts of pleasure. Researchers and artists often arrive in the tango world either with a preconceived idea of what it is all about or informed by tango men. They enter into dismissive competition with the milongueras for the favors of the milongueros, using their privileged positions as "nonnatives" to the milonga scene. I grant that the nature of the tango world aids to this effect. (Like the film industry and academia, the tango world is a macho boys' world where women play their reproductive, accommodating, and resistive tricks.) Thinking of the milongueras as irredeemable gamblers does not quite do the work of depathologizing their nocturnal doings and inclinations. Gambling, in the sense of taking unnecessary risks, is an unproductive and often addictive enterprise (see Benjamin 1969b: 177–180; Derrida 1995). However, gambling one's femininity evokes more active and less doomed images than the masochistic Freudian framing of feminine inclinations.

desires are reported through her own, her desire pouring into them. Observing and unable to fully participate in the tango world, or at least to participate the way "they" do, she includes herself as a victim of scholarly observation. Alternatively, she discovers the power of her gaze, capable of not only observing but actually also of creating the dance through interpretation. Looking for empathetic understanding while simultaneously generating a report to the academy, the dance ethnographer resorts to her familiar horizons of meaning—such as feminist theory and politics—in order to figure out (and thus disfigure) the dancers' stakes in the dance. She asks: Does the tango present a fatal macho man, or does it stage a femme fatale? Is *she* a self-defeating, manipulative woman trying to make a dent in the male homosocial tango world? Is *he* a traitorous seducer in need of maternal reassurance who mistreats those he seeks to fulfill his fantasies? Who is the victim of the tango, and who the victimizer? And whose questions are these, the tango dancers' or the ethnographer's own?

Observing, describing, interpreting, the dance ethnographer moves hesitantly back and forth until, overcome by overwhelming undecidability, she settles for an explanation that incorporates her into the picture as a victim of the dance she does not "really" dance, a victim of the dancers—now turned into a couple of victimizers—and a victim of her own desire. The tango figuras continue, prompting contradictory interpretations. As the tango comes to an end, the ethnographer discovers her own vindictive powers at play in the exercise of interpretation—that violence inflicted on the object of knowledge as the process of knowledge is developed (Foucault 1972). As the dance scholar moves from the dance floor to her desk to the academic floor, her participation in making tango an anthropological object intensifies. Writing about her fieldwork requires an effort of imagination. She wishes to report on those bodies that once moved in excess, dancing, looking for a pleasure they displayed in her presence and yet refused to put into words. She summons them back and asks them questions they have already answered in their own terms, that is, before she thought of asking; or is it the other way around, and was it actually she who scripted their answers for them, anticipating the questions she would formulate?

Her interpretations shape what she sees and hears, what she smells and senses from the fly space of the actual tango world—that reality to which she has no access, if not in (sociocultural) principle then because the ethnographic project prevents her from "belonging" to the milonga in the milongueros' terms. Her desire to know and to understand the tango and her motives for seeking to capture the tango—this object and not another one—cannot be separated from the constitution of the tango as object. Likewise, her desire cannot be disentangled from her judgments of the tango turned into object. The tango, however, objectified but not inert, transforms her as well. The milongueros, spectacularized by her interpretive presence, include the dance ethnographer in the tango spectacle. The observant ethnographer becomes a participant even when she does not move away from her speculative chair. Her thoughts, her words mimic and retrace the entangled trajectory of the dance, the abrupt stops, the sharp turns, the restlessness of the bodies in intimate embrace. The tango tension playfully erodes her manipulative attempts at thoughtful domestication.

Neither tango nor the dancing bodies in themselves should be credited for provoking this complex ethnographic situation. The most down-to-earth cultural practice or artifact participates in a similar ethnographic knower-known dynamic. Bodies are not intrinsically more mute than nations, and dancing is not necessarily more elusive than economics. The difficulty of the scholarly enterprise is more noticeable, however, because until recently dance as a field was left at the margins of the trodden paths of modern disciplinary knowledge. The lack of investment in developing a discourse to account for bodies performing seemingly unproductive movements allows these reflections on the ethnographic predicament to be revisited.

Speculations of (from) a Wallflower (Position)

[Warning: The actual performance of the wallflower starts here.]

I am pleased to introduce you today to an often invisible and mistakenly shameful character of the dance scene: the wallflower. These speculations are intended as a vindication of the wallflower. And I must confess that in doing research on tango I have frequently identified with this character. So, in speculating about "her," I have engaged in reflections about my own ethnographic undertakings. In order to elicit your sympathy, however, in a less self-indulgent tone, I will address both the dance ethnographer and the wallflower as if they were a (third person) "she."[4]

Haunted by an itch to tango, the dance ethnographer sits restlessly at the computer screen, performing her scholarly duties. She wants to dance, but she is accountable mainly as a wallflower. Wallflowering, she observes, wedges a speculative space between dance spectatorship and dance performance that allows her to observe, participate, interpret, and write. The figure of the wallflower highlights the performance of ethnography and the production of ethnographies of performance. *She writes:*

In performance and cinematic studies much effort has been devoted to the conceptualization of the production/emission and consumption/reception of cultural representations. [Note: Cite Mulvey 1988a, 1988b; Blau 1990; Nichols 1981; and others.] A wallflower potentially condenses the role of a hyperactive audience, who could but will not deliver the act of dancing; and of an ultramarginal and passive performer who can inadver-

4. On pronoun "shifters" see Jacobson 1960.

tently slip away from the dance scene (the ethnographic field) at her whim, running away with the best gossip of the evening. That is, if she can overcome a sense of melancholia, a tendency to believe that others and not she herself determine her lonesome fate. The wallflower's viewpoint complicates the dualism entrenched in these performance-audience oriented epistemologies. Through participant-observation and observant-participation, wallflowers contribute to cultural construction from a position that, although not free of *resentiment*, embraces the productive side of performative failure. *She leaves her desk, sits down in her desk chair, and starts rolling around the room while explaining:*

This wallflower, then, does not take on an identity but rather assumes a position[5] that revindicates an active aspect of some seemingly inactive undertakings, calling attention to an activity that takes place somewhere else—neither exactly on the dance floor nor completely away from it. Wallflowering is somewhat like plotting. The wallflower is characterized by a profound knowledge, investment, and even training in a performance genre, coupled with a view from the margins as an engaged spectator of that which she is ready to perform—and yet she does not. Her unpopular, often denied, but vastly practiced doings capture the embodied learning anxieties of the dance ethnographer with a specificity that the role of a participant-observer so elegantly covers up. *Still sitting and rolling around the room, she adopts extravagant positions:*

Marginality, misfitness, naiveté, awkwardness, patience beyond the call of duty, and frustration with a smile are some of the very corporeal experiences to which a wallflower-ethnographer is and accepts being subjected to in the course of fieldwork. The passivity involved in learning from others' activity will eventually deliver the strategic production of knowledge. Actually, wallflowering is somewhat prescribed by the participant-observer technique in that the desire to go native or to become totally involved in a given "culture" should be persistently frustrated by the demands of objectivity or, at least, of maintaining the distance required for the production of anthropological interpretations. But anthropologists are wallflowers with a vengeance. The tense marginality of the expert in the midst of a participatory project metamorphoses into a manipulative work of representation and interpretation as soon as the institutional, discursive field of anthropology is regained. *She stops rolling around in her chair, sits tall and still, and adopts a preachy tone, saying:*

The wallflower position is more often imposed on women than it is self-elected by us. And arguably, anyone who wallflowers, that is, who obsessively observes action while actively remaining passive, becomes feminized. It is from this feminized but not submissive position (the one of the wall-

5. See note 1.

flower who does not give up and eventually transforms the dance scene) that these performative speculations choreocritically address women's positions in the sensuous production of the tango. *She mimics the activities she describes orally:*

Sitting uncomfortably at the edge of her chair, clutching and stretching her toes captured in ankle-strap high heels ("you can't leave Buenos Aires without your tango shoes!" said Rivarola, her dance teacher–informant), the wallflower-ethnographer watches the tango scene intently. She looks for the intentionality hidden in every move. She knows that there is more to it than she can see. Her hands, placed on the small table in controlled relaxation, long for a notepad where she would record that today, Friday, March 22, 1996, she sits at the milonga El Tugurio in downtown Buenos Aires. Her manipulative work of interpretation is about to start. *The tango couple enters under a spotlight, while she continues on her chair, at a small round table. The tango couple follows her instructions*:

Figure 1: *La salida*

"Departure" or Beginning of a Tango Dance

As handsome as he can be, not because of his physical attributes but rather because he cultivates the attitude of a handsome man, el milonguero stands at an edge of the dance hall (against a wall, behind a column, next to the bar's counter, by the hall leading to the entrance) monitoring the milonga scene. His gaze wanders distractedly through the tables until it locks, abruptly, with la milonguera's look. She has been sitting there, quietly conversing (not laughing) with her female friends, since the end of the last dance set. He interpellates her with an intense nod, just one quick reverberating stroke that raises his chin and runs up through his face, lifting his eyebrows. She might deflect his invitation to dance, flashed through the room, by quietly continuing her visual search, or she will immediately move her chair to the back, stand up, and, after a brief pause, start walking toward her new tango partner as he moves toward her. An instant is enough (and the usual amount of time spent) for this intensely engaging exchange. The wallflower wonders, taking quick headnotes, "How did it happen?" She would have missed it for sure. Yet the couple is already meeting on the dance floor.

The tango music starts. They converse for a few beats of music, weighing their words, getting ready to carry each other's bodies. This is the only opportunity for verbal or even visual exchange among tango partners until the tango is over. They embrace.

The tango embrace grows rather than happens. It is carefully crafted by the two, taking hold of their entire bodies. He initiates the embrace, already a movement without displacement, by placing his upper arm under hers and pushing upward, seeking the weight of her embracing arm. The torsos move toward each other slightly as the heads search for contact, turned toward the hands that clasp, and the arms, which will lead the dance trajectory, extend. The tango bodies stretch from the waist up and down as if pulled from both ends along a slightly tilted axis, joining at the top. The balls of the feet look for groundedness. Well planted, although she is already brought to raise her heels in tension. They sense each other's balance, wondering how much challenge can they give and take in the movements they are about to perform. They quickly calculate the possibilities opened up by this firm, tight, yet flexible embrace that will structure the tango moves without asphyxiating their unmatching, improvised steps. The wallflower watches the construction of the tango embrace taking place in what feels like suspended but not empty time. Suddenly, gravity seems to pull the bodies down, the knees bend for an instant to a tango-rhythmic slash, and they slide without bouncing into a tango walk.

They just walk.

Walk together. Walk as close as necessary. So close that, at a certain point, the differences between the two of you will become essential. The need to master the other is irresistible. The resistance to being engulfed is hysterical. Keep on walking. You cannot give up. It is beyond your control. Just try to make it beautiful. Perform. Do not hide your fear, just give it some style. Move together but split. Split your roles. Split them once and for all. One should master, the other should resist. And forget that you know what the other is going through.

The interpretations of the wallflower slip into the tango scene. (Her desire?) The dance moves her imagination. Too invested in the tango to be a mere spectator, the wallflower actively spectacularizes the dance. The tango takes three rather than two: a male to master the dance and confess his sorrows; a female to seduce, resist seduction, and be seduced; and a gaze to watch these occurrences. The male-female couple performs the ritual, and the gaze constitutes the spectacle. Two performers, but three participants, make a tango (cf. Savigliano 1995). The wallflower–dance ethnographer scribbles, annoyed by her self-reflections. *She continues reciting. The tango dancers split. (No projection here; it all happens in her imagination.)* Her tango dance masters pop into the scene like talking heads, interrupting her analytical flow:

Juan Carlos Copes: "Tango is a sensual dance. It is not about sex; it is not erotic."

Carlos Copello: "Tango is not about power, it is about dancing."

Carlos Rivarola: "You think tango is machista, don't you?"

Eduardo Arquimbau: "Your right hip is crooked."

"Tango does not flow; arrest your energy"; "don't bend your knees";

"push your thighs together"; "tighten your ankles against each other before each step"; "resist my lead with the weight of your presence before each move"; "root the steps and liberate the walk, caressing the floor"; "lean on me without compromising your balance."

The tango-teachers' responses always anticipate the wallflower's thoughtfully prepared (crooked?) questions. The wallflower's research inquiries seem unnecessary. The questions are never asked. The answers are ready in advance. *The tango couple initiates another tango walk.* Tango is about guessing the partner's moves before they occur, surprising, halting the other's energy in a moving gasp. Challenge creeps into the bodies, but the tango music pulls the dancers' wills out of stiff, antagonizing entanglements. The walk continues in a tense balance, the research questions remain answered and never asked. Should the wallflower trust her skillful "informants"? They certainly think fast on their feet. *The dancers follow her instructions.*

Figure 2: *El boleo*

Throwing Something Energetically at Random;
in Tango, the Milonguera's Leg

Out of nowhere (the wallflower was distracted, lost in her thoughts), the milonguero stops the tango walk by planting his feet firmly on the ground, tightening the embrace, and pulling her slightly closer and upwards as in seeking to catch her breath . . . and the eye of the wallflower-ethnographer. Power, crooked, macho, erotic—the wallflower's imagination is triggered again. The milonguera's energy is arrested from the waist up. From the waist down, pivoting on top of a high-heeled foot, her hips quickly shake back and forth causing her free leg to make a gesture: a thrown-around [*boleo*], slack kick in the air, high or low, containing the aggressive liberating force that would throw her off balance. The rebellion, however, is there, insists the ethnographing wallflower, bringing familiar feminist understanding into the tango picture. *The dancers leave again.* The wallflower's viewpoint slips into the dancers' intimate scene. Insisting on introducing triangles to explain the circulation of desire in the tango, the wallflowering ethnographer declares that the sexual politics of tango cannot be split off from the presence of the spectator.

The wallflower gravely ethnographizes the tango situation. She produces descriptions and interpretations as she identifies the tango with her own familiar struggles. She observes, she participates, and the results are promising, pleasurable. *The tango couple starts dancing in the dark.*

Figure 3: *La sentada*

A Sitting Action

The dance couple will not clarify the issue, any issue. That is the task of the wallflower committed to ethnographic research. Where were we? Ah, yes. The torsos. Their torsos show agreement, their faces, fatalism, tied up in their tightly held hair. *The spotlight travels up and down, screening the dancers' bodies.* But from their waist down, struggle. Tango steps are developed in this context, heavily focused in the presence—the body—of the milonguera. The male imposes his reassurance, confirming his identity by sitting her, albeit briefly, on his lap. (*La Sentada* is the name given to this figure.) *The wallflower gyrates 360 degrees, holding on to her chair as if she and it were a single body. The dancers move out of sight.* She, the milonguera, has helped him to define his masculinity: Her display of resistance and difference provokes and constantly reshapes his gender identity. Her own identity, as she falls back on her feet, remains unsettled, incomplete, and on the move in those transitions between accepting and resisting subordination to his identity and his moves. The wallflower sits and writes, confirming ethnographic authority and the need for external interpretive intervention. *The dancers reappear and repeatedly perform a figure 8 in slow motion, while the wallflower mimics the milonguero's hand movements.*

Figure 4: *El ocho*

The Figure 8

In the midst of a seriously firm embrace, holding tender torsos together, the milonguero's right hand exerts a pressure on the back of his dancing partner, slightly above her waist, with a swaying movement: a wave that strikes, delicately, first with the base of his palm, signaling her to cross her legs "that way," and immediately afterward with the tip of his fingers, another small push, indicating the next crossing over, this time "this way." That way and this way, again, rubbing knee against knee, she slides one foot, almost sticking to the floor, obliquely forward; she gyrates, on tiptoe, from the hip down, *quebrando*, that is, breaking the waist, her torso always facing his, only to repeat exactly the same movement with the other half of her body—as if a mirror had sliced her in half. She brings her feet together, stretches her knees, and waits, tense, for the next *marca*, the next indication, the next gentle push, the next musical bar. *The tango dancers freeze; the wallflower continues illustrating with arm, torso, and head movements.*

The double curving lines that intersect and twist the dance trajectory complicate the structurally smooth paths of logic (thinking patterns) that should lead her to a conclusion. As the milongueros repeat the figure 8, the wallflower-ethnographer paraphrases their intricacies and doubles her understandings in entangled contradictions. Tango's figure 8 (*el ocho*) assaults her with the impossible image of two victimizers and no victims dancing: a deadly woman and a fatal man, oblivious to the presence of a victim. *The wallflower freezes*. Who is the victim if not the most engaged spectator? The wallflower swallows and sweats. *The tango dancers turn their heads and look intently in her direction. They resume dancing.*

Figure 5: *Ganchos*

Hooks

The milonguera, about to complete another figure 8, pivots on her right foot as she slides her left foot in a diagonal full thrust initiated at the thigh. Her intentions are thwarted by a slight pull the milonguero exerts on her back, moving her in the opposite direction. Startled for a split second, she recovers her balance and, facing away from her partner, redirects her free leg in a high-speed kick aimed at striking the void he has created by bending his knee. Her leg hooks dangerously onto his thigh and falls immediately back to the ground. Flashy! No wonder Madonnna adopted the *ganchos* as paradigmatic tango figures in her portrayals of a defiant Evita, notices the wallflower. The milonguero is now the victim, she asserts with relief. *The tango couple dances distractedly, bored.* The tango-woman expresses her anger . . . when the tango-man gives her the space. Whose timing was it? And how will this situation develop? *The wallflower shows excitement. The dancers start following mechanically her indications.*

Figure 6: *El giro o la calesita*

The Spin or Carousel

Taking slightly broader strides than during the tango walk, the milonguera encircles her partner, describing a quadrangular floor pattern. The embrace slackens, and the tension moves into their erect spines. The milonguero indicates a displacement that he will not follow. Nailed to one spot on the dance floor, making himself light on the ball of one foot while playfully ungrounding the other, then crossing it behind so as to turn in a twist, the milonguero provides the turning axis for *el giro*. It takes her exactly four steps to go around a full circle: legs crossing way up at the thighs, one; uncrossing, two; crossing behind, three; and free again, four.

Mechanically perfect. How can anyone see passion in this tango machine, the wallflower wonders. For an instant she saw the sacred circle and the ringmaster, at the center, trotting his favorite tamed animal around the arena. *The dancers perform a fast tango walk in a diagonal and initiate a "cradle." The wallflower runs after them carrying her chair and sits down again.*

Figure 7: *La cunita*

The Cradle

Respite. Milonguero and milonguera rock back and forth in each other's arms. They seem to offer comfort, even reassurance to one another. Each gives and takes the other's weight, alternately, by lifting one of their legs off the ground and wrapping it swiftly around the partner's opposite calf. Drop. Rock. A caress of the legs. Drop. Rock. A simple, mirrored, repeated sequence performed while turning around an imaginary axis placed between their bodies. The wallflower melts in tenderness, her back resting for the first time against the back of her chair. But she has seen enough of the tango world to know that no tango ends rocking gently like that. *The dancers perform* la mordida *vigorously under the wallflower's nose.*

Figure 8: *La mordida*

The Bite

A trap. An extended leg offering a foot, as if forgotten there on the floor, in a space that will be irremediably taken by the other dancer's body if the tango embrace is to be maintained. The projected foot lays there, tantalizing, like bait. The milonguera bites: First, she places one foot strategically along the inner edge of his foot to prevent a sidelong escape; then, she brings her whole body in a block, towering on top of the other foot, close to her partner; and finally, her feet clasp the milonguero's foot with determination and clear intentionality. She makes her arm heavy on his forearm, indicating he should stand still. He pauses in full tension. The milonguera swings a leg backward, crossing the line of her own body, twisted at the waist, until her foot reaches his far foot. She quickly strikes her target and grows back into her full stature by unwinding her contortion. The same adventurous foot is now traveling up the milonguero's calf in gentle strokes. She rests her foot on the ground by his, replaying the initial *mordida* for an instant. She removes the biting effect by crossing over his foot, leaving it free for further displacements. Awe. *The wallflower recites with difficulty, as if lacking oxygen.*

The wallflower could hardly hold her breath any longer. *The tango couple leaves the scene.* She has seen it before, but the *mordida* leading to these spectacular variations left to the female dancer's initiative always catch her by surprise. Is this the exception that confirms the (macho) rule? Or is this the telling figure, the one that shows that the rule was a misconstrued interpretation (about heterosexual dynamics)? Is this the moment of femme-fatality the wallflower has been waiting for all along in her fieldwork? *The wallflower's words pick up speed.* Are the milonguera's embellishments a mere digression, a hint of rebellion, or a spark of transgression without which it would be impossible to grasp the limits of tango's nocturnal laws? How do you distinguish the wallflowering ethnographer's desire from the milonguera's desire, or, more precisely, from the desire the milonguera performs through her tango steps? *The dancers return in a casual walk, embrace, and dance in a very relaxed manner. They continue dancing through the next scene.* Is it possible to gain access to the desire of the other, or is the desiring other caught in the act of desiring all the wallflower can hope to ethnographize? *The wallflower looks extremely agitated. She pauses for a moment and continues at a slower pace.* And when the dance scholar finally, after nights and nights of wallflowering, figures out that the puzzling question she has been trying to address concerns the formation of pleasure embedded in tango choreographies, can she pull her pleasure apart from that embodied by the tango dancers? Can her interpretations of the dancers' pleasures stand, disentangled, under control, and aloof with respect to her own watchful pleasures and displeasures? Not only the problematic and enabling pleasure of interpretation is at stake, but also the pleasure of accounting for the pleasure undergone by others who, as in tango's case, elicit the observer's complicitous spectacularization. *The tango couple anticipates the wallflower's description of the último compás and leave, oblivious.*

Figure 9: *El último compás*
The Last Beat

With the last beat of music, the perfect ending. Sharp. A full stop on the dance floor exactly at the moment the music falls silent. The tango is over. The tango bodies have been anxious all along, awaiting this trying moment. A retrospective interpretation of the whole danced tango will follow. Evaluating the corporeal communication between the dancers in the midst of a tango is a hard task. The fast exchange of challenging entanglements erupting between tense walks, the rhythmic juxtapositions played out by the feet, the arms turning from a solid to a warm embrace all amount to an undecidably harmonious yet disharmonious effect. In the end, however, regardless of the raucous or serene nature of the tango's sequential metamorphosis, the moment of dramatic effect should be marked in unison. Two high-heeled slippers facing two pointy-toed lace-up shoes, four extended knees almost in contact, the embrace suddenly grows tighter and a quivering movement ripples down the milonguera's spine until it falls in a straight line from her tailbone right down to the floor. The music ends. The two torsos release a breath. Two complicitous smiles signal the aftermath. They interrogate each other with ironic remarks: "That was not too bad." "No, not so bad." They might take the tango risk, jointly, again. *The wallflower leaves her chair and walks to her bed, located a few steps away.*

Wallflowering Gone Wild

[Warning: Readers allergic to poetic prose should skip this section.]

From her bed, she recites, yawning, sleepy: Growing wild images, creeping on the walls of the dance hall, the wallflower exudes the fragrance of all failed performances. On edge, at the verge, from the fringes, observing marginalia, the dance scholar as wallflower witnesses and records the dancing event. Wearing spikey-rimmed cat's-eye glasses—rather than spiky high heels—the tango wallflower half-sits on a chair, by the nondancers' side of the dance floor, skirting the milonga scene. She attentively watches the evening's developments. She is ready to dance. She has been practicing, she knows all the rituals: the glances, the nods, the walks, the entangled figures. And yet her performance is that of a knowledgeable spectator who fails to perform desired embodied steps. She scribbles, she interprets, she produces ethnographic writings. *She continues, turning in her bed as if having a nightmare.*

At the verge, she nervously waits to be asked to dance and she does not want to be asked, so that she can continue performing, to the point of perfection, in her daydreaming, following the movements of the actual dancers, obsessively fixing, correcting, embellishing every embrace, every posture, strategically interpreting every step. She pours drama into her writings. *She sits abruptly and reaches for a notepad located under her pillow. She jots down her ideas.*

Watching others do the dance, joining in order to learn better how to describe it, gaining a kinesthetic feel for it (an insider's point of view?), looking at how one is looked at, searching for critical intimacy while discovering complicitous criticism (begging for understanding?), the participant-observer of the dance fails to account for that part of the dance (is it what the dancers experience or what she imagines they must experience?) that continues chasing her until she sits stiffly on her tailbone, on the edge of her chair, waiting for the writing partner (the prospective dance reader?) to ask her to interpret aestheticized movements. *She looks for her glasses, finds them under the bed, and continues relentlessly taking notes.* Utterly gendered, the scholarly wallflower (who according to the Oxford English Dictionary is "a lady who keeps her seat at the side of a room during dancing, whether because she cannot find a partner or by her own choice") engages in choreo-writings: the spec(tac)ular trafficking of corpo-traces that enter the heterosexualized academic floor.

The wallflower I have in mind sits perky, alert, awake, and unnoticed. She is smart. No typical melancholy wallflower but her evil twin sister—the one who might or might not walk on spiky high-heels but certainly watches my and your steps through spiky-rimmed glasses. *She gets out of her bed and walks to her desk, located a few steps away.*

Wallflower Ecology

[Warning: Readers interested in facts (no figures) should continue here.]

The wallflower types at her computer: So far I have provided intimate close-ups of a nervously observant wallflower and of a tango couple whose steps (*figuras*) have been carefully dissected. Now I wish to create a more distanced view of the milonga scene, zooming out and panning the ecological niche where wallflowers (the "genuine" ones *and* the "perverse" ones drawn to ethnographic writing) grow and transform.

She reaches for her field notes and books as she continues writing her research report. Milongas are a harsh environment within a harsh environment. "Away from the milonga, out there, there is only solitude," say the milongueros and milongueras, but they also repeatedly proclaim that "there are no friends in the milonga." There is no secure, restful place either outside or inside the milonga world. Although the milonga, the site in which the tango passion comes to life, evokes images of a strange cult in which dance and music invoke Tango, the god, who would descend or arise, choosing well-disposed victims of possession, and despite the proliferation of ritualistic practices and codes, the tango cult does not amount to a tango "community" or to states of "communitas" (cf. Turner 1982).

In the milonga scene, each one is there for himself or herself. Associations and demonstrated interests are invested interests. These entirely personal interests, moreover, are legitimate and assumed. There is no pretense and no expectation of communal feelings beyond the common interest of maintaining the milonga scene—that is, keeping the tango dance halls open and running and continuing to produce committed tango dancers. Nor is there any real commitment to a particular tango dance hall or to an established social group of tango dancers. The milongueros and milongueras are nomadic and enjoy moving to a different milonga every day of the week. Sometimes they even make incursions into several milongas on the same night, looking for the most suitable and compatible partners.

Belonging to the milonga scene is also an unstable status. The environment is cool—not hostile, but rather loosely interested in the presence of anyone in particular, and the relationships established in the course of any one night carry on rather dimly into the next. Being a part of the milonga scene must be constantly reenacted. Having met, made small talk, or danced enraptured with someone does not warranty in any way that you will be greeted or addressed, or will dance with this person ever again. There is no social contract beyond that ephemeral incident of a one-night encounter. The milonga is cherished as a place of fortuitous and fleeting relationships, with no established loyalties or commitments, where you risk again and again the open possibility of fate putting some sweetness in your path. And you should be free and ready to take it. In entering the milonga, tango dancers step onto a highly competitive stage ruled by the laws of naked seduction.

The dance starts way before the actual dancing. The foreplay requires a considerable amount of plotting. Rules, codes, and the dance technique must be mastered. You should be noticed when you arrive, but it should not be noticed with whom you leave; you should recognize and greet only those worthy of public recognition; you should devote your energies to rapidly assessing whether there is anyone present who is worth dancing with—and if not, you will simply comment, "There's nobody here tonight," even when the dance floor is packed. You should keep your eyes panning constantly around in a state of "floating attention," ready to be caught by the glance of an interesting and interested dancer. Above all, no dancing opportunities should be overlooked. Talking—beyond making small talk or exchanging pertinent remarks—should be avoided. Engaging in conversations that take your attention away from detecting suitable dance partners is a bad sign: Either you are not interested in tango (and thus your presence in the milonga is suspect) or you are a heavy gossiper (which amounts to a serious danger for the milonguero species). The list of codes and corresponding decodifications goes on and on. Every move is informed by and conducive to seduction—a seduction that is not restricted to any one particular purpose but is open to a multiplicity of possible gains, rewards, and pleasures, from the most innocent to the most vicious. Nothing and nobody should be trusted. In the milonga everything means something else, and everyone pretends to be somebody else. Thus, everything is under scrutiny, and everyone, under suspicion. This nightmarish situation could be interpreted as collective paranoia were it not for the wide use of experientially established "tables of conversion and decodification" shared among the nocturnal milonga habitués.

Every new arrival is observed, carefully pondered, discreetly discussed, casually engaged in conversation when necessary, and, eventually, trotted around the dance floor. Every look, exchange, and invitation to dance (whether given or received) is a test. More precisely, it is a placement test for a complex and hierarchical chain of milonga initiates. It is a living chain, organized on the basis of time (marked by one's persistence in attending tango clubs and endurance at practicing the dance technique), seniority (marked by one's knowledge of the different tango styles and experience in the tango world), public recognition (such as that of professional tango dancers, renowned amateurs, or simple practitioners), age (young, middle-aged, or old), nationality (Argentine, Uruguayan, or foreigner), class (the display of classy manners being more important than the state of the bank account), and gender (men and women are the given categories; heterosexuality is the undisputed norm). The chain, however, is "alive" in that anyone can outgrow his or her initial placement. The combination of factors taken into account allows for mobility and generates competition.

The "nature" of the interest in tango is a fundamental placement datum: Are you really interested in tango, that is, are you a legitimate addict, or are your interests purely "professional," that is, financial? Do you understand the tango world, or are you simply looking for excitement? Are you seeking an exotic experience (outside your class or culture)—an affair, perhaps, or a simple squeeze—or do you really care about the perpetuation of the tango tradition? The list of tricky questions continues, ever more refined. For example, once it has been established that your interests are professional, the following inquiries (and judgments) will ensue: Are you a professional tango dancer seeking to practice traditional milonguero tango styles? (Positive.) Are you promoting yourself and/or looking for tango students? (Obvious and negative, but forgivable.) Are you stealing new tango steps for your next show? (Very, very bad.) Or are you an aspiring professional tango dancer trying to be noticed and selected? (Kind of pathetic.) The links in the chain are there, ready to accommodate each and every one. The questions are never open and direct. The string usually starts with: "I haven't seen you before. How long have you been dancing? What brought you here? Where do you go dancing? Where did you use to go? How did you learn how to dance? Who taught you how to dance tango? Where do you live?" and so forth. A night or two at the milonga is usually sufficient for experts to complete the questionnaire. You have entered the milonga food chain—a chain pulsating with anxieties about who gets the first and the best picks, who has to feed on crumbs and leftovers, what kind of bite you will make, and whether you will be tasted at all.

In 1996–1997, the milonga food chain in the downtown tango dance circuit of Buenos Aires (I must be specific here because the chain is fluid and changing) was headed by two or three professional male tango dancers who, upon entering the milonga, are quickly surrounded by a group of aspiring professional male dancers. They usually establish their headquarters near the bar and walk casually around the room, showing off and seeking prey.

The aspiring professionals follow the established pros in hopes of being included in a future tango production, and they do the work of trying out new aspiring professional female dancers. (The pros should not waste their time or expose their bodies to mistreatment in the arms of inexpert dancers.) Established and aspiring professionals (that is, stage tango dancers) also attend the milongas in order to catch the eye of spectacle impresarios—foreign and national television and film crews—and to attract tango students of both sexes. New aspiring professional female dancers, especially if young, are their favorites.

Foreign female dancers, particularly if single, are especially sought after. They provide the necessary contacts for touring and teaching abroad. In addition, foreign tango students are rich veins of cash, not because they are necessarily wealthy (as a matter of fact, wealthy visitors to the contemporary milongas are rare) but because they come to Buenos Aires with a certain amount of cash to be spent in tango training over a short span of time. To get hold of them from the beginning is essential. Foreign tango students, in turn, are given the opportunity to learn "authentic" Argentine tango styles, to mingle with "real" milongueros, and to acquire the flair of the milonga world. If they are professional dancers themselves, and especially if they are tango teachers, the milonga experience and the rubbing of elbows with renowned tango dancers adds prestige to their credentials and hence increases their enrollments back home.

You might wonder at this point about the professionally established Argentine tango female dancers, the ones who form the renowned tango couples of the staged tango. These women rarely appear on the milonga scene. Their male dance (and, frequently, romantic) partners venture into the milongas on their own. When professional tango couples split (an occurrence that is to be avoided at all costs, given the time and effort they invest in generating a successful partnership), the women have a harder time than the men in finding a replacement. Among tango pros, men tend to carry the business of advertisement, finding gigs and students. Recognized tango masters and teachers are, for the most part, male, although the gendered division of labor has been changing in the last decade. Nowadays many of the younger professional female dancers come to practice tango after years of training in ballet and modern dance. Their professional goals and lifestyles often set them apart from the "genuine" milongueras. In the tango world, these women are a special caste of artists, dancers whose whole life is devoted to the care and training of their bodies. In their case, dancing tango is not fully associated with pleasure and nocturnal adventures. Milongueros and milongueras often relate to them as if they were slick tango models, designed for stage and screen, and unavailable for everynight gaming. Occasionally they present themselves in the milongas after a late-night show or for a dance demonstration. They are admired and applauded, and after dancing with a few seasoned milongueros in a mutual gesture of acknowledgement of skills, they wallflower like the best. But they are not dancing gamblers like the true milongueras; they dance for a living and thus are seldom lured into enduring wallflowering. They have nothing to gain from it. Milongas are not their thing.

Older, experienced, traditional male milongueros (frequently including the owners or organizers of the milongas) follow the professional tango male dancers and their courts in the hierarchical chain—and they often resent it. Often these men have been informal masters, the ones who generously taught the younger professional male dancers the core of what they know. (The special dance embellishments, suitable for the stage, are often taught by older professional male dancers who rarely appear in the milongas.) The experienced milongueros, who are frequently found sitting in groups of two or three at the edge of the dance floor in visually strategic, well-located tables, are the heart of the milonga. They have seen all, and they know all, and their interest in the continuity of the tango tradition is beyond dispute. They are the figures of authority of the milonga as popular culture.

These older milongueros own most of the shares of tango's cultural capital, but they have little access to the tango's accumulation or circulation of economic capital. Experienced milongueros rarely conduct formal tango classes and rarely participate in tango shows for the stage. Old milongueros are or were great dancers. In the tango world, this means that they made original contributions to the dance vocabulary through improvisation, that they are able to master the conundrums of tango's syncopated rhythms, and, most important, that they know how to "walk" the tango (considered to be a greater accomplishment than any flashy, complicated tango "figure"). Having participated for years in the milonga scene, they have learned all the secrets of the female tango dancer's body. But they are old, old-fashioned, and slick in an outmoded way, and frequently have a lower level of education and/or sophistication than the young professionals. Their ability to seduce is based solely on their dancing skills. And they get to dance (and this is always the key to the placement in the milonga food chain: whom you get to dance with is what is at stake) with the youngest and loveliest women of the milonga. But only after the "professionals" have made their first pick.

These young women, regardless of their dancing abilities, are the trophies of the milonga night, and older milongueros make sure that the younger male dancers notice their privileged access to them. In the strong male homosocial bonding of the milonga, the competition over "spring chickens" is all-important. If the *nenas* are good or promising dancers, of course, it is better. This is, however, a statement based on my observations. In formal interviews, experienced and aspiring milongueros will insist that in the tango world looks do not matter; what counts is the skill in dancing. But they add with a smile: "Good looks, of course, don't hurt."

Young and middle-aged female amateurs, then, make up the next link of the milonga food chain, followed, in turn, by middle-aged male amateurs and some foreign male dancers, who are themselves followed by older, experienced milongueras, and, finally, a group of tango couples of diverse ages and origins who participate only sporadically in the chain's avatars—avatars ruled by those intense plays of seduction that spin around the "who gets to dance with whom" business. A man and woman who attend the milonga as a dance couple freeze their status as players in the games of seduction. As a couple they are less mobile than individual male or female dancers, in part because they are usually taken for a romantic couple as well. But only for the night; the situation is reassessed nightly. It is not unusual for members of an established romantic couple to attend milongas separately, arriving at different times and sitting at separate tables, so as to send out a clear sign about their availability—certainly for dancing, and further potential developments are left unsettled. The milonga is definitely about dancing tango, but it is also about picking up, and about pickpocketing of diverse and variable kinds. *The wallflower thumbs through her note cards in search of a precious quotation. She reads out loud in a manly voice:* "But if you can top the night by taking someone to bed, it won't hurt," *and adds:* "I was chucklingly taught by Juan Carlos, an old milonguero." *She resumes her writing.*

Let us return now to those older, experienced milongueras, those women sitting in groups of two or three, staring at the dance floor, waiting to be asked to dance. In a way, they set the tone for the female presence at the milongas, and their position condenses both the fears and the expectations of the milonga's heterosexual plays of gendered syncopation. The presence of the older milongueras is a testimony to tango's addictive powers. In their particular case, tango is beyond all doubts a passion. They *just* want to dance. Ulterior motives, whether romance, sex, company, or money, figure way down in their list of priorities. Dancing tango, they say, is what makes them feel good and alive. Few women accede to and remain in this position. In the milonga world, males usually endure much longer than females. It is said that women, after a while, fall in love (inside or outside the tango milieu), and either their jobs and domestic obligations or their lover's jealousy prevents them from coming back. Others add that for men tango dancing is more taxing and time-consuming than for women, either because men are worse "natural" dancers than women or because the male part in tango is harder. For whatever combination of reasons and beliefs, older milongueras sit there, witnessing the changes in the milonga with few complaints (in contrast to their male counterparts). They know what they are doing. Their alert sitting confirms that they are aware of where they stand in the food chain, and they are willing to pay the price: Tango is worth wallflowering for.

The Art of Wallflowering: A Gambling Theory

All women who approach the milonga scene must learn sooner or later that every time they enter a milonga, they will do so as a wallflower. Unless she arrives with her set dancing partner, every woman wallflowers (and to a certain extent, so do men). Nobody enjoys it, and some are better at it than others. In tango, wallflowering is an art.

A woman's wallflower position will be tested every single night at the milonga, no matter how good a dancer she is. The events of the night, some of which are more easily predicted than others, will bring her, more or less successfully, out of this position and closer to its opposite . . . that of the dancing femme fatale? Dancing certainly makes the difference. Most habitués of the milongas aspire to dance, and they dream of dancing all night long. If they manage to do so, milongueras leave the scene as goddesses of the milonga. And very few attain this position on any given night.

The wallflower (a dancing loser) becomes a successful milonguera (a winner of the tango-dancing game) by dancing a sufficient quantity and quality of dances. It is not enough to get to dance a lot; you have to learn to be choosy. Dancing with the best milongueros available at the club is crucial. Milongueras must learn how to discriminate among potential dancing partners. And after spotting the best, they must carefully plot how, when, and with whom they will show off their dancing skills so as to attract the attention of those potential best male partners. Accepting all invitations to dance, regardless of the partner's qualifications, are a sign of desperation and thus of low self-esteem. In addition, milongueras are judged in terms of how they get to dance in the first place. Women who ask men to dance or who approach milongueros and start long conversations in hopes they will be asked to dance definitely lose points. Issues of dignity cannot be overemphasized in anyone who wishes to be considered a successful milonguera.

In order to move out of the wallflower position, you must become an object of desire—more precisely, of tango-dancing desire, a doubly interwoven desire that includes the promise of becoming a potential vehicle for attaining the passionate tango state (that ephemeral sense of being bodily connected against all odds) as well as of generating desire on the part of those who watch the possibly sublime tango take place. For the men and women present at the milonga are the prospective femme fatale's witnesses and the men among them, her future dance partners. In their arms, tango after tango, the milonguera (or aspiring milonguera) will move from wallflower to goddess of the milonga.

Here is where I should tell you about her elaborate tricks, her ways of going about generating collective desire. But I will not. (I am contemplating writing a "Handbook for Aspiring Milongueras" where these secrets would be revealed. This, however, would amount to betraying not the milongueras —they mistrust their competitors anyway, and, needless to say, the wall-flowering ethnographer—but a longstanding milonga tradition, according to which you learn how to play the tango-dancing game as you go. Verbal instructions on or conversations about these matters are rare among true milongueras; it is expected that aspiring ones will learn through observation and experience.) For now, I will briefly address the nature of her fatale-ness or irresistible dance appeal. She might or might not be beautiful, but she must act and move with the confidence of a beautiful dancer; she must dance tango well (which does not necessarily coincide with the former); and she must necessarily be a smart risk-taker. (As I noted before, a savvy milonguera chooses her partners carefully and studies their dancing skills beforehand. She will not decline all neophytes' invitations to dance (it is understood that the milonga food chain needs them for the sake of reproduction), and she will avoid impoliteness and cruelty (watchful milongueros might avoid approaching her for fear of being subjected to the same embarrassing treatment). But she will deliver what each partner deserves. Investing too much focus and too many skills in dancing with a poor partner is unwise, causing the milonguera to lose points.) Her fascination resides in how she combines intelligence and dancing skills. She is the master of her own body's seductive dancing powers, so reassured of her mastery that she can give it away at will. A milonguera could be thought as fatal when, after making herself vulnerable by accepting a subservient wallflower position (sitting by herself in a highly visible spot, for example, is taken as a sign of admirable courage), she succeeds in becoming an object of collective tango-dancing desire (a sure sign of possessing a highly competitive gift for intelligent manipulation). A milonguera who is a winner at the tango game is a talented manager of her own resources. Sweet revenge, murmurs the dancing femme fatale of the night, knowing (and this is a sure sign of milongueras' wisdom) that she will fall back into wallflowering as soon as she steps into the next milonga.

In the tango milieu, fatale-ness amounts to dance appeal, and in that sense men are more likely to achieve that position than women. Dancing skills, attitude, and manipulation are required of both, but men are not subject to the same wallflowering requirements and judgments. Milongueros are in charge of asking women to dance, and although a woman may refuse to accept the offer, it is unlikely that a man will spend the night *rebotando* (bouncing). In addition, when men are not dancing it is assumed that they are resting and getting ready to make their next choice of a dance partner. They are choosing; women are waiting to be chosen. For milongueras, becoming a dancing femme fatale is a hard job, and an endless one, that involves not solving but rather maneuvering complex paradoxes concerning their feminine constitution.[6] The milonguera makes a puzzle out of herself. She enters the milonga as a (desiring) subject—she wishes to dance.[7] At the same time, in order to fulfill her desire, she must work at becoming an object of desire as she sits waiting for a dance. In so doing, milongueras often suspend (place "between parentheses") who they are and what they do in their daily lives and adopt a *nocturnal* feminine identity. This amounts to a milonguera's identity. They ready themselves for playing the tango-dancing game, which requires, as a gaming rule, that they risk waiting for a male dancer to identify them as desirable. This is the liminal state of the wallflower; and, as I have attempted to show throughout this essay, it is a very active take on passivity. Once she is asked to dance, and as she dances more and more in the course of the evening, her status as a (desiring) object of desire rises. In other words, her status as an object loads up to a point at which she is able to exert fatal feminine will over others. At this point, milongueros become her playthings, her objects of desire, and she can pick and choose with whom, for how long, and in what ways she wishes to dance. She is still an object of desire, but with strong desires of her own, and plenty of desiring subjects ready to become her desired dancing objects. At this point, her status as a female subject has recomposed at a different, exhilarating level compared to the one she experienced before entering the milonga—that flat and often compromised feminine agency she performs in everyday life.

The milonguera's feminine identity is taken apart each time she enters the milonga scene and it is laboriously reassembled in the course of the night. The outcome is unpredictable, although experience—tango-gambling experience—helps. Her passion for tango is a dangerous addiction that entails putting at risk, again and again, the quality of her everyday femaleness and her skills at gaming nocturnal femininity. The milonguera is more than

6. I am not following here a Freudian or Lacanian psychoanalytic approach. I am borrowing the vocabulary that is available, and twisting its conceptual connotations to fit the particularities of the tango world. Gender and sexuality are, in my view, culturally specific and fluid constructs. A particular economy ruled by a shared theory of value organizes the traffic of desire and its subject and object positions, and it establishes "worth" assessments. Desire thus becomes tangible: participants (think they) know what they desire. Women in the milongas are not interested in proving their femininity; that is, so to speak, a given—what I call here an everyday "flat" femininity. They are seeking (desiring) to become goddesses of the milonga: a goddess for a night. That amounts to femininity with a difference, and for a short amount of time, conditioned to a specific social space (the milonga). Therefore the feminine identity I am trying to analyze here falls into the particularities of what I am choosing to call nocturnal identities, constituted in dialogue with (and in opposition to) everyday sexed and sexual politics.

7. For a discussion of the uses of the concept of the "subject" at the intersection of psychoanalysis and Marxism, see Heath 1991.

a dancer whose presence is necessary for the reproduction of the tango world. She is simultaneously a (dancing) workaholic and a compulsive gambler, hooked up into both, the heavy labor of building femininity and a game called tango in which her femininity is at stake.

Milongas' politics of pleasure are puzzling, and they are often misunderstood when considered according to modern, bourgeois and, I daresay, daily daytime standards. Milongas are fantasyscapes of that parallel dimension that is the night, when nocturnal identities come out with the wildest ambitions and the most fearless desires to risk. Within this milieu, milongueros and milongueras gamble with and through each other by dancing tango. They cultivate a multiplicity of social transgressions. They enjoy crossing over socially accepted borders of age, social class, status, and even partisan ideologies. It is most definitely a gendered and heterosexual game, but the terms are quite unconventional. Milongas offer a space for unruly behaviors, out of which odd (and rather unstable) heterosexual couples result. When judged according to modern everyday bourgeois standards, true milongueros and milongueras do not fit heterosexual gender prescriptions. Men are patriarchal and authoritarian, but are also often economically dependent and obsessed with their looks and seductive skills. Women are frequently wealthier, better educated and more entrepreneurial than their partners, but forgiving and blinded by romance . . . until they become fed up and leave the men for a better catch or a more restful existence. Milongueros confirm their theories about the female species and await freshly arrived prey in the milonga niche. Milongueras tend to abandon the scene altogether with a telling tango story of wallflowers and femmes fatales, often with a twist: The true femmes fatales of the milonga are actually men. *The wallflower leaves the writing scene on this taunting note, betting on the tangoesque allure of delivering always less than it seems you could.*

On a projected computer screen rolls the following list of maestros y maestras, danzarines y bailarinas, milongueros y milongueras *whom she wishes to thank* de todo corazón: Lidia Ferrari, José Luis Lussini, Enriqueta María Palencia, Susana Cannataro, Raúl Bravo, Omar Correa, Eduardo Capussi, María Edith, Juan Carlos Muiño, Ana Postigo, Ana Gómez, Dina, Brenda, Cinthia, Blanquita Carozzi, Lawrence Leetz, María Teresa, Eduardo Aguirre, Ernesto Guerrero, Jorge Gallo, Angel Cristaldo, Bocha y Lidia Migale, Esther "Pichi" Pinelli, Liliana, María Emilia, Pedro y Ana Monteleone, Eduardo Arquimbau, Graciela González, Celia Blanco, Juan Carlos Copes, Verena Voucher, Carlos Copello, Gustavo Naveira, Héctor Chidichimo, Puppi Castello, Guillermo Cunha Ferré, Alejandra Quiroz, Brigitte Winkler, Nicole y Ricardo, Omar Vega, Suzzana, Nicolás, Danel y María, Jessica, Esteban, Carlos, Antoñito, Toto, Cacho, Susana Miller, Marcelo Pareja, Hans Muller, Fernando, Walter, Héctor, y Natalia Hills.

Exhibit B
Writings Attributed to Manuela Malva

Prueba B
Escritos Atribuidos a Manuela Malva

Librettist's Note

In my libretto, Manuela Malva plays the part of an Argentine émigré who meets Angora Matta in a Buenos Aires café where Manuela has been invited to sing a song she wrote. She bonds with Angora over émigrés' sorrows, and she is asked by a stranger to hand Angora the third instruction, the one that will lead Angora to her victim. Again, XYa claims that she collected the following writings from Manuela's friends or family, and she wishes to present them as documents attesting to Manuela's real—as opposed to fictive—nature. I dispute this assertion. Moreover, overcoming a state of deep confusion brought about by my apprenticeship to XYa, I was able to establish that I actually wrote these film reviews myself, seeking to understand the biting personality of Manuela (the character). Having lived abroad for a considerable time, Manuela is obsessed with the ways in which Argentine-ness is misrepresented and disfigured through exotic tangoesque clichés. In her analyses, the concept of culture is problematic in that it enables historical decontextualization as well as an artificially drawn isolation from world politics. In her writings, "cultures" are products of politicoeconomic plays of interculturality that dangerously shape ideologies by making them present through apparently innocuous artistic expressions.

Evita

The Globalization of a National Myth

Have you seen *Evita* (Parker 1996a)? Not Eva, not Eva Duarte, not Eva
Perón, but a version of her historicomythical character in the diminutive;
not just a foreshortening, but a downsizing, right from the beginning, to
situate spectators comfortably, to help them take a close look at a tamed
Eva, an Eva made familiar. This is not the Evita addressed by her *descamisados*, who used the diminutive as a term of endearment, to evoke the
proximity of a shared past of deprivation—their empathy a product of her
demonstrated refusal to forget her origins.[1] This is a different Evita. Another Evita myth, no doubt, that acquaints the audience with the story of a
woman who makes her way up to a position of great power, not just because
she is so special (after all, we know many women like her, with her kind
of aspirations and her abilities to manipulate) but rather because she was
lucky enough to live her life in a wealthy banana republic, somewhere
down there, in one of those places where golden tanks, macho boots, corrupt bureaucrats, and a mysteriously emotional religiosity (based on Ca-
tholicism's connections with primitive superstitions) ensure that the people
are adoring masses or persecuted victims. A Hollywood-made Evita myth

---

1. Evita's origins, marked by her birth out of wedlock as well as by the class
ascription of her maternal family, has been a matter of much debate among both
her contemporaries and more-recent biographers. Evita's own attempts at manipulating information on her birth and her family's status have been extensively
discussed in Fraser and Navarro 1996 and Dujovne Ortiz 1995. In a recent presentation at the UCLA Center for Latin American Studies (April 1997), Tulio
Halperin Donghi observed that it is false to consider Evita's maternal family as
low class, given that both her sisters married professional Argentinean men (one a
lawyer, the other a military officer). Thus, Evita's alignment with the poor and
working-class *descamisados* seems to have been more of an ideological choice on
her part than a situation laid on her by the circumstances of her birth and/
or family status. This remark introduces a denaturalizing distance concerning
Evita's class alliance, opening up a space for a political, rather than psychological, analysis of her historical figure.

requires no more than these elements to convey a clear image of the engines of history at work over there, in such places as Argentina, at any given time.

In this *Evita*, Evita's controversial role in history is presented in a dramatically undisturbing way, and it becomes moving because her public political figure is thoroughly personalized and thus banalized. *Evita* is a melodramatic remythologization and conforms to the narrative conventions of melodrama identified in Brooks 1980. It tells a tale of a self-made woman who, like many women of her time and place, beds her way up through men and is sensitive enough to exert grand-scale token charity among her people but not sensible enough to restrain herself from indulging in Diors and costly furs and jewelry. Finally, she must face the limits of power as she faces the limits of her body; she must renounce the vice presidency and she must die—like a woman, and more specifically, like a femme fatale of film noir (see Kaplan 1980; Doane 1991). The controversy is over from the very beginning, by showing the audience a glamorized, fascinating woman's death, but the tale continues: She was loved, then and now. Take a look at those interminable lines of dark faces in sorrow, that tango musical lament and danced mourning, and if you did not get it, the song is there to remind you: "You must love me."

But this recent $60 million remythologizing of Evita could not have been successful without the entangled workings at also remythologizing Argentina's national history. For that purpose, it is sufficient to present a few glimpses of a quasi-mute Juan Perón, some dazzling flashes of mobilized military equipment, street violence and corpses now and then, the masses, and a balcony. After all, *Evita* is about Evita, is it not? So why bother complicating her myth with the nation's history? Familiar snippets are enough to trigger all the corresponding stereotypes, situating the viewer, comfortably, in the mythical terrain of those kinds of nations' histories. And if you did not get it, a Che narrator figure will fill you in with all the necessary gossip, that is, anti-Peronist gossip, so you do not fall prey to Evita's intricate charms like so many of those down there did. This Che is also subjected to a careful remythologization. He is not a revolutionary conscience (such as one would expect of Che Guevara), but the voice of "reason," the voice of a sensible Che (as Argentines are referred to by other Spanish-speaking nationals) haunting Evita like a ghost, warning her and us, the spectators, against an easy romanticization of Evita's life. What makes his point of view privileged and authoritative is that he speaks from all possible class positions, as a participant and observer of Evita's most eventful interventions in Argentine history. His tone is both accusatory and disdainful, and he brings into question Evita's modus operandi both from a moral point of view and from the perspective of an experienced skeptic who can foresee, from the beginning, her destruction.

This *Evita*, then, is this ubiquitous Che's interpretation of Evita, as myth, and of her role in the making of history. And he is reporting to a transnational audience from a pseudoliberal, "universally" bourgeois perspective that amounts to an anti-Peronist perspective. But his rationalist anti-Peronism is not the self-interested anti-Peronism of the oligarchy, responding in confabulatory choruses to Evita's attacks on their properties and values. This waiter, journalist, student, factory worker, bartender, valet, peasant, and occasionally tuxedoed Che is a transclass, cultural translator whose ideology and interests can be pinned down only in his gender specificity and heterosexual appetites. For no matter how much we learn about Evita's promiscuous sexual adventures, her eroticism is absent and displaced in the form of desire for power.[2] Perón is a fatherly figure or a teammate in a passionate pursuit of power, and the only erotically invested romance seems to be in the realm of Evita's dream, in which she dances a frantic, tangoized waltz with an attractively defiant Che, who manages, like no one else, to put her in her womanly place. In his arms Evita is sincere. But this is a dream, a fantasy, a delirious moment entered simultaneously by Evita and el Che when they meet in a state of lost consciousness (she collapses in a church, he faints after being beaten up in a student demonstration). And it seems as though this moment was what Evita longed for all along: true romance.

The Madonnification of Evita

The casting of Madonna as Evita and the presence of tangoesque dance scenes throughout the film contribute to produce a version of Evita's history that engages with a personal politics suitable to globalization. Madonna the superstar definitely shapes the ways in which Evita's image and story reach the film audiences. There are obvious reasons for this: Madonna is a star commodity, meaning that she is a contemporary cultural product that aggressively circulates in the entertainment market (see Bordo 1993; McClary 1991). In addition, and unlike traditional film stars, Madonna offers a surface of great visibility on which it is possible to project a variety of personalities and styles. Film stars usually cultivate a strong presence that pervades all the characters they represent onscreen. Contrarily, Madonna is referred to as a superstar because of her *lack* of depth. Her flatness is precisely what allows her image to shine brightly as an icon (see Tetzlaff 1993). Madonna,

2. On the desexualized image of Evita and its resexualizing moments, when Madonna takes the leading role in the film, particularly in the dance scenes, I have been following Richard Dyer's analysis of the ideological and cultural functions of star images and their relations to the construction of film narratives, characters, etc. (Dyer 1992a).

also in contrast to character actresses, does not inhabit or perform different characters. Madonna is, to be sure, malleable, passing from one persona to another throughout her career, but rather than inhabiting the characters she performs, she appropriates them. Madonna's ability to put on, uncompromisingly, whatever suits her at the moment imbues her with an aura of power signaled by success and manipulation. It is this chameleonlike, superficial versatility, combined with the power she has accrued through the management of her fame, that creates a tense connection between Madonna and Evita. Madonna as an all surface and screen superstar projects an unspecific image of Evita, invading Evita's own strong personality, historical depth, and cultural characteristics with a spectacular blurring of boundaries. Madonna dissipates Evita's national and historical specificities as she renders visible a transcultural Evita of universal womanness.

Once Evita is Madonnified as a female superstar, Madonna and Evita seem to become a perfect match, joined by ambition, manipulation, and celebrity. Despite their quite different aims and circumstances, they both stand for "women with power" and thus enter hand in hand into the pantheon of femmes fatales. Feminist theorists interested in the visual arts, frequently making use of psychoanalytic understandings, insist that "woman" as a concept and woman's body as a construct offer a privileged surface on which to project (male) sexual fantasies and fears (see Doane 1991; Hart 1994; Allen 1983; Dijkstra 1986; Rose 1986). By definition, woman is the unknown and unknowable dark continent. Women cannot be pinned down. Always enigmatic, women are all the same and yet constantly changing. This capacity for multiciplicity, already mentioned in Madonna's case, is replicated in the controversies surrounding Evita's personality while she was alive and her contrasting mythifications after her death: Evita the saint, the whore, the revolutionary, the powermonger (J. Taylor 1979). Evita as depicted through Madonna in this film fits point by point the characteristics of the femme fatale, that dangerous side of femininity always threatening to take over women who step aside from the taming rules of patriarchy: she is determined and aggressive, she manipulates men masterfully, she is childless and narcissistic. All of these features amount to self-centeredness and egoism. The femme fatale is confirmed as a love object, an object offered for adoration. Narcissism, as an erotic self-investment that defies emotional attachments to men and to the male-centered social world, connects Evita's image to Madonna's contemporary version of femme fatality, transcending cultural and historical differences.

Madonna, and not Evita, however, seems on several accounts to be the main beneficiary of this universalizing operation. Madonna, who eagerly pursued the role of Evita in Parker's film, appropriates Evita's charisma and looks in order to give depth to her own superficial "material girl" image. Evita serves Madonna in her transition to motherhood. Madonna's

Evitism, adopted beyond the film sets, cultivates the conservative femininity of her time: romantic, fragile, caring, wrapped up in delicate fabrics,
wearing toned-down make-up, and excelling in costly bourgeois good taste.
Evita's own image as a strong, foul-mouthed, independent woman of her
times is thus subdued in Madonna's representation, where spectators instead see a softened Evita, looking for Perón's approval after every public
performance, leaning on his shoulder for protection, smiling gently at the
poor as she distributes kitchenware and money, or naively moved by her
own words as she addresses the crowds. In Madonna's characterization,
Evita is romanticized and unthreatening. Evita's dangerousness as a femme
fatale becomes contained before her death, and not by her death (the destiny reserved for fatal women, who, in the end, always bring fatality to
themselves).

It is interesting to analyze Parker's *Evita* from this point of view, because the film's narrative is saturated with death and destruction. Evita's
death opens and closes the narrative, tightly containing her disruptive
powers as a warning or moral lesson that serves as a backdrop to any potential seduction effected by her transgressive doings, even when they are
presented in a tamed version, as in this case. But what I find most remark-
able, going back to the Evita/Madonna connections and disjunctions, is
that while Evita actually dies (paying the price for her femme fatality), Madonna, the star, acts (that is, she pretends) to die as Evita only to resurrect
herself as the star who played the coveted Evita role. Evita gives new thrust
to Madonna's career. *Evita* inaugurates and in big letters announces Madonna's metamorphosis from pop idol to mature actress.

Audiences, critics, and Madonna herself work hard at blurring the differences between Evita the historical figure and Madonna the star. They
compare their lives and their looks, stressing their parallels from the lurid
stories of rags to riches to the bleaching of their hair (see, e.g., Ayerza
1996; "Dos mujeres, dos destinos" 1996; Martínez 1996; Escribano 1996;
"Madonna: 'Soy igual que Evita'" 1996). And yet, *Evita*, the film, constantly wrestles with the presence of two main female leads, namely, Madonna *and* Evita. The Evita/Madonna juxtaposition amounts to a tense
competition between two spectacular identities in which Evita becomes awk-
wardly Madonnified and Madonna cultivates Evitism. One, Evita, plays
the dramatic role engaged with historicity; the other, Madonna, becomes
paramount in the scenes that provide the lyrical, transhistorical component to the film (see Dyer 1992a).

Tangoizing Argentine Identity

The dance sequences are precisely the sites where the globalization of
Evita takes place and where the Argentine national myth becomes trans-

nationalized. Madonna, portraying a dancing Evita, is able to produce an intensely personal, intimate, and thus universal representation of Evita as a "woman."[3] This is a place that the real Evita rarely inhabited in her life (see Mayer 1996). Producing these tangoesque images of Evita, Madonna projects a universal image of a femme fatale, devoid of specificity, except for that frivolous exotic touch (the tango) that makes femmes fatales fascinating in their difference and yet recognizable or easy to identify with as the generic "woman in power." The spectacularization of a seemingly banal national cultural trait such as the tango both expands the stereotypical and erases all other specificities that would work against easy universalistic assimilations.

The relationship between tango and Argentine national identity is complex (Savigliano 1995). Tango was not considered a national dance in Argentina until after the European elite identified it as such. Even then, the upper and middle classes in Argentina resented their representation by tango, for they considered it a poor one in both senses of the word: Tango was a lower-class dance, a dance of the poor, and it represented the nation as a whole poorly, that is, inaccurately. Eventually, however, many Argentineans accepted the European view of Argentina, of tango, and of the connections between the two. The internalization or reproduction of the European point of view can be understood as "auto-exoticism": seeing oneself as an exotic other. These days, not very many Argentineans actually dance tango. Yet most Argentineans would identify tango as a key component in Argentine national identity.

Eva Perón was one of many Argentineans who did not dance tango. In fact, both she and her compatriot Che Guevara were renown for their lack of dancing skills. For example, Cabrera Alvarez includes the following passage in his biography of Che:

> There is a dance that night, and the friends decide to go. It's a bustling crowd, and the couples seem to multiply on the dance floor. Ernesto ["Che" Guevara] approaches his friend and tells him in a low voice, "Runt, listen well. I'm going to dance, but you know. . . ." Alberto [Granados] doesn't need any kind of explanation to know that his

3. Linda Williams (1989) argues that pornographic films as well as musicals strive to represent that which cannot be directly seen or that which has been previously invisible. Women's desires, motives, and impulses thus figure prominently in these genres, striving to become visible. I wish to argue that dancing provides precisely that space within the film narrative for historicity and cultural specificity to be-come subsumed under a generizable imaging of "expressions" and "true feelings." Dancing as a code for accessing the plot's essential meaning acquires an explanatory power that usurps the relevance of other complex information.

friend is incapable of distinguishing a military march from a *milonga*. "When they play a tango," Ernesto requests, "kick me, then I'll know what it is. Agreed?" More or less every other piece played by the improvised band is a tango, but for some reason they suddenly play a Brazilian *shoro* entitled "Delicado." Granados remembers the song was popular at the time his friend began to court Chichina, and wishing to remind him of that time, taps him with his foot. Ernesto takes a young woman out to dance. The tempo of the *shoro* is quick, but he doesn't hear it. He dances to the beat of a tango, marking off his steps with mathematical precision. (Cabrera Alvarez 1987: 77)

There are similar stories about Evita's incompetence as a dancer, including an account of why the famous actress and tango singer Libertad Lamarque slapped the lesser-known Evita during the filming of *La cabalgata del circo*:

According to the testimony of Sergia Machinandearena, the scene of the slap or of the heated discussion between the true star and the starlet with "clout," took place during the rehearsal of a *pericón*, a folkloric dance that does not require special talent and that all Argentine schoolchildren know how to dance. But despite how fine and delicate her feet were, Evita did not manage to adapt them to the demands of the rhythm. And Libertad, who danced very well, finally reacted. According to her own testimony, she did not slap Evita on the cheek but she did tell her off completely. How she was fed up with Evita's absurd hours and had it up to here with the forementioned *pericón* for which they had to hire a dance professor to try to untangle Evita's feet. (Dujovne Ortiz 1995: 87)

Evita and Che, however, following the conventions of Broadway and Hollywood musicals, perform several dance scenes in *Evita*. In fact, Evita dances significantly more in Parker's film than she did in stage productions of the musical, where tangos performed by professional dancers appeared almost only as a backdrop to provide the Argentinean cultural ambience. The filmed *Evita*'s extra dancing is an example of how Madonna, the music-video diva, takes over the historical character. The Madonnification of Evita spectacularizes the female body and its desires, as it is engaged in recognizably stylized movements that reveal its enigma in the form of a "natural" code. Madonna/Evita's tangoesque dances, as such, are a lyrical relief, where the corporeal and the emotional ask spectators to abandon the search for intellectual appraisals of Evita's life. The dancing moments appeal to the logic of the senses, a logic that allows gaps, contradictions, and fragmentations to run smoothly on a totalizing register where specificities become mere formal details. From a cinematic point of view, dancing familiarizes Evita, focusing on her generic femininity, while diverting attention from her politics. The tango dances are coded in either tropical, Hispanic, or waltzed styles, providing a cultural reference to be interpreted according to stereotypes of more-familiar dance genres. Thus, Evita's tango-rumba—performed on a crowed city bus when she first arrives in Buenos Aires—announces her contagious, irresistible excitement, which promises to turn the metropolis into her territory and dance floor. Her first incursion into a rowdy bar is signaled by a couple performing a tango-flamenco, announcing the dark, rowdy, alcohol- and smoke-ridden underworld into which she will immerse herself and pay the price for her ambition. The tango-waltzes she dances in the arms of El Che and Perón show her classy, conflicted arrivals at the pinnacle of power. Evita/Madonna's most tango-like tangos, small snippets of which are offered to the viewers, stand for her most debased stages of prostitution: she dances in close embrace with rough-looking Latin men in dusty dance halls. Tango's allusion to excessive eroticism has frequently been coupled in filmic uses to destructive, antisocial appetites for power—tango as a fascist dance. Parker's *Evita* makes use of these tango resonances, politicizing Evita's personal desires and neutralizing the politics at play in the configuration of national and cultural stereotypes. Indeed, one of the most important ways in which the film marks Madonna's Evita as Argentinean is by showing her dancing tango. *Evita* tangoizes Argentina as a nation and Evita as a national myth, thereby drawing on a familiarly exotic cultural reference laden with political implications that package Argentine otherness for global consumption.

Madonna/Evita dances both the most gruesome and the most sublime landmarks of her biography, and her dances always indicate some kind of social mobility. She dances her first arrival in Buenos Aires fleeing from the prospects of a dull future in Junín, a small town where as a bastard she would have faced an inescapable fate. She dances night after night in slummy bars and dance halls, in the arms of older working-class or raffish-looking Latin men. (These professional Argentine tango dancers are not mentioned by name either in the film credits or in the captions of Parker's book *The Making of Evita* [1996]. They are Pedro Monteleone, Guillermo Cunha Ferré, and Luis Salinas.) These shady tangos, recognizable by the inclusion of *ganchos* and other paradigmatic *figuras* such as *ochos* and *cepilladas*, mark the shameful but obstinate path Evita/Madonna takes to the top by manipulating machismo (associated with tango). These tangos stand for sexual favors, and the tango dance halls become fancier and her dancing partners whiter and better dressed as she endures this tangoesque rite of passage from destitute prostitution to a more rewarding and even legitimate prostitution in the arms of Perón.

Madonna/Evita's dance scenes with Perón signal their first encounter (a brief slow dance in which the shots focus on their faces as they study each other, culminating in a striptease of Evita's gloves (reminiscent of Rita Hayworth's *Gilda*, another woman in Buenos Aires trying to escape her past). A dance also marks Evita's triumphal entrance, after her wedding to Perón, into the circles of political power. Like a queen, all in white, Evita/Madonna climbs the stairs of a monumental palatial building and waltzes with old generals, diplomats, and public figures; she leaves the scene in Perón's arms, always dancing, in graceful transition to her prominent (and yet inexplicable) place in history.

The dances of sorrow, the slow-paced tango laments performed by somber Argentines in dimly lit indoor and outdoor settings, with the camera zooming in on grave, suffering Latin faces of all ages, indicate Evita's passage from life to death to immortality. The death-dance scenes, which prominently feature María and Roberto (a well-known professional tango couple also ignored in the film credits), open and close the film narrative, making tango an exotic, ritualistic dance of mourning, one associated with a strange religiosity. Thus, Argentine tango, being a national symbol of Argentineness, renders an aura of primitiveness and alterity to Evita's mythification and to the mores and customs of the Argentine people. Evita and her people are carefully exoticized so as to establish the distance necessary to generate fascination in the global spectator. At the same time, and in tense contradiction with this exoticizing thrust, Evita's doings and especially her personal motives and psychological traits are presented in terms familiar enough to elicit a transnational audience's identification.

The Banalization of the Political

Popular psychoanalytic interpretations (what Freud called "wild psychoanalysis") slip into this *Evita* in an attempt to explain her fascinating personality. Beyond historical, political, and social circumstances, what seems to be important for the audience to know is that this very special woman's life story can be understood only from the point of view of the psychic consequences of a sad and wounded child's development. The lack of a legitimate father and the presence of a morally corrupt mother amounted to the constitution of a female subject obsessed with compensating for the degrading status of being a bastard. Her beauty, determination, and aggressive personality allowed her to craftily manipulate her way to the top, but she could not come to terms with her success, for at the very bottom she felt either undeserving or unsatisfied or both, and so she overworked and overextended her ambitions until she reached her own bodily limits. She had to pay the price. She died.

"Don't cry for me, Argentina"—because I got what I deserved, because (as you can see after this interpretive account) my death makes perfect sense. And also because I lived my life this way so that I would be remembered, don't you see? I plotted my own mythologization! This is the kind of path along which the audience is led through the presentation of a highly personalized and psychological version of Evita's life. Politics and the sociohistorical background are there (not very carefully researched or worried with accuracy, but that is another topic), spectacularized in dazzling shots that convey this movement of starting from the surface, the appearances, the muddled noise of contextual information, in order to reach the depth, the kernel, the dark continent of Evita's unconscious. The result is both convincing and undisturbing. A grand story but a sad one; an exhausting career and a spectacular end. Adored and hated forever. She got away with it. And we are left wondering if this is the fate of women who engage fully in the world of politics.

Attending primarily to the personal, as this Evita encourages audiences to do, we are immersed in a moral riddle trying to figure out how to deal with justified or unjustified causes, means, and ends. Did the causes justify her means? (Did her illegitimacy as a child justify her defiant and aggressive behavior toward the dominant classes?) Or did her ends justify her means? (Did her pursuit of social justice justify her authoritarianism and her fanaticism?) Or did her causes justify her ends, whatever her means? (Did her early experiences of deprivation justify her hunger for power, regardless of the personal and social costs?) Or were her means unjustified no matter what the causes and ends? (No matter what traumatic experiences struck her in the beginning, nor what egotistical or noble social concerns moved her to act, her demagogic and calculating manipulations in the political arena wronged others and Argentina's history.) This *Evita* will not deliver an answer or the necessary elements to allow for an informed assessment precisely because of the uneven treatment given to the personal and psychological story vis-à-vis the political and sociohistorical context. Not only is there not enough context (which raises the question of how much would be enough) but the context provided is not complex enough, not blurred enough, creating the illusion that the context is just that, a frame that should serve to illuminate the personal picture, the personal picture of a historical and mythical political figure.

Like a modern fable, a soap-operatic moral tale, this *Evita* offers a universally applicable lesson beyond place and time. Looked at from the point of view of the projection of the image of a femme fatale onto Evita, a point on which I have been insisting, it seems as if Parker's *Evita* would code all political and historical information as a series of catastrophes (earthquakes, social upheavals, political repressions) unknowingly brought about by the mere presence of Evita—who, as a stereotypical femme fatale, has it in her nature to bring about trouble.

This *Evita* fails to construct a public persona on both accounts, the mythical and the historical. The aesthetic treatment of the political scenario, carried out mainly through images of great visual impact but scant analytical or explanatory power, and the treatment of Evita's personal motives and desires, addressed insistently through lyrics fully loaded with the interpretive power of words, generate the effect of two parallel, contrasting scores that never amount to a syncopated rendering. In this *Evita*, the political happens and the personal speaks, or rather sings, even when it talks politics. In addition, the musicality of the words, regardless of their content, creates a climax of intimacy and a transcendental, intersubjective bridge, prompting a rush across cultures, nations, and history (see Dolar 1996).

The singing voice, a major feature of musicals, is dangerously powerful in that it appeals to emotions that provide synthetic judgments not readily available to critical ponderings. The voice beyond the words, like the stylized movements of the dancing body (beyond necessary pragmatic activity), is taken for a senseless play of sensuality. These are fascinating forces, pregnant with excessively moving and intricate meanings and yet, in themselves, considered empty and frivolous. I tentatively suggest that, at least in contemporary Western and westernized cultures, the singing voice and the dancing body exhibit a dimension that runs counter to self-transparency and to sensibility, as if their pleasurable corporeality operated against the logos and the physicality associated with labor and the production of meaning: singing and dancing as the other of production, its radical alterity. And yet, music, song, and dance constitute powerful discursive registers that operate, in conjunction with the image, in the production of signification. They allocate points of view, points of hearing, and points of kinesthetic identification that alternately reproduce and challenge hegemonic perspectives (see Shohat and Stam 1994). Alan Parker, in his book *The Making of Evita* (1996), recognizes the challenges posed by filming a historical account in which all the words are sung. He declares his intention of producing an "objective," "balanced" account of Evita's controversial life at the same time he acknowledges that the screenplay is based on the libretto of the British musical *Evita* of the 1970s (which was probably inspired by Perón's return to Argentina after eighteen years of exile). The lyrics are from Tim Rice, as in the stage version. They were based on a book by María Flores, *The Woman with the Whip*. María Flores was the nom de plume of Mary Main, an Anglo-Argentine historical novelist who returned to Argentina in the early 1950s, at the height of Evita's interventions into politics. The book was published in New York in 1952 and was translated into Spanish and published in Buenos Aires only in 1955, after Perón's ouster. It provided a magnificent collection of elaborate anti-Peronist gossip (Fraser and Navarro 1996: 199 n. 11). Parker's *Evita* tries to compensate with images for some of the historical background missing from the staged version of the 1970s, but the lyrics (being roughly the same) bend all the complex information toward a seamless narrative of oppositional politics coded as an analysis of a personality type: Evita as the woman with the whip, resentful, power hungry, and so on. As Evita's "problematic" personality becomes more and more paramount, the ideological and political motives that guided her behavior (such as the redistribution of wealth) become less and less relevant. We are being taught a lesson about a woman who misbehaved, a universally applicable lesson. That she misbehaved with Peronist goals in mind and that her misbehavior contributed to Peronist political ends becomes superficial.

The Politics of Apolitical Myth-Making

The final scenes of Parker's *Evita* clearly direct the viewers' attention away from historical specificities and beyond ideological considerations. At the majestic site of Evita's wake, endless lines of sorrowful Argentines, one by one, slowly approach the glass-topped coffin. Perón watches the scene, gloomily, standing by the corpse, which seems to symbolize the death of his source of power. The presence of El Che by the coffin suddenly catches Perón's and our attention. El Che defiantly places a last kiss on Evita as he directs an intense look in Perón's direction. Perón returns the look, puzzled at first and then with growing suspicion. Above the woman's dead body, two powerful men exchange menacing looks. Black-out, the end. It all comes down to another exemplary story of machismo. The audience is prompted to wonder: What would have happened if Evita had met and fallen in love with El Che? The suggested response in the film is romantically apolitical: Perón would have been jealous. Either in Che's or in Perón's arms, Evita would have been no more (and no less) than a woman whose passionate doings unfailingly nurtured rivalry among men—a drive stronger than history, stronger than politics. Evita's ending seems to imply that sexual politics would clue us into a universally applicable answer to the question of what politics is—a masterfully depoliticizing take on politics.

The seemingly depoliticized take on Evita, however, is a remarkably effective political move, given that all the stereotypical knowledge about the political atmosphere that surrounded Evita's Argentina then percolate down to the Argentina of today. Evita, and especially Perón and Peronism, were matters of great international attention and political concern toward the end of World War II. The international press reported on Perón's and other military officers' sympathies if not connections with Franco, Hitler, and Mussolini, and on Peronism's alleged resemblances to Nazism and fascism, as well as stories about corrupt dealings with officers from these totalitarian and genocidal regimes who sought asylum in the vast pampas. The truth of these reports is still being debated in international scholarly circles. The association between Peronism and fascism, or, for the more prudent, between Peronism and totalitarian, nationalist, populist, demagogic, personalistic regimes that respond to antidemocratic ideological inclinations is accepted, in general, as a given. Add to this a superficial knowledge about the successive military dictatorships of the 1960s and the 1970s, equally assimilated under the rubric of fascism, and you get a picture of sorrowful victims and victimizers who could never learn the lessons of democracy. The intervention of the United States in Latin American affairs during these decades, seeking either to overthrow or consolidate these regimes, is frequently left out or underestimated. But my point is that this information, or the impressions left by this segmented information, are still at play, and moreover are actively unsettled, doing their work as they remain unaddressed on the screen.

It could be argued that this *Evita* is a spectacle. I agree, so long as by "spectacle" we understand an artistic, creative rendering of a story, in this case a life story, that in providing a synthetic, condensed view of a complex and often puzzling historical phenomenon (which is precisely the source of artistic interest and public appeal) fully engages the political and ideological terrains (see Dyer 1992a, 1992b; Nichols 1981). Spectacles that address the interstices between a nation's history and its myths, produced for a transnational audience, effectively do political work. As the artist, in this case the director, chooses what to keep and what to discard, what to stress in the plot, which connections to establish and which ones to leave out, an aesthetic rendering comes to life, not so different from the world of myths, with their symbolic power and effectiveness.

Myths are beliefs, not specifically true or untrue, certainly invested with the power of representing something worth knowing. They are particularly interesting in that they effect representations between the real thing and its interpretations—in other words, between the historical and the historiographic. An artistic production of this kind, a cinematographic spectacle, works also in an in-between, neither documentary nor fictional narrative. Spectators, especially when not well informed, are left either skeptically dangling or totally enraptured, and frequently both. This one masterfully crafted impressionistic interpretation is the only information most viewers will ever have the time or interest to get about Evita. Evita thus enters the transnational scene through a powerful medium that generates a new myth capable of reproducing old myths about Latin American history, of reinforcing universalistic connections via subjective identifications, of reinstating the morality of fear and fascination surrounding the explosive womanpower equation, and of generating a whole new global packet of "Evitist" commodities including Evita fashion, jewelry, cosmetics, coffee-table and academic books, and even $1,500 seven-day Evita tours (e.g., Chacón 1996; "Madonna's Moment as Evita, Mother, and Fashion Force" 1996; "Buenos Aires: The City of Evita" 1997).

The Menemization of Evita

And so, "Have you seen Evita?" I am repeatedly asked—not "what do you know about her?" but "have you seen," not "her," obviously, but her most recent, spectacular and highly publicized representation, followed by "What do you think?" And it takes me some time to sort out and choose a referent (what I think about Evita, the historical figure, pleading with or agitating the masses at the balcony, or the nomadic, embalmed corpse now locked up at a mausoleum in La Recoleta; about Evita, as portrayed in other recent films; about Madonna's performance of Evita; or about the film, *Evita*, directed by Alan Parker, as a whole, a work of cinematic art or a piece of entertainment). And how should I respond? As myself, a regular viewer and cinema fan; as a cultural translator; as a responsible scholar; as a delegate of the Argentines (and if so, of which ones? The Peronistas or the anti-Peronistas? The right- or left-wing Peronistas? The nationalist or liberal (Menemist) Peronistas? Or the ones above and beyond these disputes, who welcome any representation of Argentines in a Hollywood production, calculating that it is better to be there, identified even if misrepresented, in a global culture, than to be totally erased and ignored?) Who or what is Evita and whom or what do I represent when I talk or write about Evita?[4]

None of my colleagues or friends has the time, interest, or patience to let me go carefully through this entangled checklist before I respond. Therefore, I have come up with an answer that gives me some room to complicate things: "Yeah, I've seen both of them." The initial surprise at this doubling of Evita allows me some time to assemble a combination of responses, trying to address all these issues, synthetically, at once. This is my opportunity to protest the Evita question, and to attempt to unravel and reweave what seems to be a simple, straightforward question. In order to focus my thoughts somewhat, I have addressed the present remythologizing of Evita, the historical figure and the myth, through the intervention of the Hollywood screen apparatus. My intention has been to relate this cinematic production to the transnational spectacularization of third-world historical figures and to the global circulation of Latin American national myths. I would like to conclude with some reflections on the Argentine responses to the decision to produce a Hollywood version of Evita, though not to the film itself because it had not yet been shown in Argentina when I was last there.

4. Similar questions have been confronted, directly or indirectly, by several Argentinean fiction writers and playwrights such as Copi (1970), Tomás Eloy Martínez (1995), Néstor Perlongher (1986), Leónidas Lamborghini (1972), Luisa Valenzuela (1983), and Rodolfo Walsh (1986). Issues of power and sexuality surrounding the erotics of nationalism are at the center of these works. The analysis of their strategies of representation and self-representation are beyond the scope of this essay.

These early responses are concerned in one way or another with issues of cultural imperialism.

It has been widely argued that culture, and especially popular culture —including not only music or dance but also myths—nowadays circulate globally, despite their obviously local or national original production. But discussions have engaged more fully with the mechanisms (the "hows") of transnationalization—the rapid flow of information and overall mass-mediatization of culture—than with the politics of cultural piracy or appropriation. The local Argentine reactions to the Hollywood production of *Evita*—culminating in an Argentine filmic counter-version (*Eva Perón*, 1996) with at least two more films planned ("Tres películas en marcha y otros dos proyectos en duda" 1996)—fully engage the political dimension of these transnational undertakings and demonstrate resistance not only to what is perceived as the unethical or irresponsible use of national symbols or icons but also to the persistence of unequal power relations between nations and constituencies within so-called globalization and transnationalism.

Whose perspective on Evita is more likely to become transnationalized, and whose representation of Evita is more likely to achieve the status of a globally circulated myth? Argentines have a clear, consistent opinion on that, despite their own differences, which have produced competing histories of Evita and contrasting Evita myths (see the contributions of Marcos Mayer, Pablo Chacón, Gabriela Bolognese, Horacio González, and Antonio Cafiero in *El nuevo porteño* (1996)). No one seems to doubt that the Evita Argentine children will know will be the one represented by Madonna in Alan Parker's Hollywood film, and they resent it. *Evita hay una sola, y es nuestra* (There is only one Evita, and she is ours), proclaimed the posters plastered through Buenos Aires as the international film crew arrived at the international airport. This is, of course, wishful thinking (see the contributions of Juan Pablo Feinmann, María Saenz Quesada, Alicia Dujovne Ortiz, Abel Posse, and Marysa Navarro in "Tema: santa o hereje: quién fue Evita?" 1996).

There have been many myths of Evita in and outside of Argentina, but this time something different seems to be at stake. The Hollywood re-mythification of Evita fits almost too well the trend of spectacular politics introduced by the recent Peronist government under Menem. Menemism, as critics of the social costs embedded in this government's free-market policies brand this refashioning of Peronism, has retained nothing but the memory of what once moved hopeful masses of Argentines: the ideals of social justice, economic independence, and political self-determination. Hollywood's *Evita* evokes precisely Menem's understanding of a Peronism suited to current times: spectacular, frivolous, and depoliticized. The film *Evita* recalls the past glories of Peronism and reveals its unviable utopianism. The memory of Evita's willingness to give up her life for the cause of her *descamisados* still helps win elections in the midst of a generalized confusion brought about by Menem's use of Peronist slogans and symbols to implement neoliberal policies.

Argentines have no doubt that this Hollywood remake of Evita's myth will have a global impact on the representation and interpretation of Argentine history, an impact that some welcome and others resist because of its political implications. Globalization is well under way, and the new empire is one in which very few Argentines will have a say about the kind of history or the myths that will explain our past or guide our future. Antonio Negri, an Italian Marxist political philosopher, suggests that, at this point, we would do better to move beyond the problem of figuring out how to resist global imperialism (Negri 1996). We should rather focus on what kind of empire we want.

Cinematic Sex Tours

On Potter's The Tango Lesson *(1997) and Saura's*
Tango, no me dejes nunca *(1998)*

I have been puzzled for many years now by this question: Why are outsiders to the tango world attracted to the tango? What are they looking for in the tango experience? What pleasures does the tango offer them? And how do these outsiders know what is in a tango and in the tango world for them? I could have settled for an enigmatic, transcendental answer, like so many tango lovers who point to the seductive powers of the dance, the music, the poetry—the mysteries of art. I have not. So this is another attempt at understanding what tango conveys and, specifically, how these tangoesque desires are produced and disseminated.

For this purpose I have chosen to look at the uses of tango in contemporary narrative cinema and at the sophisticated ways in which spectators are invited to engage in a particular kind of pleasure that I will call "cinematic smart sex tourism"—by which I mean sex tourism with a "cultural" edge. Two recent tango films, *The Tango Lesson* and *Tango, no me dejes nunca*, clued me into this: "Culture" (understood as "difference") rather than sex, or, better, the erotics of "cultural difference" structures non-*tangueros'* tango pleasure—a pleasure that anticipates the tango experience per se, that is to say, a pleasure already generated and contained in the desire to enjoy the pleasures experienced by "others"—the pleasure of "difference."

In these two tango films the erotics of "cultural difference" is constructed through the collaborative and conflictive efforts of contemporary Argentine and international artists. The making of a tango product for transnational and transcultural circulation is their common goal. The marketing strategy: to appeal to a global audience interested in cultural difference and invested in experiences (whether cinematic or live) of smart tourism—that is, tourism with in-depth information of the host culture. These tango films, thus, bring spectators—I will call them "cinematic tourists"—down south to Buenos Aires and present them with tangoesque scenarios of deep emotional involvement, creating a space for subjective connections across and beyond cultural difference. The message: Immerse yourself into the culturally other and, despite the shock and traumas you will endure, you will emerge enriched and inspired. My purpose: to explore how the commodification of "culture"—in this case of tango—serves to hide the economic exploitation of the other through benign or benevolent liberal values such as uncritical cultural relativism coded as celebratory multiculturalism. "Culture" has become a comfortable way to talk about "difference" and to leave inequality out of the picture. The telling point for me has been the fleeting appearance of the milongueros and especially the milongueras (those rather unglamorous, everynight inhabitants of the Buenos Aires tango world for whom tango is an alternative source of identity to the globalized dominant bourgeois way of life that they cannot afford). Their marginal presence in the films, depicted as a legitimizing referent to authenticity and tradition, forecloses their crucial participation not only in the making of tango—what it is and what it stands for—but also as active, generous teachers and consultants of the artists (foreign and "native") who have the privilege of tapping into the tango in order to tell us (spectators and cinematic tourists) their own moving stories. A final note: As a consequence of this revival of tango cultural appropriation (in which, I repeat, sectors of the "native" and of the culturally thirsty of the world collaborate), a new wave of "folklore criollo" (music and dances associated with rural areas and with "pre-tango" national roots) is gaining popularity among young Argentines seeking yet another artistic expression capable of conveying the "difference" (unemployment, increasing inequality in the distribution of wealth, and the International Monetary Fund's neoliberal policies, which reproduce underdevelopment while promising development) that resides under the motto *civilización o barbarie* (civilization or barbarism), a paradigmatic false opposition that has guided Argentine history since the birth of the nation. But this is a different discussion. (Although Valentino dancing tango dressed in gaucho robes—something like a cowboy dancing hip-hop—is still there, in the exotic imagination, telling us that this difference does not really matter.)

Tangos have attracted foreign (by which I mean non-Argentinean and non-Uruguayan) film producers and directors since at least the 1920s and, I will venture to say, to the same *effect* all along.[1] (I will not guess their intentions.) The strangely syncopated tango music has been used to generate

1. On Argentinean themes (including tango) in Hollywood productions, see Diego Curubeto 1993. On tango in film history, see Jorge Couselo 1977.

thrilling climaxes. Tango songs (whether the Spanish words are understood or not) convey melodrama, and tango dance suggests sexy power struggles. Visual and aural snippets of the tango genre (the art) are interspersed in narratives of illicit adventure driven by excessive ambitions (involving sex and money) that generate emotional upheaval. A little bit of tango in both Hollywood cinema and cinema *d'auteur* has come to symbolize transgression (that is, the exploration of ethical limits; see Foucault 1977) and to announce some kind of containment, a promised return to the familiar with gained wisdom, a moral. Tangos are there, in the story, to convey a dangerous flirtation with the dark side of desire generated by an existential crisis (aging, a boring marriage, a lack of inspiration) or to signal the tragic existential consequences of an unsought circumstance (unemployment, immigration, war) on its victims. In either case, ambition makes things go wrong for oneself or others, and tangos are there to sensualize the victims' fall at the hands of the victimizer—who in the end also turns out to be a victim of the invisible hands of desire and/or fate. Cinematic dramas and comedies use tango noises and images to evoke grand subterranean forces of the inner or outer world, their power when unleashed, and their dangers when out of control. (Dramas such as *The Four Horsemen of the Apocalypse* (1921), *Sunset Boulevard* (1950), *Gilda* (1946), *Isadora* (1968), *Last Tango in Paris* (1973), *Alice* (1990), and *Scent of a Woman* (1992) take the tango-esque dark forces to heart; comedies such as *Some Like It Hot* (1959), *Addams Family Values* (1993), and *The Mask* (1994) use tango grotesquery to laugh at the invisible powers.) Tango sounds pour into the audience's ears, announcing liminal moments and transitions into dangerous terrains. Tango images are always danced; bodies are left to themselves and abandoned to pleasure, frequently behind closed doors, in enclosed spaces, at night, creating intimacy even in the presence of others. From that space of captivity tangos, exotic and erotic, threaten and inspire life and make of life an art.

Foreign film spectators (meaning those who do not "belong" to the Latin American tango lands) hum a little tango and try a tango step in their minds as they leave the theater. Bits of tango here and there, the mere mention of the word "tango" in the title or music credits, and fascination rushes in with its contradictory impulses: You need some tango in your life; but you should not overdo your tangos. Tango has operated since the early twentieth century as a metaphor of crisis and enrichment adequate to bourgeois sensibilities (in film tango music, the sad melody elegantly tames the pounding rhythm; filmed tango dances are always sleek and glamorous, containing loads of energy created and communicated through silky moves). Tango is a cultural spice for mature audiences, and film directors have promoted and made use of this by-now "universal art" with little interest in its sociopolitical moorings. Tangos have become ingredients of self-reflection, workings-out of interiorities. They belong to the "human condition." Tangos are urban and urbane enough, they are white enough, they are classy enough, they are sensual rather than sexual, and they are heterosexual.

Tangos are by now a civilized tradition (a toying with the past and with a culturally specific origin), conservative with a touch of wilderness. In tangos colonialism is long over, assimilated and forgotten. Global imperialism and postcoloniality have brought north and south to a neutral terrain where free-floating "culture" bits circulate as fetishes of a passé exotic threat, now nurturing multiculturalism (the celebration of cultural difference without politics). Now the natives want to be like the tourists, but they will work at keeping "difference" (read *as* culture) alive for the sake of bartering their entrance into the world strata of the privileged by offering "cultural" services.

Multiculturalism is a form of exoticism that implies the pleasure of sampling worldwide "authentic" *experiences* (collecting objects is not enough). Natives (those identified as different, no matter how hybrid) must share and teach selected customs and manners (the ones designated as "culture" by preservationists and survivalists) to make a living. ("Cultures" are valued commodities under north-south transactions.) Since the end of the twentieth century it has been safe and sound to be a cultural tourist in tango land. You can count on the native's collaboration; natives appreciate multiculturalists' interests, and we have our specialists (artists and scholars) working at "culture" to that effect.

So now you have it. Sally Potter and Carlos Saura, two artistic cultural survivalists, launch cinematic tango tours to Buenos Aires almost simultaneously (1997 and 1998). They initiate a new era in tango film history. These are whole films about the tango culture (not mere snippets of the artistic genre.)[2] The metaphoric uses of tango are set into its cultural context, and spectators are transported down Argentine way to live a tango adventure led by the hand of an enlightened cosmopolitan traveler, an *artiste.* In each case an artist (film director) immerses herself or himself in the tango world of Buenos Aires (the original tango location) and lives an intense tango story as her or his life becomes entangled in intimate sexual relationships with tango natives—that is, tango specialists, artists among the natives, the only culturally significant natives worthy of a tourist's time. (Tourists follow the path of traditional ethnography; they also make use of "key informants.")

From the outset, both films show the excruciating labor, the craftmanship of the auteur wrestling to tell the story of the tango culture (like an

2. An earlier, unsuccessful attempt was Leonard Schrader's *Naked Tango*, released in 1989.

ethnographer invested in accurate observations and descriptions) while searching for insightful inspiration in the tango personal experience (again, like the ethnographer involved in participation and self-reflexivity). Both films start at the desks of the cultural specialists (the film directors), who are scripting and pondering over scripting their tango stories and who cannot avoid putting themselves at the center. (This of course will be attributed to tango and tangueros' irresistible seductive powers and tango's culturally distinctive ability to provoke or reveal existential wounds.)

Sally, the protagonist of *The Tango Lesson* (played by Sally Potter herself), is a successful British film director who struggles over her next film script and finds respite from her hardworking, lonely days as an artist in dancing ballroom tango. Work and pleasure at the moment are split in her life, and she suffers a crisis of inspiration. Mario, the protagonist of Carlos Saura's *Tango* (played by Miguel Angel Solá), is a conflicted, nomadic artist (born in Argentina and raised in Spain, he has come back to Buenos Aires after a long interval to find his friends disappeared under political repression), and he is undergoing a mid-life crisis. These are postfeminist, enlightened artists: he is attuned to his emotions and to how his personal life (a love affair gone astray) affects his work; she is wary about her work and the loss of her feminine sensibilities, her split subjectivity as it affects her ability to create and enjoy her art, which should be one and the same with her life. The fact that she is single at the time of her crisis is not an issue. For Mario, however, life, no matter how successful his art, makes no sense without a love/sex relationship.

Sally Potter's *The Tango Lesson* is an autobiographical traveler's account ready-made for established single professional women undergoing the typical midlife crisis of a daughter of the women's liberation movement. Her film follows the outline of a tango tourist's handbook specially designed for liberated, heterosexual women. It contains actual tango dance lessons (costly private ones, and sometimes with two or three male dance masters at her disposal), and lessons that warn prospective women tango tourists about the emotional minefield that awaits them in Buenos Aires. Sally's lessons expose her liberal feminist vulnerabilities. She is searching for the lost Woman in the form of a *tanguerina* (tango ballerina), a dance genre that can accommodate her aging and her imperfections and that values "life experience." In tango she has found a (hetero)sexy but elegant dance that promises dangers she has had the courage to face, and now to share with her spectators. Tango, as an experience of multiculturalism, can teach.[3]

3. On the uses of experience as testimonies and documents see the contrasting and informed viewpoints of Joan Scott 1992 and Judith Oakley 1992. See also Walter Benjamin's provocative discussions of the concept of experience throughout *Illuminations* and especially in "On Some Motifs in Baudelaire" (1969b).

Spectators are invited to a postfeminist consciousness-raising session. *The Tango Lesson* is a step program for female wannabe tangoholics, and when offered on screen, as a spectacle, it generates that same strange fascination for the pathetic that talk shows elicit in order to exploit. *The Tango Lesson*, however, lacks the sense of humor of this genre of entertainment; Potter controls the dangers much too well. Sally learned the tango lesson (she mastered the tango men in a way the native women can never do), and now she can teach tourists and natives.

Rewind. Sally is a talented, successful artiste in a tough, no longer so patriarchal world that has lost its feminine, soft side. She is out to explore that vein of "herself" in exotic lands with exotic men—she hardly acknowledges the presence of women in the tango world except as unthreatening rivals with whom she never engages. Set in a time of postcolonial dislocations, exoticism happens wherever tango people go. Sally's tango adventures move between London, Paris, and Buenos Aires and are carried through a mélange of languages. She suffers confusion. Dazzled by Pablo's (Pablo Verón) tango performance at the Folies Bérgères, she decides to start a transaction with a "cultural" native that will turn her world upside down. Sally wants to be a dancer (to reestablish the severed connection with her body, which stands for her "inner" and "true" self, according to Potter's script notes), but she will not let go of her power as a film director.[4] She wants to feel like a "real" woman, and, to no one's surprise, she ends up falling in love with a macho young tango man.

Sally seduces Pablo by presenting herself as a film director who can make him a star in exchange for his tango lessons. Tango lessons include (surprise, surprise) a sex/love affair. He plays the lover, fulfilling her fantasies, until they run into a wall. Having dumped his tango dance partner, Pablo invites Sally to perform in a tango show. Sally is in tanguerina heaven. The tango training sessions and the show itself turn out to be disastrous. She is not a good enough tango dancer, supposedly because she is not a submissive enough woman for that. The fact that a few technique lessons, no matter how strenuous, cannot prepare her for a tango show is never mentioned; what is clear, instead, is that a female partner in tango is an underdog, and that is something she cannot accept. She cries. The limitation on their relationship is cultural, inscribed in the tango. Sally cannot be a tango woman; but can she be a woman?

Fast forward. Sally and Pablo shout over the telephone to each other in French:

Pablo: "You know nothing about tango."

Sally: "And you know nothing about me."

---

4. "All my director's instincts were stimulated. It was his presence I knew I could work with. . . . I was falling in love" (Potter 1997: ix).

Pablo: "Maybe I don't want to know anymore."

Sally: "Then I suppose it's over between us."

Pablo: "What is? . . . You have been using me to live out your little fantasy."

Sally: "No. No. It's you who's been using me. You never really wanted to dance with me. . . . You have been humoring me, so that one day I might put you in a film and make you a star."

The record is set straight. They decide to keep "the personal and the professional" separated. Pablo proposes to "sublimate."[5] So his desire is there? So he has not been deceiving her? Or is he deceiving her again so that she does not replace him with another tango dancer? He and she have seen them lurking around like sharks. . . . There are many like him (tango men) but very few like her (established filmmakers interested in tango.) There are also famous actors who would be willing to fill his role—Antonio Banderas comes to mind. Her agent cannot believe Sally will not take the opportunity of casting a famous actor to make her tango movie a big success. Sally is disappointed, but she will not betray Pablo. As we will soon learn, she is on a mission.

At this point the erotics of power changes gears: Sally will assume her role as film director, boss Pablo around, and teach him and his fellow tango men (still no tango women) how to be actors. She writes the story, sells the story, casts herself in it as prima tanguerina, sings, and acts as herself. (In the introduction to her published script she mentions her decision to tell this story from "the inside out" (Potter 1997: ix).) But Sally will not turn into a male entrepreneur. She is a powerful boss with a difference: she is a woman. She does not resent Pablo; she takes charge of her own confusion, her misleading desires. She will stay emotionally connected to him, now no longer as a lover but as a mother figure. She will show him his own vulnerability and guide him out of his pain. Sally is wise and charitable, a hardworking woman. Pablo will be her work of art. (Potter's introduction to the film script concludes: "Pleasure—taken to its extremity—becomes work. And work—taken to its extremity—becomes love.")[6]

Rewind. The scene of epiphany: Sally and Pablo meet after bitter quarrels at the Church of St. Suplice in Paris. In the background we see Eugène Delacroix's painting of Jacob wrestling with the Angel. "When doing the tango—Sally explains to Pablo and to the audience—Pablo was the Angel and she was Jacob, struggling with him" (or with herself, she then ex-

5. The inclusion of psychoanalytic terminology in a tango dancer's casual conversation might seem out of place, but it actually calls attention to psychoanalysis's widespread popularity among Argentineans.

6. Potter 1997: xii; see also p. ix: "Was it love or work? Had I perhaps fallen in work?"

plains). Pablo and Sally assume the wrestling poses *qua* demonstrators. "It's a Jewish story. . . . Jacob realized—Sally continues—that he could never defeat the stranger . . . because . . . perhaps Jacob had simply been wrestling with himself." And then, "I've been following you in the tango, Pablo. But to make a film, you have to follow me."

Fast forward. Now, in Buenos Aires, Pablo confesses he is lost. He no longer finds himself at home; he doesn't belong anywhere. Pablo is a tango artist, but no longer an inhabitant of the Buenos Aires tango world. Sally understands his sorrowful wanderings because she is Jewish; Pablo has forgotten his Jewishness, a spiritual anchor that could orient him through life. We are in the final scene. Pablo asks: "Tell me Sally, what does it mean to feel like a Jew? . . . I don't really belong in France, but I don't belong here anymore either. I am afraid. . . . I'm afraid I will disappear without leaving a trace." He insists on knowing what brought them together, what made their roads cross. "Why have we met?" he asks, eyes full of tears. Wanting to be a film tango star and to make a successful tango film is not enough. Sally had already told us spectators that she wanted more; now we learn that so does he—following her script. He is a macho man, but he is also vulnerable; and he did not manipulate Sally's feelings after all— which would make her look like a dupe. So Sally gives him a lesson: Stardom is not enough. (She knows it: she is a star.) His quest is the human quest: to leave a trace in the world after you are gone. And she has given him that. Pause.

The Tango Lesson is Sally and Pablo's (somewhat incestuous) child: a product of their imperfect love, marked by missed encounters. In the end, Sally sings a lullaby to him, the father and the child of her own tango. Privileged women of the world, this you can find in a tango tour if you pull rank, wisdom, and professional contacts: You get to play the tanguerina; you get to have sex with young, athletic, ambitious, macho tango men; you get to fall in love and to make them fall in love with you and your power (and you will never know the true proportions of the equation); you get to cry and feel victimized (you might have been missing your vulnerable feminine spot); you get to show generous understanding and even offer some advice to the guy (poor thing, he doesn't know any better); you can leave Buenos Aires with a profitable and glamorous tangoesque product ready to sell (for example, I came up with a tango film; you see what you can do), and with a tango story (sad and endearing, but sexy and full of "libidinal force") to share with your friends and eventually tell to your grandchildren. If you are looking for a tango adventure, here is the handbook. Stop. Eject. Change tapes.

Play Saura's *Tango*. In Saura's film, spectators have to do more work. *Tango* (in the Spanish release the film's title is *Tango, no me dejes nunca* —Tango, Never Leave Me) is not a handbook for tourists but an instruction manual for artists—artists as ethnographers.[7] In Saura's film, spectators witness all the technical steps (edited and glamorized, of course) undertaken in the making of a tango spectacle that is simultaneously being filmed. (*Tango* begins and ends with shots of a panopticon-like camera, unnoticed by those being filmed.) Film spectators are thus privileged viewers of a double show: The film is about making a film about making a tango show. The audience is addressed both as film spectators and as the prospective tourists for whom Mario (the artistic director, played by Miguel Angel Solá) is preparing a tango show. Pause.

Spectators of *Tango* are positioned as amateur ethnographers (be they artists, tourists, or a combination thereof) who have the privilege of watching the making of a piece of transcultural cinema, an ethnographic film (a fictionalized documentary with a strong subjective voice) of an "other" culture made into a work of art with the participation of native artists.[8] Saura's Mario is the artist as "native" ethnographer (a native distanced from his culture, reporting on his culture to outsiders interested in "other" worlds). Sally would be Saura's ideal spectator, but she would not have ever met Mario, the maker of the tango show. Sally and the cinematic tango tourists she addresses will come down to Buenos Aires to attend tango shows like Mario's (they are made for tourists), but she would have not taken interest in or looked for anyone like him. Mario's tango world is not authentically "native" enough. In Buenos Aires, the setting of Saura's *Tango*, Mario's world would cross with Sally's as artist colleagues—not enough tango for him or her. Despite the cultural divide and the north-south divide (remember, she is British, while he is Argentinean), their paths do not cross in a tango story. They are too much of the same class. They are looking for the same "other" thing, and they are not other enough for each other.

Saura's *Tango* is thus self-reflexive about filmmaking and self-reflexive about an artist's search for inspiration as he digs up the roots of his own culture in Buenos Aires with a "world" (as in "world art") audience in mind. Play. Mario is undergoing a midlife crisis. As he reads the tango screenplay that will set him to work, he becomes profoundly depressed. Spectators *qua* amateur ethnographers soon learn that his sorrow is personal and political. Upon returning to Buenos Aires he finds a city in denial after the military dictatorship. His old friends are dead and (fast forward) the producers of his tango show do not want to remember the sad past.

7. See Hal Foster's provocative "The Artist as Ethnographer" (1996) and Joseph Kosuth's collection of quotations-meditations on the subject in "The Artist as Anthropologist" (1993).

8. For a discussion of the differences between ethnographic film and documentaries as well as a critical treatment of transcultural cinema, see Taylor 1998; Devereaux and Hillman 1995; Tobing Rony 1996.

Rewind. He has broken up a sex/love relationship with Laura (Cecilia Narova), a professional native tango dancer. A quasi-rape scene develops between the two, where Laura reminds Mario that she not only has another lover but is happy with him. (We will understand, if we manage to put the disjointed pieces together, that Mario's violent reaction to Laura's rejection is related to his rage over the political repression of the past and the current widespread denial he encounters.)

Fast forward. Mario limps on a broken leg (he has had a car accident) while he watches Laura and Carlos (her new lover, played by Carlos Rivarola) rehearsing a passionate *tango de fantasía* (a highly choreographed tango) for the show he is directing. Pause. Mario (as we are informed by his limp), unlike Sally, does not aspire to be a dancer. He does not need to "embody the experience" of a native; he is a (broken) native. He hires tango dancers for his show and picks his lovers from among them. Tango dancers are the native artists (professionalism affecting their true native's nature, but we must keep in mind that artists are the "cultural" specialists among the natives) who will guide (actually work for) Mario in his culturally marked existential journey. Mario is worried about aging, and he seeks to confirm his masculinity in the company of beautiful female tango dancers who are supposed to have sex with him, fall in love, and be happy with him. Stop. Eject. Change videotapes. Back to Potter's *The Tango Lesson*. Play.

Pause. Why would Saura's Mario and Potter's Sally, two artists exploring the tango world, not end up with each other? Mario would not be interested. Sally is not vulnerable, young, sexy, or dangerous enough. She does not *belong* to the tango world. Mario's new love object, Elena (Mia Maestro), does qualify in that she combines all of the above. Unlike Sally, Elena is a tango femme fatale waiting to be tamed (and saved) by Mario. There is an interesting twist here concerning femme fatality that deserves further attention. Elena, Mario's chosen object of desire and potential restorer of his broken masculinity, is dangerous because she is kept by an older mafioso. (This powerful mafioso is a Spaniard—his accent is clearly distinguishable from that of the rest of the cast, typed as Argentineans—and thus represents the former colonial power through its sexualized exploits of the natives.) Thus Elena's fatality (her fatal attraction for Mario) responds to her intimate association with a man who is doubly worthy as a rival (mafioso and colonizer) for Mario—who is seeking to confirm his native masculinity. It seems as though native women would, at least in this context, qualify as femmes fatales when they are under the shadow of dangerous men. If, as in this case, that man stands for colonialism, her fatalness increases, as does her attraction. The presence of dangerous men by femme fatales seems to apply to nonnative women as well when the story takes place in a colonial or neocolonial setting. Consider, for example, Rita Hayworth in *Gilda* (1946). Look for *Gilda* in the video rack. Eject Potter's *The Tango Lesson*. Play *Gilda*.

Enough. Pause. Gilda is the object of dispute between two foreign men: a German owner of a Buenos Aires casino with Nazi affiliations, and an American adventurer lost to gambling and stranded in the South American harbor. Johnny, the American, agrees to work for the illicit German entrepreneur as Gilda's bodyguard. Although the plot differs greatly from that of Saura's *Tango* (Gilda and Johnny happen to be former lovers whom the Nazi casino owner and arm trafficker unwittingly reconnects, thus launching a masterful noir love triangle), both films coincide in presenting their femmes fatales as being kept by older and dangerous men who, at first, facilitate the women's encounters (or re-encounters) with the young and troubled men who will become their romantic lovers and who will then play as paramount male rivals to the young losers seeking confirmation of their masculinity. Gilda and Elena, the femmes fatales, act in both stories as heterosexual pawns of a patriarchal, homosocial game. Buenos Aires stands in both films for an exotic and thus barbaric world location, where illicit activities accumulate at all imaginable levels (political corruption, arms trafficking, gambling, and sexual exploits) and where human ambitions have no institutional or ethical restraints. The natives serve, with few exceptions, as backdrops. (In *Gilda*, Gilda's maid and the casino's male restroom attendant serve as paradigmatic voices of moral soundness, a privilege of their humble occupations; in Saura's *Tango*, dance masters are shown dutifully performing their artistic task with no psychological or political quarrels, the latter being a privilege reserved to Mario, the broken native.)

The main female characters and femmes fatales of the stories, Gilda and Elena, are emblematic figures caught at that particularly ambitious time of life when they are enjoying the perks of having been chosen as love objects of powerful men whom they do not love and who thus do not bring them happiness. Both women are presented as having to make existential choices within the set parameters of a patriarchal world, that is, between two men who represent opposite poles of power and riches versus love and care (the latter not without conflicts). Gilda and Elena, both cast as artists (one, a seasoned singer and dancer; the other, an aspiring professional tanguerina), play the feminized part of the neocolonial encounter (Gilda as an American, Elena as an Argentinean), struggling with different options for accommodating to imperialist, capitalist patriarchy. Their transgressions never amount to potential breaks with or daring resistances to the well-established world order. Their best bets (which convey the "happy ending in both films) are contained within the limits of romantic heterosexual love, the only thing that really matters. (Gilda will return to the United States in Johnny's arms; Elena will be rescued by Mario, the returning and enlightened diasporic native.) What artistic genre could convey this passionate trap better than a tango? What body could corporealize this conflictive drive better than a Latina dancer? Who could rival these stereotypical composites, their resounding redundancy, their by-now tamed exoticism, their settled evocative power (surely that of trouble and conflict, but typed and thus kept at bay as in a nonconflictive conflict) more successfully than these dancing women ready-made to restore damaged senses of masculinity? Stop. Eject. Back to Potter's *The Tango Lesson*. Play. Pause. A Sally cannot restore a Mario's masculinity. She does not need what he has (money, genius). She is a competitor; she is too much of a man (age, status, and success, in which last she is aided by her contacts in Hollywood—those are also mentioned in her film). Stop. Change videotapes. Play Saura's *Tango* again.

Mario is looking for a woman who can deliver the cultural specificity he has lost; he needs a native tango artist. He tries two of them, a mature one and a young one, in the course of the story. Elena, the younger one, will deliver. Innocence makes the female native artist a notch more native and a notch closer to untampered-with femininity. Pause. And Mario, he is not "authentic" enough for Sally. There are plenty of men like him in her regular world. She didn't come all the way to Buenos Aires for that! Mario's leg is broken! He can't dance. She can't be his victim. He is too enlightened and politically correct. She has nothing to offer to rescue him either. (He does not need her money, prestige, or success.) Mario, like the tango women in Sally's film, is invisible. Broken native artists like Mario and women native artists like the professional tango dancers are not adequate for Sally's intended financial, sexual, and spiritual transactions. Marios and Sallys exist in the tango world, but they do not see each other because they are looking for the same thing, which they both lack. (In Lacan's words: Woman (1985).) Stop. Eject. Change videotapes. Play *The Tango Lesson*.

Pause. Sally wants to become Woman herself by finding a real man who will make her live like one (and those men live in another world, turned feminine by the doings of her world). She has in mind a world like the tango world where men enjoy dancing with each other—and she makes them dance for her. (Queue up. Play. Scene of the male tango trio. Pablo (Verón), Gustavo (Naveira), and Fabian (Salas) dance playfully and wildly until Sally intervenes. She, the tanguerina, passing from one's hands to the other, establishes order and beauty over all-male anarchy.[9]) Sally wants a man who is both macho *and* vulnerable: a wild child. She wants a tango dancer, a native artist. Stop. Eject. Change videotapes. Play Saura's *Tango*.

Pause. Saura's Mario, contrarily, does not even try to dance. He hires the men who dance with the women with whom he is in love. He watches the women in their arms, fuels his desire, and takes them straight to bed. Tango is a foreplay, a warm-up that other (tango) men do for him so that he can have

9. "Turns and jumps and lifts. It [the dance] becomes wild and anarchistic and athletic. Their [male dancers'] energy, frustration, competitiveness and exuberance finally finding form [with Sally's participation.]" (Potter 1997: 74).

sex. He does not put his body at risk (at stake) through the tango. Mario stays away from dancing tango from the very beginning. He is aware that his body limps. Mario knows he cannot compete with tango dancers on their own turf. Remember that although they are all native artists, Mario is a broken one. (He sees the tango men; Sally did not see the tango women.) But Mario believes that his fantasy, his desire, and his genius surpass (and are more valuable than) what his aging body can show. Native artists embody "culture"; broken native artists like Mario create "world art." He does not want to make a spectacle out of himself; he makes spectacles. He will not even think of dancing. Professional tango dancers, male and female, are the repository of Mario's sexual fantasies and the matter of his work.

Queue up Carlos Rivarola and Julio Boca's tango duet and the all-male group choreography on a checkerboard floor. Play. Male tango dancers figure even more prominently in Saura-Mario's film/spectacle than in Sally's. Male tango dancers frequently dance with each other not only in group choreographies, but also in duets, where their "professional" skills as dancers surpass their tangoesque erotic connotations.[10] The camera shoots from a distance, capturing the dancers' full bodies, following their movements' trajectories over an open, bare space. Fast forward.

Advance frame by frame. Saura's all-female tango scene, in clear contrast to his all-male ones, focuses on pseudo-lesbian erotics (women seducing and even kissing each other).[11] The camera zooms in on the tanguerinas' lingerie, make-up rituals, lavish 1920s wardrobes, long cigarette holders, and lusting faces rather than on their dancing. Pause. (No all-female tangos in Potter's film.) Play. But Saura-Mario's tanguerinos show that they can dance. Mario personally trains two of them for a knife fight (not a tango) so that their and his masculinity is clear of doubts. (Spectators and tourists should not be confused.) In this scene, Mario's only intervention as choreographer, he also establishes his expertise in native culture that, as a broken native artist, is broader and wiser although less authentic (a lesser form of knowledge) than the culturally specific skills of the tango dancers. Pause. Mario's fantasy about (native) men is that when left in men's hands (male duets) they will fight over life and death. Heterosexuality is a must. (Here Mario and Sally are in agreement.) And so is homosociality. When heterosexuality and homosociality do not work hand in hand, all hell breaks out.

Rewind.

Play. Mario detects his next prey in a traditional tango club. Here spectators *qua* amateur ethnographers and cinematic tourists get their one and only glimpse of the "authentic" tango world, populated by old, unattractive, plain tango dancers, and they are instructed through the actors' con-

10. Choreographed by Julio Boca and Carlos Rivarola.
11. Choreographed by Ana María Stekelman.

versations on how to appreciate the elegance and serenity of the popular tango. (These are the real natives at dance; they are the ones whose culture the native artists represent.) Elena, wearing a tight white minidress, is a *nena* (chick). She dances absentmindedly in the arms of an old tango dancer. (At this point, Elena is a real native dancer; Mario, with the help of his choreographers, will transform her into a native artist.) A Spanish mafioso, the owner of the tango club, asks Mario to audition Elena, his lover, for his upcoming tango show. Mario is forced into treason. The love war over Elena is silently declared as he starts coaching her specially for the show.

Mario seduces Elena by making her a tanguerina. Pause. (Sally's dream come true! But I already explained why Sally and Mario were not meant for each other.) Fast forward. After resisting for a while, Elena moves into the studio with Mario. The negotiations between a broken cosmopolitan native artist and a newish native tango artist—mediated through the heterosexual encounter—begin. The mafioso's hitman lurks at the door. And Mario's happiness is assaulted by nightmares of big "P" Politics. He cannot forget the dirty war and its casualties. He decides to include a choreographed tangoized scene of a concentration camp into his tango show.[12] The producers of the spectacle (local entrepreneurs, men and women), following the law of the market, reject his idea and advise him to deliver what the public wants: pure tango entertainment. (They mention that this is an audience that is used to television and is thus stupefied.) Pause. The presence of capital globalizes the narrative, and the exploitation of cultural fetishism becomes evident. Enter the artist as messiah. The same path trodden in Sally's case, although she was less grandiose. Unpause.

Mario, the artiste, rebels against capital's mandate and reveals the dark side of history ("the military played tangos loud while torturing to suffocate the screams of the victims"). He will not represent tango isolated from the sociopolitical context that informs the art and the tragedy it expresses. Stop. Rewind. Play. The scene in the concentration camp begins as he lies in bed with Elena. Mario explains to her (and thus to the new generation of native artists) the relevance of keeping the sad memories alive. Elena jumps into the scene running and covering her ears in terror. She cries. All the victims of the military torture dance scene are women. All victims are women. All women are victims. Mario, the responsible artist, postpones being a responsible lover in order to complete his mission. He is the self-appointed keeper of the memory of power. Mario struggles to separate the personal and the political, his fantasies and the real world, but his artistic mind keeps bringing them together. Women are victims. Fast-fast forward.

The final scene of Saura/Mario's *Tango* depicts the arrival of immigrants

12. Choreographed by Ana María Stekelman.

in the Buenos Aires harbor around 1880. Extras in historical costumes fill the scene. Spectators learn that these natives are dislocated hybrids, like Mario and like many of them. The mafioso's hitman has been hired for the scene. In the midst of an early tango dance scene celebrating the (hybrid) origins of tango, the hit man as immigrant stabs Elena, also cast as an immigrant. (Spectators learn that humans, not only natives, are savage. We are all victims of our nature.) This is Mario's opportunity also to become a responsible lover. He runs to her rescue from the "murder scene" to confirm this is just a performance and assure himself (and herself) that she is alive and that he loves her. Happy ending, responsible artiste, humanity reunited in its pain, and he gets to keep the girl. Stop.

Saura's film is about production: the production of a film (the camera is present, traveling, reflected in mirrors); the production of a tango spectacle (the work of the artistic director, set designers, choreographers, dancers, singers, musicians, producers, et cetera); and the production of artistic creation. Sally joins Saura's Mario at this point in their roles of embodying the conundrums of making art with an interest in cultural specificity (in this case, tango) at the service of world, transcultural, and humanistic impulses. Mario and Sally are positioned as artists capable of interculturalism, that is, of creating informed and enlightened cultural understanding.

Exerting acrobatic mediations, they grapple with exoticism and alterity (Sally with her ancestral Jewishness and British colonialism; Mario with his knowledge of how foreign tactile eyes[13] approach his own culture); they also grapple with auto-exoticism (their own—Sally is tempted to go "native," Mario to heal his "broken" nativeness—as well as that of the native artists who sell themselves as representatives of "authentic" culture); and they grapple with the highly emotional political and personal investments that artistic inspiration requires. Sally and Mario are aware of the doings of capital and its ordering of the world. (She knows of her power as a British filmmaker vis-à-vis an Argentine tango man; he, Mario, knows that his contacts as a cosmopolitan artist situate him as an artistic director vis-à-vis the native artists he employs for the tango show.)

They cannot, however, make sense of how that difference (that part of the difference that is not "cultural" and that marks exploitation) affects their personal relationships and compromises their art. On both accounts, love/sex and work, they settle for a universal perspective—a move of Hegelian *aufhebung* (sublation). In the end, spectators, now informed cinematic tourists or amateur ethnographers, learn that difference—heterocultural and heterosexed—ignites passion in life (privately in their beds, and publicly at work) and that that is the human condition. That is the universal message of art and of the artist. It is a tango! Full circle. The spectators,

13. On optical "tactility" see Benjamin 1969c.

now educated and informed as to what tango at bottom "expresses," are readily equipped for a tango sex tour of Buenos Aires. And they will make tourism a work of art.

In conclusion, the so readily accepted and pervasive paradigm of "art as universal" works, in Jacques Derrida's (1981) terms, as a *pharmakon* (a drug that cures as it poisons). Potter and Saura, each in his or her own way, work hard at creating "culturally sensitive" tango stories. (Sally follows a postfeminist agenda; Saura follows a postmodern, historico politically informed agenda.) However, the necessity of reaching the spectator through personal and psychological identification—a humanistic recipe in the arts—ends up undoing all that painstaking work of pointing out the politicoeconomic underpinnings of so-called cultural difference. Situating themselves at the center of these tango stories as protagonists and cultural translators and thus pushing to the margins the actual protagonists of the tango world (the milongueros—whose looks and behaviors are harder for cinematic tourists to digest), Potter and Saura invoke universalism through art. Thus art becomes that outworldly space where "understanding" is possible. I am inviting readers to undergo the exercise of revising this pervasive logic that suggests that "cultures" are out there, in the world, for us—privileged, smart tourists/ethnographers/artists—to grab. That nowadays, identifying "cultures" is, from the start done with appropriation in mind. And that the idea of Art—as the sign of the sublime and universal—helps to mask the dark side (exploitation, domination, and inequality) of "cultural difference" that we do not wish to face: the privileges we refuse to recognize and to be accountable for.

Exhibit C
Writings Attributed to Angora Matta

Prueba C
Escritos Atribuidos a Angora Matta

Librettist's Note

Angora Matta (the name) came to me after a long night of philosophical discussions about death. Her name preceded her tale and demanded a crime story that would have a Latin American femme fatale as the protagonist. (I had been working on this to me enigmatic stereotype of femininity for many years.) Manuela Malva and Elvira Díaz were already in the making; Angora had to meet them, and she would as she returned to Buenos Aires. sAngora's personality (her thoughts, her voice, her everyday life) remained opaque to me; she carefully concealed her preoccupations and motivations. No wonder, I thought, since she is an assassin for hire. Getting to know her would mean exposing her vulnerabilities, endangering her life. Thus, it comes as no surprise that XYa would find only a few, rather hermetic, documents attributable to Angora. Death, evil, ambition, and a knife under a pillow populate her yellow walks between the north and the south.

Edgy Meditations/ Meditaciones Filosas

(O.) Emotional Mapping [Mapas emocionales]

Nostalgia is beautiful; denial mutilates.

When I am pressed to define beauty, not as a thing out there, but as a feeling regardless of what or where or how it is initiated, I can think only of pain. The very beautiful hurts and saddens. Sadness is sweet. Bitterness is ugly. Anger is bittersweet, a sharp longing for beauty that resists sadness.

Angora Matta, 23/2/2000

(T.) Mapas emocionales [Emotional Mapping]

La nostalgia es hermosa; la negación mutila.

Obligada a definir lo bello, no como cosa distante sino como sensación independientemente de qué, dónde o cómo se origina, sólo se me ocurre pensar en el dolor. Lo muy bello lastima y entristece. La tristeza es dulce. La amargura es monstruosa [horrible]. La rabia es dulciamarga, una añoranza filosa que extraña lo bello y se resiste a la tristeza.

Angora Matta, 23/3/2000

(O.) Error

Sólo la inexperiencia (o la arrogancia) permite creer que la locura es inversamente proporcional a la racionalidad.

Angora Matta, s. f.

(T.) Error

Only lack of experience (or arrogance) enables the belief that madness is inversely proportional to rationality.

Angora Matta, n. d.

(O.) Cantan

Las palabras son sonoras, y en la intimidad, cuando pienso o escribo cualquier mamarracho, me hacen música.

Angora Matta, 14 de deciembre de 2000

(T.) They Sing

Words are sonorous, and in intimacy, when I think or scribble, they make music for me.

Angora Matta, December 14, 2000

(O.) Pasó un conejo blanco

De alguna fábula aprendí que el mundo se dividía en dos clanes: el de los zorros y el de los conejos. Un día de nubes signadas, distraída de lo importante y puesta al trabajo, más que ver intuí una inquietud pelusona cruzando decididamente de izquierda a derecha. No interrumpí mi quehacer. De derecha a izquierda, entonces, cruzó otra vez con blanca insolencia. Tuve que tomar nota. Esa noche lo seguí en un sueño entre paredes lisas y pastizales altos. Nos enfrentamos en el codo de la escalera que formaba un claro muy estrecho, los dos agitados. Primero húmedo y rosado, mazcullaba algo, tembloroso. Me atrapó su mirada negra y fija. Me acerqué a olerlo y trastocó su dimensión. Las orejas, dos cuchillos gigantescos; los bigotes, quince punzones amenazantes. Entendí que desde su estatura me advertía rabioso que entre los conejos también hay asesinos. El mundo se me complicó.

(T.) A White Rabbit Passed By

Some fable taught me that the world was made up of two clans: that of the foxes and that of the rabbits. On a day of portentous clouds, distracted from what is important and set to work, I intuited more than saw a fuzzy restlessness crossing decidedly from left to right. I did not interrupt my doings. From the right to the left, then, it crossed again, with its white insolence. I had to notice. That night I followed it in a dream between plain walls and tall grasses. We faced each other where the staircase turns into a very narrow open space, the two of us agitated. First, pink and humid, it mumbled something, trembling. Its black and fixed look trapped me. When I came closer to smell it, its dimensions transformed. The ears became two gigantic knives; the whiskers, fifteen threatening puncheons. I understood from its height that it was warning me angrily that there are also assassins among rabbits. The world became more complicated.

(O.) Muerte Entera

T.) La muerte entera sólo puede vivenciarse a través de sus efectos sobre los otros. (Cuando alcanza al sujeto ya es demasiado tarde para ser vivida como experiencia.) Por eso la muerte es incomprensible y materia de creencias. (O.) Los que no creen en la muerte (entera) suelen creer en la reencarnación y hasta en la resurrección. Creo que esos son los que creen en lo que se ve y se toca. Yo creo en lo que me dicen al oído. Y por eso le creo a la muerte que me pide entrar de la mano del cuchillo. (T.) La experiencia más cercana a la muerte es la de matar. Se la evita porque se cree que es contagiosa (la sustancia de la muerte reptando del matado al matador).

(T.) Death Entire

(O.) Death entire can be experienced only through its effects on others. (When it reaches the subject it is too late to be lived as experience.) That is why death is incomprehensible and a matter of belief. (T.) Those who do not believe in death (entire) tend to believe in reincarnation and even in resurrection. I believe those are the ones who believe in what can be seen and touched. I believe in what is spoken into my ear. And that is why I believe death when it asks me to enter holding hands with my knife. (O.) The closest experience to that of death is killing. It is avoided because it is believed to be contagious (the substance of death creeping from the killed into the killer).

(O.) La secta de los ambiciosos

Una de las lógicas más imposible de seguir es la de las conveniencias. No atiende a explicaciones razonadas, ni apela al entendimiento. Pero es la lógica prístina y abrumadora de los intereses implacables. (T.) Intereses dispares, incongruentes que se juntan por un instante, el de la loca decisión, para después iniciar la lenta corrida en dirección a la garganta del otro incapaces de reconocer el malentendido original (habiendo todos acordado a hacerse los ciegos): éste es el modelo coreográfico que practica la secta de los ambiciosos.

(T.) The Sect of the Ambitious

One of the most impossible logics to follow is that of convenience. It does not attend to reasoned explanations, it does not appeal to understanding. But it is the pristine and overwhelming logic of implacable interests. (O.) Disparate, incongruent interests coming together for an instant, that of the mad decision, after which they start running slowly at each other's throats unwilling to acknowledge the original misunderstanding (to which all agreed to be blind): this is the choreographic pattern followed by the sect of the ambitious.

(O.) El mal y la maldad

No son lo mismo. El mal anda por ahí. No es erradicable. Parece ir y venir, buscando víctimas inocentes o conscientes. En verdad no busca nada, ni pide ni da nada. No es cosa ni verbo; es nada de nada. (El mal precisa el auxilio del hacer.) El mal es un espejo de la intencionalidad perniciosa que le es ajena. Como todo sustantivo que hace objeto de una acción, debe ser sospechado. (En ese sentido merece el mismo tratamiento crítico que el bien.) Pensándolo bien, ¿qué hace el mal (o deja de hacer) cuando no se lo practica? Ocupa el espacio de lo paranoico. Acecha. Amenaza. Atemoriza. Pero sólo se lo conoce a través del ejercicio de la maldad, malevolente o benevolente. El mal entonces existiría antes de ser cometido; luego del acto, nos enfrentamos a la maldad. Siempre llegamos a saber de la maldad por sus víctimas.

Es fácil identificar al objeto de un acto de maldad (la víctima), no así a su sujeto o victimario. De allí que hasta los más malvados suelan dar lástima. Se entiende mejor el sufrimiento, ya sea el de la víctima (sentimiento por el cual nos enteramos que se ha cometido el mal) o el del perpetrador de la ignominia. (En este último caso, algún sufrimiento profundo y/o pasado justifica la maldad.)

No recomiendo este ejercicio: ¿qué aprenderíamos si en lugar de quedarnos del lado de la lástima nos corriéramos al lado del odio? Esto se me ocurre porque veo en amplia práctica otro ejercicio, tal vez más escabroso: pasarse de la lástima, y de un ligero gemido o lagrimeo, al costado de la apatía. El odio (que no aconsejo) al menos se resiste al olvido. Y mientras no se convierta en resentimiento, otro sentimiento estupefaciente, retiene la alerta. Siempre y cuando se consiga transformar la naturaleza, la calidad caliente propia del odio recién nacido, injertándole una dosis de sangre fría. Algo así como una represión calculada, elegida. (Esto no sería una sublimación; sería una oda al trauma y un jugueteo con sus síntomas.)

Yo guardo mis odios con gran cuidado; tengo muy pocos. No los comento con extraños. Prefiero que queden claros, definidos, y con el peso propio. En mi experiencia, al relucir los odios se oxidan. No así las armas de la venganza. Este cuchillo, que duerme bajo mi almohada, pide salir de día, con sol en lo posible, al bosque sin abismos. Ahí evaluamos lúcidamente los componentes de cada crimen potencial. (Nunca escojas un arma halagadora y ni siquiera generosa.)

(T.) Evil and Evilness

They are not the same. Evil runs around. It cannot be uprooted. It seems to come and go, looking for innocent or conscious victims. In truth it does not look for anything, nor does it ask or give anything. It is neither a thing nor a verb; it is nothing about nothing. (Evil needs help from the verb "to do.") Evil is the mirror of a pernicious intentionality that is alien to it. Like all nouns that make an object out of an action, it must be suspected. (In this sense it deserves the same critical treatment as the good.) Carefully considered, what does evil do (or fail to do) when not practiced? It occupies the space of paranoia. It lurks. It threatens. It scares. But it is known only through the practice of evilness, malevolent or benevolent. Evil thus would exist before it is exerted; after the doing we confront evilness. We always get to know evilness through its victims.

It is easy to identify the object of an act of evilness (the victim); not so the agent or victimizer. Hence even the most evil tend to elicit pity. Suffering is better understood, whether that of the victim (the feeling through which we learn that evil has occurred) or that of the perpetrator of the ignominy. (In the latter case, a profound and/or past suffering justifies doing evil.)

I do not recommend this exercise: What would we learn if rather than staying on the side of pity we were to move onto the side of hatred? I think of this because I see the vast practice of another exercise, perhaps scarier: To move from pity, and from a light moan or welling of tears, to the flanks of apathy. Hatred (which I do not advise) at least resists forgetfulness. And when prevented from being converted into resentment, another stupefying sentiment, it retains alertness— whenever it is possible to transform the natural, the hot quality characteristic of newborn hatred, by implanting into it a dosage of cold blood. Something like a calculated, chosen repression. (This would not amount to sublimation; it would be an ode to trauma and a toying with its symptoms.)

I guard my hatreds with great care; I have only a few. I do not discuss them with strangers. I prefer that they stay clear, defined, with their own weight. In my experience, when aired, hatreds rust. This is not the case with the weapons of vengeance. This knife that sleeps under my pillow asks to come out in the light of day, under the sun, when possible at the forest without abyss. There we lucidly ponder the components of each potential crime. (Never choose a flattering weapon and not even a generous one.)

Costurero para escribir

revés de puntada
de punta alfiler
mostrar la hilacha

Sewing Kit for Writing

understitch
pinpoint
show the loose threads

(O.)

Caminares Amarillos

Camina sobre terreno tomado.
Camina, la cabellera hosca.
Camina olfateando con los pies.
Camina como un domador de suelos mordedores.
Camina con un dejo de zapatos mojados.
Camina con los deseos en el dobladillo.

Camina con las mangas hipnotizadas.

Camina con la esperanza en las rodillas.

Camina dejando pespuntes en el cemento fresco.

Camina con tobillos de esponja estrujada.

Camina a contraluz y en declive.

Camina acomodándose los anillos.

Camina con la mirada en los bolsillos.

Camina con el vientre apelmazado.

Camina con la arrogancia de la ley de gravedad.

Camina al ritmo de sus clavículas.

Camina con suspiros en el escote.

Camina con todos los huesos y desdeño muscular.

Camina con las ancas olvidadas.

Camina con los muslos angustiados.

Camina sobre piso siempre nuevo y siempre roto.

Camina con las ideas roncas.

Camina al paso de los gritos pelados.

Camina con perfume de huracán colorado.

Camina entre los ojos del que la mira.

Camina rompiendo el estado de sitio.

Camina de espaldas a la traición.

Camina sin alma.

Camina bajo tres sombras.

Camina rozando helechos.

Camina esquivando pedradas transparentes.

Camina sobre murmuraciones maledicentes.

Camina a pesar del manotón aciago.

Camina, la boca fresca.

Camina, los labios de palabras entreabiertas.

Camina en dirección bifurcada.

Camina. Las paradas le quedan impúdicas.

Camina contra las esquinas. Camina enfrente.

(T.)

Yellow Walks

Walks over taken terrain.

Walks, the hair rough.

Walks sniffing with the feet.

Walks like a tamer of biting grounds.

Walks with a hint of wet shoes.

Walks with desires in the hem.

Walks with the sleeves under hypnosis.

Walks with hope in the knees.

Walks leaving tidy stitches on fresh cement.

Walks with ankles of squeezed sponge.

Walks backlit and in decline.

Walks refitting her rings.

Walks with the look in the pocket.

Walks with a scowling belly.

Walks arrogant of the law of gravity.

Walks to the beat of her clavicles.

Walks with sighs at the cleavage.

Walks with all the bones and with muscular disdain.

Walks with the buttocks forgotten.

Walks with the thighs in anguish.

Walks on flooring always new and always broken.

Walks with hoarse things in mind.

Walks in step with the roaring shouts.

Walks with the scent of the red hurricane.

Walks in between the eyes of the beholder.

Walks breaking the curfew.

Walks back to betrayal.

Walks without a soul.

Walks under three shadows.

Walks brushing ferns.

Walks missing transparent stone throws.

Walks over nasty rumors.

Walks despite the fateful grasp.

Walks fresh in the mouth.

Walks, lips with words torn open.

Walks in a forked direction.

Walks. Standing still feels indecent.

Walks against the corners. Walks across.

(O.) Final para Cuento Espeluznante

Books covered her bed. The knife under the pillow.

(T.) Ending for a Thriller

La cama cubierta de libros. El cuchillo bajo la almohada.

References Cited

Writings

Allen, Virginia. 1983. *The Femme Fatale: Erotic Icon*. Troy: Whitston.

Appadurai, Arjun. 1991. "Global Ethnoscapes: Notes and Queries for a Transnational Anthropology." In *Recapturing Anthropology: Working in the Present*, edited by Richard G. Fox, pp. 191–210. Santa Fe, N.M.: School of American Research Press.

Apter, Emily and William Pietz, eds. 1993. *Fetishism as Cultural Discourse*. Ithaca: Cornell University Press.

Archetti, Eduardo P., ed. 1994. *Exploring the Written: Anthropology and the Multiplicity of Writing*. Oslo: Scandinavian University Press.

Arendt, Hanna. 1969. "Introduction: Walter Benjamin, 1892–1940." In *Illuminations*, edited by Hanna Arendt and translated by Harry Zohn, pp. 1–58. New York: Schocken Books.

Arlt, Roberto. 1993. *Aguafuertes porteñas: Buenos Aires, vida cotidiana*. Buenos Aires: Alianza Editorial.

Avelar, Idelber. 1999. *The Untimely Present: Postdicatorial Latin American Fiction and the Task of Mourning*. Durham, N.C.: Duke University Press.

Ayerza, Laura. 1996. "Cara a cara con Madonna." *Gente*, February 1, 22–34.

Bakhtin, M. M. 1981. *The Dialogic Imagination*, translated by Caryl Emerson and Michael Holquist. Austin: University of Texas Press.

Barthes, Roland. 1977. *Sade, Fourier, Loyola*, translated by Richard Miller. Baltimore: Johns Hopkins University Press.

Baudrillard, Jean. 1984. *Las estrategias fatales*, translated by Joaquín Jorda. Barcelona: Editorial Anagrama.

Benjamín, Walter. 1969a. "The Task of the Translator." In *Illuminations*, edited by Hanna Arendt and translated by Harry Zohn, pp. 69–82. New York: Schocken Books.

———. 1969b. "On Some Motifs in Baudelaire." In *Illuminations*, edited by Hanna Arendt and translated by Harry Zohn, pp. 155–200. New York: Schocken Books.

———. 1969c. "The Work of Art in the Age of Mechanical Reproduction." In *Illuminations*, edited by Hanna Arendt and translated by Harry Zohn, pp. 217–252. New York: Schocken Books.

Blau, Herbert. 1990. *The Audience*. Baltimore: John Hopkins University Press.

Bordo, Susan. 1993. "'Material Girl': The Effacement of Postmodern Culture." In *The Madonna Connection: Representational Politics, Subcultural Identities, and Cultural Theory*, edited by Cathy Schwichtenberg, pp. 265–290. Boulder, Colo.: Westview.

Borges, Jorge Luis. 1984. *Evaristo Carriego: A Book About Old-Time Buenos Aires*, translated by Norman Thomas di Giovanni. New York: E. P. Dutton.
———. 1989. "El Puñal." In *Jorge Luis Borges: obras completas, 1923–1949*, pp. 156. Buenos Aires: Emecé Editores.
———. 1989. "Borges y yo." In *Jorge Luis Borges: obras completas, 1952–1972*, pp. 186. Buenos Aires: Emecé Editores.

Braudel, Fernand. 1981. *The Structures of Everyday Life: The Limits of the Possible*, translated by Siam Reynolds. Vol. 1 of Civilization and Capitalism, 15th–18th Century. New York: Harper and Row.

Briand, René. 1972. *Crónicas del tango alegre*. Buenos Aires: Centro Editor de América Latina.

Brooks, Peter. 1980. "The Mark of the Beast: Prostitution, Melodrama, and Narrative." In *Melodrama*, edited by D. Gerould, pp. 125–140. New York: New York Literary Forum.

"Buenos Aires: The City of Evita." 1997. *Honolulu Advertiser*, January 5.

Butler, Judith. 1993. "Critically Queer." *Gay and Lesbian Quarterly* 1, no. 1: 17–32.

Cabrera Alvarez, Guillermo, ed. 1987. *Memories of Che*, translated by J. Fried. Secaucus, N.J.: Lyle Stuart.

Castilla, Eduardo S. 1969. "Tiempo de Tango Fuera de Tiempo." In *El tema del tango en la literatura argentina*, by Tomás Lara and Inés L. Roncetti de Panti, pp. 437–438. Buenos Aires: Ediciones Culturales Argentinas.

Chacón, Pablo E. 1996. "Evita fashion." *Nuevo porteño* 1, no. 4: 38–39.

Copi [Raul Damonte Taborda]. 1970. "Eva Perón." Unpublished manuscript.

Cortázar, Julio. 1993. "Las puertas del cielo." In *Bestiario*, pp. 117–137. Buenos Aires: Editorial Sudamericana.

——. 1996. "Bruja." In *Cortázar: cuentos completos*, vol. 1, pp.66–72. Buenos Aires: Aguilar, Altea, Taurus, Alfaguara S.A.

Couselo, Jorge. 1977. "El tango en el cine." In *Historia del tango*, vol. 8, *El Tango en el espectáculo*, pp. 1289–1328. Buenos Aires: Corregidor.

Curubeto, Diego. 1993. *Babilonia gaucha: Hollywood en la Argentina, la Argentina en Hollywood*. Buenos Aires: Planeta.

Dalle Vacche, Angela. 1992. *The Body in the Mirror: Shapes of History in Italian Cinema*. Princeton: Princeton University Press.

Da Matta, Roberto. 1991. *Carnivals, Rogues, and Heroes: An Interpretation of the Brazilian Dilemma*, translated by John Drury. Notre Dame: University of Notre Dame Press.

de Certeau, Michel. 1984. *The Practice of Everyday Life*, translated by Steven Rendall. Berkeley: University of California Press.

——. 1988. *The Writing of History*, translated by Tom Conley. New York: Columbia University Press.

Deleuze, Gilles. 1988. *Spinoza: Practical Philosophy*, translated by Robert Hurley. San Francisco: City Lights Books.

——. 1989. *El pliegue: Leibnitz y el barroco*, translated by José Vázquez and Umbelina Larraceleta. Barcelona: Ediciones Paidós.

——. 1991a. *La imagen-movimiento: estudios sobre cine 1*, translated by Irene Agoff. Barcelona: Ediciones Paidós.

——. 1991b. *Coldness and Cruelty*. New York: Zone Books.

——. 1996. *Crítica y clínica*, translated by Thomas Kauf. Barcelona: Editorial Anagrama.

Derrida, Jacques. 1981. "Plato's Pharmacy." In *Dissemination*, translated by Barbara Johnson, pp. 61–172. Chicago: University of Chicago Press.

——. 1988. "Signature Event Context." In *Limited Inc.*, translated by Samuel Weber and Jeffrey Mehlman, pp. 1–24. Evanston, Ill.: Northwestern University Press.

——. 1995. "The Rhetoric of Drugs." In *Points . . .* , edited by Elizabeth Weber and translated by Peggy Kamuf et al., pp. 228–252. Stanford: Stanford University Press.

——. 1998. *Monolingualism of the Other or the Prosthesis of Origin*, translated by Patrick Mensah. Stanford: Stanford University Press.

Derrida, Jacques, et al. 1985. *The Ear of the Other: Otobiography, Transference, Translation*, edited by Christie McDonald and translated by Peggy Kamuf. Lincoln: University of Nebraska Press.

Devereaux, Leslie, and Roger Hillman, eds. 1995. *Fields of Vision: Essays in Film Studies, Visual Anthropology, and Photography*. Berkley: University of California Press.

Dijkstra, Bram. 1986. *Idols of Perversity: Fantasies of Feminine Evil in the Fin-de-Siècle Culture*. New York: Oxford University Press.

Doane, Mary Ann. 1991. *Femme Fatales: Feminism, Film Theory, Psychoanalysis*. New York: Routledge.

Dolar, Mdlar. 1996. "The Object Voice." In *Gaze and Voice as Love Objects*, edited by Renata Salecl and Slavoj Žižek, pp. 7–31. Durham, N.C.: Duke University Press.

"Dos mujeres, dos destinos." 1996. *Clarín*. January 28, 41.

Douglas, Mary. 1984. *Purity and Danger: An Analysis of the Concepts of Pollution and Taboo*. London: Routledge.

Dujovne Ortiz, Alicia. 1995. *Eva Perón: la biografía*. Buenos Aires: Aguilar.

Dyer, Richard. 1992a. "Entertainment and Utopia." In *Only Entertainment*, pp. 18–34. London: Routledge.
———. 1992b. "Four Films of Lana Turner." In *Only Entertainment*, pp. 65–98. London: Routledge.

El nuevo porteño. 1996. "Dossier: Si Evita Viviera." December, 35–53.

Escribano, José Claudio. 1996. "Procura la actriz mimetizarse con Eva." *La nación*, January 23, 5.

Fabian, Johannes. 1983. *Time and the Other: How Anthropology Makes Its Object*. New York: Columbia University Press.

Fernández, Macedonio. 1990. *No todo es vigilia la de los ojos abiertos*. Buenos Aires: Ediciones Corregidor.

Ferrer, Horacio. 1995. "Les Tangos Vagabonds," translated by Pierre Monette. In *Tango nomade*, edited by Ramón Pelinski, pp. 11–16. Montreal: Triptyque.

Flores, María [Mary Main]. 1952. *The Woman with the Whip*. Garden City, N.Y.: Doubleday.

Foster, Hal. 1996. "The Artist as Ethnographer." In *The Return of the Real: The Avant-Garde at the End of the Century*, pp. 171–204. Cambridge, Mass.: MIT Press.

Foucault, Michel. 1972. *The Archaeology of Knowledge, and the Discourse on Language*, translated by A. M. Sheridan Smith. New York: Pantheon Books.
———. 1977. "A Preface to Transgression." In *Language, Counter-Memory, Practice: Selected Essays and Interviews*, edited and translated

by D. F. Bouchard and S. Simon, pp. 87–111. Ithaca, N.Y.: Cornell University Press.

Fraser, Nicholas, and Marysa Navarro. 1996. *Evita: The Real Life of Eva Perón*. New York: W. W. Norton.

Freud, Sigmund. 1962. *Three Essays on the Theory of Sexuality*, translated and edited by James Strachey. New York: Basic Books.

García Canclini, Nestor. 1968. *Cortázar*. Buenos Aires: Editorial Nova.

González Tuñon, Enrique. 1967. *Tangos*. Buenos Aires: Centro Editor de América Latina.

Gramsci, Antonio. 1971. *Selections from the Prision Notebooks*, edited and translated by Quintin Hoare and Geoffrey N. Smith. New York: International Publishers.

Greimas, Algirdas J., and Jacques Fontanille. 1993. *The Semiotics of Passions: From States of Affairs to States of Feelings*, translated by Paul Perron and Frank Collins. Minneapolis: University of Minnesota Press.

Grosz, Elizabeth. 1990. "Sexual Relations." In *Jacques Lacan: A Feminist Introduction*, pp. 115–146. London: Routledge.

Harris, David. 1992. *From Class Struggle to the Politics of Pleasure: The Effects of Gramscianism on Cultural Studies*. London: Routledge.

Hart, Linda. 1994. *Fatal Women: Lesbian Sexuality and the Mark of Agression*. Princeton: Princeton University Press.

Heath, Stephen. 1991. "The Turn of the Subject." In *Explorations in Film Theory: Selected Essays from Ciné-Tracts*, edited by Ron Burnett, pp. 26–45. Bloomington: Indiana University Press.

Heller, Agnes. 1979. *A Theory of Feelings*. Assen: Van Gorcum.

Jacobson, Roman. 1960. "Closing Statements: Linguistics and Poetics." In *Style in Language*, edited by Thomas Sebeok, pp. 350–377. Cambridge, Mass.: MIT Press.

Jameson, Fredric. 1983. "Pleasure: A Political Issue." In *Formations of Pleasure*, pp. 1–14. London: Routledge.

Kaplan, E. Ann, ed. 1980. *Women in Film Noir*. London: British Film Institute.

Kosuth, Joseph. 1993. "The Artist as Anthropologist." In *Art After Philosophy and After: Collected Writings, 1966–1990*, edited by Gabriele Guercio, pp. 107–128. Cambridge, Mass.: MIT Press.

Lacan, Jacques. 1985. "God and the Jouissance of the Woman." In *Feminine Sexuality: Jacques Lacan and the Ecole Freudienne*, edited by

Juliet Mitchell and Jacqueline Rose and translated by Jacqueline Rose, pp. 137–148. New York: W. W. Norton.

Laclau, Ernesto, and Chantal Mouffe. 1999. *Hegemony and Socialist Strategy: Towards a Radical Democratic Politics.* London: New York.

Lamborghini, Leonidas. 1972. "Eva Perón en la hoguera." *Partitas.*

Lara, Tómas, and Inés L. Roncetti de Panti. 1969. *El tema del tango en la literatura argentina.* Buenos Aires: Ediciones Culturales Argentinas.

Lebrun, Gerard. 1987. "O conceito de paixão." In *Os sentidos da paixão,* pp. 17–34. São Paulo: Funarte, Editora Schwarcz.

Limón, José E. 1994. *Dancing with the Devil: Society and Cultural Poetics in Mexican-American South Texas.* Madison: University of Wisconsin Press.

"Madonna's Moment as Evita, Mother, and Fashion Force." 1996. *Vogue.* October.

"Madonna: 'Soy igual que Evita.'" 1996. *Caras.* January 24.

Martínez, Tomás Eloy. 1995. *Santa Evita.* New York: Vintage Español.
———. 1996. "Lo que no se perdona." *Página* 12, February 7, 3.

Mayer, Marcos. 1996. "Planeta Evita." *El nuevo porteño* 1, no. 4: 36–45.

McClary, Susan. 1991. "Living to Tell: Madonna's Resurrection of the Fleshly." In *Feminine Endings: Music, Gender, and Sexuality,* pp. 148–166. Minnesota: University of Minnesota Press.

Mercado, Tununa. 1996. *La madriguera.* Buenos Aires: Tusquets Editores.

Mercer, Colin. 1983. "A Poverty of Desire: Pleasure and Popular Politics." In *Formations of Pleasure,* pp. 84–100. London: Routledge.

Mulvey, Laura. 1988a. "Visual Pleasure and Narrative Cinema." In *Feminism and Film Theory,* edited by Constance Penley, pp. 57–68. New York: Routledge.
———. 1988b. "Afterthoughts on 'Visual Pleasure and Narrative Cinema' Inspired by 'Duel in the Sun.'" In *Feminism and Film Theory,* edited by Constance Penley, pp. 69–79. New York: Routledge.

Negri, Antonio. 1996. "Después de la globalización, el imperio." *El nuevo porteño* 1, no. 4: 85.
———. 1999. *Insurgencies: Constituent Power and the Modern State,* translated by Maurizia Boscagli. Minneapolis: University of Minnesota Press.

Nichols, Bill. 1981. *Ideology and the Image: Social Representations in the Cinema and Other Media.* Bloomington: Indiana University Press.

Oakley, Judith. 1992. "Anthropology and Autobiography: Participatory Experience and Embodied Knowledge." In *Anthropology and Autobiog-*

raphy, edited by Judith Oakley and Hellen Callaway, pp. 1–28. London: Routledge.

Parker, Alan. 1996. *The Making of Evita*. New York: Collins.

Perlongher, Néstor. 1986. "Evita vive (en cada hotel organizado)." *Cerdos y Peces*.

Potter, Sally. 1997. *The Tango Lesson*. London: Faber and Faber.

Puertas Cruse, Roberto. 1959. *Psicopatología del tango*. Buenos Aires: Editorial Sophos.

Rose, Jacqueline. 1986. *Sexuality in the Field of Vision*. London: Verso.

Sanjek, Roger, ed. 1990. *Fieldnotes: The Makings of Anthropology*. Ithaca: Cornell University Press.

Sartre, Jean Paul. 1956. *Being and Nothingness*, translated by Hazel Barnes. New York: Washington Square Press.

Savigliano, Marta E. 1995. *Tango and the Political Economy of Passion*. Boulder, Colo.: Westview Press.

Scheper-Hughes, Nancy. 1992. *Death without Weeping: The Violence of Everyday Life in Brazil*. Berkeley: University of California Press.

Scott, Joan. 1992. "Experience." In *Feminists Theorize the Political*, edited by Judith Butler and Joan Scott, pp. 22–40. New York: Routledge.

Shohat, Ella, and Robert Stam. 1994. "Stereotype, Realism, and the Struggle over Representation." In *Unthinking Eurocentrism: Multiculturalism and the Media*, pp. 178–219. London: Routledge.

Spinoza, Benedict de (Baruk). 1989. *Ethics, Including the Improvement of the Understanding*, translated by R. H. M. Elwes. Amherst, N.Y.: Prometheus Books.

Spivak, Gayatri. 1980. "Revolutions That As Yet Have No Model: Derrida's 'Limited Inc.'" *Diacritics* 10, no. 4: 29–49.
——. 1993. "Politics of Translation." In *Outside in the Teaching Machine*, pp. XX. New York: Routledge.
——. 1999. *A Critique of Postcolonial Reason: Toward a History of the Vanishing Present*. Cambridge: Harvard University Press.

Stallybrass, Peter, and Allon White. 1986. *The Politics and Poetics of Transgression*. Ithaca, N.Y.: Cornell University Press.

Taylor, Julie M. 1979. *Eva Perón: The Myths of a Woman*. Chicago: University of Chicago Press.

Taylor, Lucien, ed. 1998. *Transcultural Cinema: David MacDougall*. Princeton: Princeton University Press.

"Tema: santa o hereje: quién fue Evita?" 1996. *La Maga*. January 31, 1–7.

Tetzlaff, David. 1993. "Metatextual Girl: Patriarchy-Postmodernism-Power-Money-Madonna." In *The Madonna Connection: Representational Politics, Subcultural Identities, and Cultural Theory*, edited by Cathy Schwichtenberg, pp. 239–263. Boulder, Colo.: Westview Press.

Thomas, Nicholas. 1996. *Out of Time: History and Evolution in Anthropological Discourse*. 2d ed. Ann Arbor: University of Michigan Press.

Tobin, Jeff. 1998. "Manly Acts: Buenos Aires, 24 March 1996." Ph.D. diss., Rice University.
———.1999. "A Performance da Masculinidade Portenha no Churrasco." *Cadernos pagu* 12: 301–329.

Tobing Rony, Fatima. 1996. *The Third Eye: Race, Cinema, and Ethnographic Spectacle*. Durham, N.C.: Duke University Press.

"Tres películas en marcha y otros dos proyectos en duda." 1996. *La Maga*. January 31, 5.

Trías, Eugenio. 1991. *Tratado de la pasión*. México D.F.: Editorial Grijalbo.

Turner, Victor. 1982. *From Ritual to Theory: The Human Seriousness of Play*. New York: PAJ.
———. 1987. *The Anthropology of Performance*. New York: PAJ.

Valenzuela, Luisa. 1983. *Cola de lagartija*. Buenos Aires: Bruguera.

Walsh, Rodolfo. 1986. "Esa mujer." In *Los oficios terrestres*, pp. 9–19. Buenos Aires: Ediciones de la Flor.

Williams, Linda. 1989. *Hard Core: Power, Pleasure, and the "Frenzy of the Visible."* Berkeley: University of California Press.

Films

Addams Family Values. 1993. Directed by Barry Sonnefeld, characters by Charles Addams, starring Anjelica Huston, Raul Julia, and Cristina Ricci. Paramount (United States).

Alice. 1990. Directed and written by Woody Allen, starring Mia Farrow, Joe Mantegna, and William Hurt. Orion (United States).

La cabalgata del circo. 1945. Directed by Mario Sofficci, screenplay by Francisco Madrid and Mario Sofficci, starring Hugo del Carril, Libertad Lamarque, and Eva Duarte. (Argentina).

Eva Perón. 1996. Directed by Juan Carlos Desanzo, screenplay by José Pablo Feinman, starring Esther Goris as Eva Perón and Víctor Laplace as Perón. Aleph Producciones (Argentina).

Evita. 1996. Directed by Alan Parker, screenplay by Alan Parker and Oliver Stone, lyrics by Tim Rice, music by Andrew Lloyd Webber, starring Madonna as Evita, Antonio Banderas as Che, and Jonathan Pryce as Perón. Hollywood Productions (United States).

The Four Horsemen of the Apocalypse. 1921. Directed by Rex Ingram, screenplay by June Mathis; starring Rudolf Valentino and Alice Terry. Metro (United States.)

Gilda. 1946. Directed by Charles Vidor, screenplay by Marion Parsonnet, starring Rita Hayworth as Gilda, Glenn Ford as Johnny Farrell, and George MacReady as Ballin Mundson. Columbia Pictures (United States).

Isadora. 1968. Directed by Karel Reisz, based on *My Life* by Isadora Duncan, starring Vanessa Redgrave as Isadora, Jason Robards, and Ivan Tchenko. Universal (United States).

The Mask. 1994. Directed by Chuck Russell, screenplay by Michael Fallon; starring Jim Carrey and Cameron Diaz. New Line Cinema (United States.)

Last Tango in Paris. 1973. Directed by Bernardo Bertolucci, screenplay by Bertolucci and Franco Arcalli, starring Marlon Brando, and Maria Schneider. PEA Artiste Associe/ United Artists (Italy/ France).

Naked Tango. 1989. Directed and written by Leonard Schrader, starring Mathilda May and Esai Morales. Scotia International (United States.)

Scent of a Woman. 1992. Directed by Martin Brest, screenplay by Bo Goldman, starring Al Pacino, Chris O'Donnell, and Gabrielle Anwar. Universal (United States.)

Some Like It Hot. 1959. Directed and written by Billy Wilder, starring Tony Curtis, Jack Lemon, Marilyn Monroe, and Joe E. Brown. United Artists (United States.)

Sunset Boulevard. 1950. Directed by Billy Wilder, screenplay by Wilder, Charles Bracket, and D. M. Marshman; starring Gloria Swanson and William Holden. Paramount Pictures (United States.)

The Tango Lesson. 1997. Directed and written by Sally Potter, starring Sally Potter and Pablo Verón. Sony Pictures Classic.

Tango, no me dejes nunca. 1998. Directed and written by Carlos Saura, starring Miguel Angel Solá, Mia Maestro, and Cecilia Narova. Sony Pictures Classic.

Music/Culture

A series from Wesleyan University Press
Edited by George Lipsitz, Susan McClary, and Robert Walser

About the Author

Marta Elena Savigliano is the author of *Tango and the Political Economy of Passion* (1995), which received the Congress of Research on Dance Award for Outstanding Book 1993–1996. She is an anthropologist and political theorist, and Professor in the UCLA Department of World Arts & Culture.